Commission on the Bicentennial of The United States Constitution

808 17th Street, N.W. ● Washington, D.C. 20006-3999
(202) USA-1787 / FAX (202) 653-5219

Warren E. Burger
Chairman

Dear Librarian:

The Commission on the Bicentennial of the United States Constitution is making available to your library this copy of Jeffrey St. John's book, <u>Constitutional Journal</u>. The book is written as a journalist's eyewitness day by day account of the Constitutional Convention in Philadelphia. St. John's book draws on James Madison's notes and correspondence and other writings of delegates to the Convention.

I urge you to encourage its use as part of the Bicentennial celebration.

Cordially,

Warren E. Burger

CONSTITUTIONAL JOURNAL

CONSTITUTIONAL JOURNAL

A Correspondent's Report from the Convention of 1787

Jeffrey St. John

Jameson Books, Inc.
Ottawa, Illinois

Jameson books are available at special discounts for bulk
purchases for sales promotions, premiums, fundraising or
educational use. Special condensed or excerpted editions can
also be created to customer specification.

For sales information and catalog requests write:

Jameson Books, Inc.
P.O. Box 738
Ottawa, IL 61350

815-434-7905

10 9 8 7 6 5 4 3 2   90 89

Printed in the United States of America.

Distributed to the book trade by Kampmann & Company.

CONSTITUTIONAL JOURNAL is
available on audio tape. Write the publisher for information.

ISBN 0-915463-42-3

Library of Congress Catalogue Card Number 87-83130

*To Kathryn,
an animating force in this work and
in the author's life.*

CONTENTS

★

FOREWORD

★

The Bicentennial of the Constitution has stimulated an outpouring of popular writing and serious scholarship on the Constitution and how it came to be. Mr. St. John's account, both serious and popular, was first published in the *Christian Science Monitor* as a series of columns from May to September 1987. His *Constitutional Journal* reveals the magnitude of the task the 55 delegates to Philadelphia undertook, as well as the uncertainty of its outcome.

We know, of course, that the meetings of the delegates were closed, "secret" meetings which, among things, made it easier for members who had taken a position one day to change it later without embarrassment. So firm was this rule of secrecy that in one of his few statements as Chairman, George Washington severely scolded some unknown delegate who had carelessly left some of his notes on the debates—later found on the floor by the clean-up crew.

St. John's device of simulated "daily reports" enables the reader to share in the tension of the occasion. It also allows us to behold the transformation of the sessions from a meeting authorized "for the sole and express purpose" of revising the Articles of Confederation to a Constitutional Convention that became a great milestone in world political history. These 55 men sat down together and devised—constituted—a new government unlike any in all human history. They did not invent all the ideas but drew on the great thinkers of Greece, Rome, France, England and Scotland.

Mr. St. John frankly concedes that no one except the delegates was allowed in the meetings, but takes the reader through the debates, day by day, in an entertaining style that succeeds in conveying both the historical facts and the emotion and drama of the debates. To do so he drew, of course, on James Madison's voluminous notes which were not made public until 1840, four years after his death, along with other writings of the post-Convention period. Slowly, through bargain and compromise, the framework of the new government emerged, guided more by young James Madison than any single delegate. Beyond the mere erecting of a frame—the organic law—of government, the delegates foresaw and resolved countless details as to how the new government was to be run.

Matters which we take for granted today as well-settled, such as the prohibition on members of Congress being appointed to office by the President, were the subject of debate and controversy. Any number of such issues, if they had been resolved differently, would have had a significant impact on the structure and functioning of our government. This book illuminates the uncertainty of the outcome as to issues facing the delegates and allows us, from the vantage point of over 200 years, to behold the providential foresight of the Founders. We have taken the Constitution too much for granted, as though our country's course through uncharted waters was foreordained.

It is clear that until the end the product of the convention was far from certain and George Washington, James Madison, Ben Franklin and others attributed the result to Divine guidance. Thomas Jefferson, at first skeptical, later called the men who drafted the Constitution "demi-gods." As the *Journal* shows, the delegates' task was far from easy; Washington and others called the result a "miracle."

The *Journal* demonstrates the political culture of the 13 states operating under the Articles of Confederation but also their willingness to abandon the "firm league of friendship," as their union was described in the Articles. States jealously guarded their own perceived interests. Conflicts between the large states, such as Virginia, Pennsylvania, Massachusetts and New York, and the smaller states—Delaware, for example—were inevitable. The South, long dependent on the evil institution of slavery, was fearful of the mercantile, abolitionist North and of farmers who worked their own fields.

This conflict emerged in the Northwest Ordinance of 1787 which prohibited slavery in the new territories. For a time the outcome of the Convention was in serious doubt. But the Convention's ultimate success, as Mr. St. John ably demonstrates, was largely attributable to the skill and statesmanship of the delegates in dealing with what seemed at the time to be intractable problems. Heated interchange and vigorous disagreements were constant throughout the Convention, but the spirit of compromise and unsurpassed creativity and ingenuity ultimately prevailed.

That creativity and ingenuity sprang from the minds of extraordinary men. The *Journal* conveys a sense of the personalities of the delegates. We are able to witness the quiet leadership of George Washington as the crises of the Convention unfolded and were resolved. Young Madison, in many ways the driving intellectual and synthesizing force behind the Constitution, is presented as a staunch advocate of his home state's interests, yet also as a statesman concerned with a true federal union of the states. The *Journal* also presents lively portraits of delegates perhaps less recognized in the history books, but nonetheless crucial to the framing of the Constitution. Gouverneur Morris and James Wilson of Pennsylvania, and Roger Sherman of Connecticut are three names that come to mind.

This is a book the Commission on the Bicentennial is placing in the library of every high school and college in the country—and in other libraries. And adding to the value of this original version is an appendix of hard-to-find copies of the Articles of Confederation and the Northwest Ordinance of 1787.

Young Americans and their teachers will find this volume very useful to an understanding of our great Constitution—and how difficult it was to get it.

Warren E. Burger — Chairman,
Commission on the Bicentennial of the U.S. Constitution
Chief Justice of the United States, 1969–1986

PREFACE

★

The Constitutional Time Machine

How would the Constitutional Convention of 1787 have been
influenced or affected if the secret sessions had been leaked to
and reported by the news media of 1987?

How would a newspaper or broadcast correspondent have
covered the most complex, and critical, political story in
American history if he or she had inside information about the
daily debates, and access to personal diaries and letters of the
delegates?

This work is one reporter's answer: 124 *Journals* of the day-
to-day debates of the Constitutional Convention in Philadelphia that officially met from May 25 to September 18, 1787.
Each is written as if this author were transported back to
Philadelphia in a time machine to the summer of 1787. Using
modern reportorial techniques, the Convention that created
the U.S. Constitution is treated like an evolving news story
not much different from the debates the author has covered in
the U.S. Congress.

For instance, the reportorial techniques used are: "a
source says" ... "this correspondent has learned" ...
"a copy obtained by this correspondent" ... "an observer
notes" ... "allegedly" ... "James Madison is reported...".
The *Journal* is written in the present tense and spellings in
direct quotes are carefully retained to preserve further the
reader's sense of reading "today's" news. Personal opinions
and interpretations of the "correspondent" have scrupulously
been avoided; all interpretations by "observers" are foot-

noted. Each day's closing comment is a journalistic touch used in contemporary times, but it is often suggested by possible forthcoming events during the Convention.

The *Journal* was almost two years in preparation and is based on the documented record of the Convention debates and supplemented by scholarly works. Seventeen published works on the Convention were used and over forty additional histories of the period and biographies were consulted.

As a print and broadcast journalist during the last thirty years, I have covered in Washington, D.C., the political institutions created by the Convention and concretized in the Constitution. Having written on historical subjects for print and broadcasting, I came to realize that I had only a superficial knowledge and understanding of the origin of the political institutions that daily affect my life and the lives of millions of Americans. I soon found that I was not alone. Most Americans know there was a Convention in 1787 and know about the Constitution it produced, but know almost nothing of the process that went into the Constitution's creation.

Professor Michael Kammen in *A Machine That Would Go of Itself: The Constitution in American Culture* (Alfred A. Knopf, 1986) maintains that most Americans do not understand the Constitution and many equate it exclusively with the U.S. Supreme Court. The subject of the Constitution, Dr. Kammen insists, is too often poorly taught in the schools and textbooks on the subject tend to be unclear, superficial, inconsistent and even inaccurate.

"For almost two centuries," writes the Cornell University historian, "it has been swathed in pride yet obscured by indifference: a fulsome rhetoric of reverence more than offset by the reality of ignorance."

The Constitutional Convention of 1787 is a difficult and demanding story to tell, largely because it involves a multitude of elements, ideas, issues and personalities. One historian has estimated that if a verbatim transcript had been made of each session of the four-month Convention in the summer of 1787, consisting of some four hundred hours, it would probably fill at least fifty volumes.

In this century dozens of books devoted to the Convention and the Constitution have been published, most of them of a scholarly nature. Many of these works I have relied on in creating the *Journal*, describing the daily process of the Convention in a reportorial style much as I have done in covering the national conventions of both American political parties since 1960. The reason I chose this approach was to try to produce clarity out of complexity, providing the accurate essence of what transpired and at the same time show the delegates' ordeal of summer statecraft as a profoundly human, as well as historical, drama that changed American and world history.

The *Journal* is an effort to provide a concise composite of one of the most important news stories in history—a complex and compelling political drama that remains relevant today. By using modern journalistic techniques and writing as if I were in Philadelphia two hundred years ago, the story takes on a reality that sometimes is lost when cast in the context of an event two centuries ago. It also reads like a mystery, as the reader moves swiftly through each *Journal*, wondering what might happen next. The reader will discover, as did the author, that the Convention might easily have turned out entirely different from the way it did. It could have ended in failure for half a dozen reasons, narrowly escaping dissolution during angry disagreements.

We should also remember that the Framers of the American Constitution had none of the modern tools of communications that our current political leaders—and press—take for granted. The Framers, for example, did not have access to lending libraries, computer data systems, high-speed printing presses, radio and television, nor even the telephone and telegraph, tools that might have assisted them in creating a document that has endured for two hundred years. When viewing their achievement in this context, one has to stand in absolute awe of how they achieved so much, in so short a span of time, by their collective human intelligence.

The Framers brought to their ordeal of creating a new government an understanding of the past, a commonsense view of the possible in 1787, and the profound belief that it was possible for human beings to create a framework of freedom that might endure in the future. The Convention was as much a drama of human reason as it was an act of faith that personal liberty and the rule of law, not of men, could serve their own time and future generations of free Americans.

Initial research for the *Journal* was underwritten by a grant from the National Endowment for the Humanities to the American Studies Center, Washington, D.C. The entire series has been reviewed by a panel of eight scholars and historians for historical accuracy and integrity.

The *Journal's* original goal was achieved when the *Christian Science Monitor*, one of America's most respected daily newspapers, took the unprecedented step of publishing during the weekdays of the 1987 bicentennial summer 81 of the 124 *Journals*.

"I doubt that the *Christian Science Monitor* has ever made a commitment for so many articles in a single package as the Constitutional Journal," wrote Mrs. Katherine Fanning, editor of the *Monitor*. "Mr. St. John has caught the spirit of the Constitutional Convention so well we felt it deserved the large commitment of space for daily articles from May 22 through September 15. We are delighted that all his lively, human, carefully researched pieces are being preserved in book form."

With the additional syndication of the daily *Journals* to other newspapers across the country by the *Monitor* News Service, my goal of reaching Americans with the news story of the Convention has more than been reached.

Behind the achievement of creating a document that has endured two hundred years are hidden complex sets of ideas, issues and clashes of interests. By understanding this constellation of conflicting elements, the reader may have a clearer understanding of how the Constitution was forged.

Reading the document in its completed form reveals what was resolved. Reading the *Journal* may provide an insight into how and why the delegates created a framework of freedom for "We the People . . ." of the future.

JEFFREY ST. JOHN

Randolph, Virgina

ACKNOWLEDGMENTS

★

James Madison in 1834 declined credit as the sole "Father of the Constitution," in writing to an admirer. "This was not like the fabled goddess of wisdom, the offspring of a single brain. It ought to be regarded as the work of many heads and hands."

While the author is the sole writer of this work, and assumes full responsibility for its contents and presentation, many heads and hands were helpful, even indispensable, in its creation and finalization.

First and foremost is my wife and editor Kathryn Boggs St. John, who stubbornly refuses to share coauthorship of this and other, previously published works, although she richly deserves such recognition. The *Constitutional Journal* is clear, concise and comprehensible because of her diligent and dedicated professionalism. She not only performed the initial editing and typed every single *Journal*, but checked and rechecked every quote and source for accuracy and saw the *Journal* through its many stages. The *Constitutional Journal* bears this writer's name but the work is also the product of Kathryn's clear and unerring editorial eye.

The *Constitutional Journal* was the outgrowth of "Headlines & History," a newspaper and broadcast series on American history. The series was first broadcast over the Voice of America in English and translated into twenty-three languages on a daily basis in 1982–1983. Frank Scott, then with the VOA's English Language Division, was instrumental in giving "Headlines & History" its worldwide forum.

Beginning in 1983 a weekly broadcast version of "Headlines & History" was heard nationwide over the Mutual

Broadcasting System and overseas on Armed Forces Radio. Application to the National Endowment for the Humanities for a modest research grant was proposed after a futile effort to secure funding for the *Journal* project from major American corporations. Denise Liebowitz, then with the American Studies Center, was crucial in helping secure the NEH grant and assembling the panel of eight constitutional scholars and historians to review the *Journal*.

The author is particularly grateful to the panel of scholars who offered valuable insights and suggestions, considerably strengthening its historical integrity. They are: Dr. Lance Banning, History Department, University of Kentucky; Dr. George Billas, American History Department, Clark University (Worcester, Mass.); Dr. Richard Brown, Department of History, University of Connecticut; Dr. Morton J. Frish, Department of Political Science, Northern Illinois University; Dr. James Hutson, Chief, Manuscript Division, the Library of Congress; Professor Pauline Maier, Department of Humanities, Massachusetts Institute of Technology; Dr. Robert Weir, History Department, University of South Carolina; and Dr. Gordon S. Wood, Department of History, Brown University.

Although the *Journal* was initially conceived as a broadcast series for the bicentennial of the Philadelphia Convention, as a contributor of historical articles to newspapers, I thought it appropriate as a newspaper series during the bicentennial and as a book.

John Hughes, friend and former editor of the *Monitor* and now director of the *Monitor's* broadcasting services, was instrumental in bringing the *Journal* to the attention of the paper's editor, Mrs. Katherine Fanning, and to Managing Editor David Anable and Feature Editor Roderick Nordell, and recommending that it be given serious consideration.

I am particularly appreciative that these three took the time to read all 124 *Journals* before making a decision— which was to publish 81 *Journals* between May and September 1987. I am grateful for Mr. Nordell's quiet and patient professionalism in preparing the series for newspaper publication. I wish also to thank Chris Needham of the Christian Science Monitor/Los Angeles Times News Syndicate for her work in preparing the *Journal* for syndication to newspapers nationwide.

Three libraries, in addition to my personal library, were critical in the research of the *Journal*: the Martin Luther King Library, Washington, D.C.; the Joseph DuPuy Eggleston Library, Hampden-Sydney College (interestingly, James Madison was one of its founders); and the Dabney S. Lancaster Library, Longwood College, Farmville, Virginia. Mrs. Martha Le Stourgeon, librarian at Longwood, was particularly helpful, as was Catherine Pollari, reference librarian at Hampden-Sydney.

THE CONVENTION DELEGATES

★

The total number of delegates who served at the Convention was 55. There were others who did not serve, including Patrick Henry of Virginia and the Rhode Island delegation. Of the 55, not all were in Philadelphia during the entire summer; some arrived late (New Hampshire's delegation for instance), others left early, a few stayed only briefly, some were temporarily absent for business or personal reasons, a few were serving simultaneously in the Continental Congress. When the U.S. Constitution was finally adopted, the State delegations unanimously voted their approval, and 39 delegates that final day affixed their signatures to the document. Three delegates refused to sign.

The 55 men are listed below, by State delegation North to South, an asterisk indicating those who were not present on September 17; the three who were present but refused to sign are in italics.

New Hampshire
John Langdon
Nicholas Gilman
Massachusetts
Elbridge Gerry
Rufus King
Caleb Strong*
Nathaniel Gorham
Connecticut
Roger Sherman
William Samuel Johnson
Oliver Ellsworth*
New York
Alexander Hamilton

John Lansing, Jr.*
Robert Yates*
New Jersey
William Paterson (Patterson)
William Livingston
Jonathan Dayton
David Brearly (Brearley)
William Churchill Houston*
Pennsylvania
Benjamin Franklin
Robert Morris
James Wilson
Gouverneur Morris
Thomas Mifflin

George Clymer
Thomas FitzSimmons
   (Fitzsimons, FitzSimons)
Jared Ingersoll
Delaware
John Dickinson
George Read
Richard Bassett (Basset)
Gunning Bedford, Jr.
Jacob Broom
Maryland
Luther Martin*
Daniel Carroll
John Francis Mercer*
James McHenry
Daniel of St. Thomas Jenifer
Virginia
George Washington
James Madison
George Mason

Edmund Jennings Randolph
James Blair, Jr.
James McClurg*
George Wythe*
North Carolina
William Richardson Davie*
Hugh Williamson
William Blount
Alexander Martin*
Richard Dobbs Spaight, Jr.
South Carolina
John Rutledge
Charles Cotesworth Pinckney
Pierce Butler
Charles Pinckney III
Georgia
Abraham Baldwin
William Leigh Pierce*
William Houstoun*
William Few

CONSTITUTIONAL JOURNAL

Friday, May 18, 1787

All roads leading to Philadelphia have become rivers of mud in the last week.[1] James Madison of Virginia believes the bad weather prevented a majority of delegates from being present on May 14[2] to attend what newspapers here are calling a "Grand Convention." Last February, Congress in New York set May 14 as the date for the thirteen States to meet in this port city.[3] The Convention is to consider revising the Articles of Confederation that have determined the political relationships among the thirteen States since 1781.

Mr. Madison is one of the leading critics of the Articles.[4] He is also one of the major advocates for holding this Convention. The 36-year-old scholar-legislator was one of the first of the Virginia delegates to arrive here from New York after attending sessions of the Continental Congress. Mr. Madison is reported to have brought with him a trunkload of books, shipped from Paris by the U.S. Minister to France, Thomas Jefferson. The books are primarily the histories of the ancient world which he intends to use in Convention debates to bolster his arguments for reforms.[5] Sources close to the Virginia delegates have informed this correspondent that the delay in the start of this Convention has been used by the Virginia Congressman to refine his proposals and to plan political strategy with his fellow delegates.[6]

Mr. Madison is relying heavily on the prestige of fellow Virginia delegate George Washington to counter any opposition to his plans. General Washington arrived on May 13 greeted by cheering crowds, ringing church bells and a military honor guard.[7] The 55-year-old hero of the American War of Independence was reluctant to attend this Convention and decided to do so only after intense pressure from Mr. Madison and others.[8]

3

After his arrival, General Washington paid a courtesy call on the 81-year-old Dr. Benjamin Franklin. The former U.S. Minister to France returned from Paris two years ago and was elected president of the Executive Council of Pennsylvania. Dr. Franklin has called this Convention an "assembly of notables." Although he suffers from a painful bladder stone and chronic gout,[9] Dr. Franklin held a dinner at his home two days ago for General Washington and all the other delegates. Dr. Franklin is reported to have told a friend later that a cask of porter was consumed by the delegates—making for a mellow consensus.[10]

Observers believe that Dr. Franklin's role at this Convention will be to reconcile differences by his wit, charm and political astuteness, which he displayed while in Europe. He reluctantly agreed at his age to participate in the Convention to silence rumors in Europe that the thirteen independent States are heading for certain political shipwreck.[11] Dr. Franklin's concern is reflected in this statement on the Convention:

> Indeed, if it does not do Good it must do Harm, as it will show that we have not the Wisdom enough among us to govern ourselves; and will strengthen the Opinion of some Political Writers that popular Governments cannot long support themselves.[12]

No wonder the Old World watches what is happening here in the New World with doubt. The political experiment being shaped on this side of the Atlantic does not exist in Europe or elsewhere.

Saturday, May 19, 1787

Rhode Island has flatly refused to send a delegation to this Philadelphia convention to consider revising the Articles of Confederation.[1] The news has produced an outpouring of denunciations against the tiny State. Rhode Island mavericks in control of the State government believe they can continue a policy of issuing inflated paper money, from which some benefit politically and financially. If they participate in this Convention they might be forced to end such a policy.[2]

Rhode Island's refusal has underscored a major weakness of the Articles of Confederation. Any revisions must have unanimous agreement of all thirteen States. With Rhode Island's boycotting the Convention, it remains a serious question whether any revisions adopted can be considered legally binding.[3]

Sources close to General George Washington report he is furious at Rhode Island's action, calling it "scandalous conduct."[4] The General was pleased, however, by the arrival yesterday of his former close military aide during the War of Independence, Colonel Alexander Hamilton of New York. The 30-year-old lawyer and legislator is, along with James Madison, responsible for making this Convention possible.

In March 1785, General Washington hosted a conference at his Mount Vernon plantation. The delegates from Virginia and Maryland reached agreement on regulation of the Potomac River and also recommended to their respective State legislatures that a larger conference should be convened to consider the nation's commercial problems.

Mr. Madison seized on their recommendations to persuade the Virginia legislature to invite the twelve other States to send delegates to a second conference at Annapolis, Maryland, in September of 1786.[5] Nine States accepted the invitation, but only five sent delegations. Colonel Hamilton represented New York and it was he who drafted a report calling for the current Convention here in Philadelphia to revise the Articles of Confederation.[6]

The lack of concrete results at the Annapolis meeting served as a stepping stone to bring the current Convention into being.[7] The behind-the-scenes role played by both Colonel Hamilton and Mr. Madison in engineering this Convention marks them as major players for power here in Philadelphia. And they have had support for their plan from George Washington, adding to their power.

Rhode Island's refusal to attend has given General Washington worry. He made this statement:

> I very much fear that all the States will not appear in Convention, and that some will come fettered so as to impede rather than accelerate the great object of their convening which . . . would place me in a more disagreeable situation than any other member would stand in.[8]

The General's concern for possible damage to his public prestige, if the Convention fails, is viewed by observers here as puzzling. The high regard in which he is held by all Americans for his past service could never be damaged by his standing in the present,[9] no matter how many failures he were to support.

Sunday, May 20, 1787

A revolutionary plan that would go beyond the official purpose of this Convention was disclosed today by a member of the Virginia delegation. Colonel George Mason, in a letter written to his son, a copy obtained by this correspondent, says that the Virginia delegation has been meeting in secret, for up to three hours a day.

What has emerged from these meetings, according to Colonel Mason, is a plan for a strong *national* government that would radically reduce the power and independence of the separate States. The plan also calls for the proposed new national government to have absolute veto power over all State laws. The Virginia proposal is a potential political powder keg. Colonel Mason conceded the proposal would encounter problems:

> It is easy to foresee that there will be much difficulty in organizing a government upon this great scale, and at the same time reserving to the State legislatures a sufficient portion of power for promoting and securing the prosperity and happiness of their respective citizens. . . .[1]

This revolutionary proposal is reliably reported to have been drafted by James Madison and was shown to General George Washington for his approval over three weeks ago, before he arrived in Philadelphia.[2]

The General not only has attended the daily closed meetings in Philadelphia of the Virginia delegation, but is using various social functions to sound out other delegates about just how much of the revolutionary plan they might accept.[3]

Clearly, the General and the Virginia delegation run the risk of being charged with flying under false colors. Virginia has been the principal advocate of a convention for the sole purpose of revising the Articles of Confederation.[4] The Virginia proposal for a new and powerful national government would replace the Articles and doubtlessly anger some State delegations who might feel they have been misled.[5]

One of several justifications for the revolutionary proposal is what has happened in Massachusetts in the last nine months. A former captain in General Washington's army, Daniel Shays, led armed mobs—made up mostly of farmers—against state courts. The mob action delayed court collection of debts owed by the farmers to creditors.[6] The disorders, from General Washington's viewpoint and that of others who favor this Convention, demonstrated the need for a stronger government to deal with any future violent disorders.[7]

However, some observers believe that the mob violence, led by Captain Shays, has been used by James Madison and others to justify radical revision of the relationships among the States, which is now surfacing here in Philadelphia.[8] The recent election of John Hancock as the new governor of Massachusetts, by an overwhelming majority, is at the same time viewed as an indication that peaceful conciliation in the State will replace armed confrontation.[9]

The Shays Rebellion has had a dramatic impact on General Washington and many delegates to this Convention. However, Dr. Benjamin Franklin has taken less seriously the scattered violence in Massachusetts. One month ago he wrote Thomas Jefferson in Paris predicting the rebellion would be put down permanently.[10] Dr. Franklin may prove to be a better prophet than General Washington.

Monday, May 21, 1787

A potential political storm is gathering force at this Convention before it is even formally convened. Delegate George Read of Delaware is reported to have dispatched an urgent letter home today to his fellow delegate John Dickinson. The letter, a copy obtained by this correspondent, urges Mr. Dickinson to proceed to Philadelphia without delay.

Mr. Read reports that he has in hand a draft copy of the plan drawn up by Virginia for a consolidated national government. Mr. Read expressed to Mr. Dickinson the fear that the Virginia proposal puts at political risk the power of small States like Delaware. He told Mr. Dickinson:

> I suspect it to be of importance to the small States that their deputies should keep a strict watch upon the movements and

propositions from the larger States, who will probably combine to swallow up the smaller ones by addition, division, or impoverishment. . . .[1]

Both Delaware delegates strongly favor overhauling the Articles of Confederation and they agreed to serve at this Convention for that purpose. However, the credentials issued by the State of Delaware clearly forbid them to agree to any revision of the Articles that denies the small State equality of voting in a national congress.[2]

Mr. Read points out in his letter that under the Virginia Plan Delaware would have only one representative out of eighty, with the majority held by the larger, populous States like Virginia. [3] Ironically, Mr. Dickinson was one of the initial authors of the Articles of Confederation, an alliance among the thirteen States since 1781. The Confederation was formed primarily as a "firm league of friendship"[4] and the Articles considered by its authors the constitutional expression of the Declaration of Independence.[5]

The Articles left ultimate power to the States, and the central government was given specific, sharply circumscribed power.[6] A single national Congress, based in New York, was created with each State having one vote. The powers given to Congress to administer the affairs of the Confederation can only be exercised with the approval of at least nine States.[7] In the last six years, deadlock, indecision and drift have been terms used by the critics of Congress and of the Confederation. Demands for reform of the Articles began from the time they were ratified, particularly in matters of domestic commerce and foreign trade.[8]

This Convention is the climax of a six-year campaign waged by the critics of the Articles. The leading critic and advocate of reform has been James Madison of Virginia. He can be expected, when the Convention begins, to deliver up an indictment of the Articles, based on his own service in Congress. As a scholar in politics, he is also reported to have drawn up a 41-page pamphlet titled *The Vices of the Political*

System of the United States. As the title implies, it is said to be a critical examination of the Confederation under the Articles.[9]

However, delegates like Mr. Read and Mr. Dickinson of Delaware have apparently very early become alarmed about and alerted to what Mr. Madison and others have in mind. It is not reform; it is a political revolution.

Tuesday, May 22, 1787

Rains and roads mired in deep mud are reported as the major reason why this Convention has now experienced its eighth day of delay. General Washington revealed today that the North Carolina delegation made an appearance at the State House here in Philadelphia.[1] However, this brings the total number of States only to five, two short of the seven required to conduct convention business. General Washington is known to be growing impatient and irritated:

> These delays greatly impede public measures, and serve to sour the temper of the punctual members, who do not like to idle away their time.[2]

Most of the delegates who have arrived in this city of 40,000 are staying at the Indian Queen Inn. Colonel George Mason of Virginia is surprised that it costs him only 25 Pennsylvania shillings a day for his room, a groom for his horse, and a Negro servant.[3] The servants' hair is powdered white, which accentuates their dark complexion.[4]

Colonel Mason's approval of his accommodations at the Indian Queen does not extend to the social life of Philadelphia. Accustomed to the informal but elegant life at his Virginia plantation, Gunston Hall, the 61-year-old Virginia planter complains of having grown "heartily tired of the etiquette and nonsense so fashionable in this city. . . . It would take me some months to make myself master of them." [5] This is Colonel Mason's first trip to Philadelphia. Almost his entire career as a political statesman has been spent in his own State. He is credited with inspiring the Declaration of Independence by his authorship of the Virginia Declaration of Rights. Thomas Jefferson has called him a man "of the first order of greatness."[6]

Since the Declaration was signed here in 1776, Philadelphia remains the largest city in the thirteen States. The city fathers and its newspapers are particularly proud that the Convention is being held here and not in New York. As a port city, its waterfront teems with cargo vessels from Europe, some discharging white indentured bond servants who will be sold to the highest bidders. On market days, stern buckskin-clad frontiersmen rub elbows with sad-eyed Shawnee Indians, German farmers, and sailors speaking a dozen different tongues.[7]

Most of the Southern delegates to this Convention find Philadelphia a rude contrast to their life of quiet comfort at neat manor houses and cultivated plantations. The cobblestone streets here are crowded with people and animals producing a symphony of sound. The warm days of May bring to a visitor's nostrils odors of sewage from the Delaware River mixed with the smell of horse manure that is a feast for flies. Swarms of flies in the streets are joined by wind-borne mosquitoes from nearby stagnant water pools, making the city a candidate for fresh outbreaks of malaria and yellow fever.[8]

However, it is a political fever that is coursing through every class in this city. The longer the Convention is delayed, the higher the fever rises, and with it the feeling that, in the words of General Washington, "a great drama" is about to begin.[9]

Wednesday, May 23, 1787

The single most critical concern of delegates at this Convention, next to its delay in starting, is whether it can come to grips with the real, or imagined, economic problems facing the thirteen States. No issue has done more to bring this gathering of prominent and wealthy delegates together than the question of domestic and foreign commerce.[1]

While General George Washington, Alexander Hamilton and James Madison speak openly of the need for revising the existing political relationships among the States, behind their words lurks the economic equation.

Mr. James Monroe, a member of the Continental Congress until last year, is reported to have stated to Mr. Madison in a communication dated today that in his view this Convention is the axis on which the future of the country might turn. Mr. Monroe, a 29-year-old lawyer who is currently a member of the Virginia House of Delegates, wrote Mr. Madison from Fredericksburg, Virginia:

> We all look with anxiety to the results of the convention in Phil. Indeed it seems to be the sole point on which all movements will turn. . . . Yet it may, by some be thought doubtful, . . . that it will be impossible to adopt any plan that will make concurrence of all the States.[2]

Mr. Monroe during his three years in Congress was unsuccessful in persuading the 13 States to grant Congress the power to regulate domestic and foreign trade and to levy duties on imports as a revenue-raising measure. Rivalries between Northern merchants and Southern planters defeated the proposal.[3]

In 1785 Mr. Monroe was also unsuccessful with a proposal to amend the clause in the Articles of Confederation that prohibits Congress from concluding treaties of commerce with foreign nations if such treaties denied individual States the right to impose their own duties.[4]

The economic difficulties since the end of the War of Independence and even depression in foreign trade last year have been blamed on the weakness of the Articles to give power to a central authority to regulate and control domestic and foreign commerce. It has been this argument that the advocates of a convention have successfully employed to bring this Convention into being.[5]

However, this argument is being challenged by the economic recovery that has been well under way in most of the States. Even General Washington conceded as early as last month that economic recovery in the States was accelerating and that people are "more industrious than they were before the war."[6]

But recent mob violence in Massachusetts by debt-ridden farmers convinced General Washington and others that this Convention is necessary for national salvation despite the growing economic good times. The farmers are victims of a depression in foreign trade, high taxes, and swift retirement of debts. The initial evidence at this time suggests that the General and others overreacted to the mob violence.[7] If there was an overreaction that caused a stampede of support in the States for this Convention, there is also a fear that the good economic times of the present will not continue in the future without guidance from a central government.[8]

Thursday, May 24, 1787

The delay of 10 days at this Convention may be at an end. South Carolina's delegation arrived today here in Philadelphia, and Massachusetts delegate 32-year-old Rufus King reports that he expects the State of New Jersey will arrive tomorrow. This means that seven States will make up the necessary quorum for conducting Convention business. Mr.

King also revealed that delegates have apparently agreed to elect General George Washington president of the Convention.[1]

The 55 men from 12 States who are expected to attend this conclave are from the planter, merchant, and professional classes. Over half of the delegates are lawyers, and 44 of the 55 have served in the Continental Congress.[2] Eight of the delegates signed the Declaration of Independence, six signed the Articles of Confederation, and 21 are veterans of the recent war with Great Britain. Six have served, or are serving, as governor of their respective States. The average age of the delegates is roughly 43.[3] (Dr. Franklin's age of 81 raises the average considerably.) As a group, therefore, they represent the educated, successful and wealthy leaders in the 13 States.

One elected delegate has refused to serve. He is Patrick Henry of Virginia. Mr. Henry, when asked his reasons for refusing to serve, is reported to have replied, "I smelt a Rat."[4] Behind this colorful but blunt comment are two issues that have agitated the 51-year-old Mr. Henry.

First, most delegates believe that whatever this Convention creates, the States will remain independent. But Mr. Henry contends that any new constitution would represent a hankering after glory and riches, rather than liberty.[5] The second issue is that Mr. Henry is reliably reported to believe that whatever is concluded here in Philadelphia will be at the expense of personal liberty and sovereignty of the independent States. He is also reported to believe that industry and a prosperous economy are the solutions to current problems, not a new set of political rules.[6]

The Virginia delegation is deeply troubled over the impact Mr. Henry's absence will have on public opinion.[7] James Madison had this cutting comment:

> I hear from Richmond with much concern that Mr. Henry has positively declined his mission to Philadelphia. Besides the loss of his services, there is danger I fear that this step has

proceeded from a wish to leave his conduct unfettered . . . .
where the result of the Convention will receive its destiny from
his omnipotence.[8]

Mr. Madison's assertion of ego playing a part in Mr. Henry's
opposition is not entirely true. The former governor of Virginia was deeply alarmed by recent negotiations in which
John Jay, the Confederation's secretary of foreign affairs,
proved willing to agree with Imperial Spain's closing the
Mississippi River to U.S. trade. Although Congress has not
approved the treaty, Mr. Henry still fears a sellout to Spain to
benefit business interests in the Northern States.[9]

Mr. Madison warned General Washington late last year
that Mr. Henry would oppose this Convention if Congress did
not reverse its appeasement of Imperial Spain.[10] Ironically,
the threat of Imperial Spain provides Mr. Madison additional
justification for holding this Convention, as it does for Mr.
Henry's opposing it.

Friday, May 25, 1787

A driving rain beat against the high, wide windows of the
State House here in Philadelphia today as General George
Washington was unanimously elected president of the Convention.[1] The heavy rain and illness kept 81-year-old Dr.
Benjamin Franklin away from the first formal Convention
session today, after New Jersey provided the necessary quorum of seven States.[2] Dr. Franklin was expected to propose
General Washington for president. Instead, Robert Morris of
Pennsylvania, one of the richest men in North America, nomi-
nated the 55-year-old General. John Rutledge of South Carolina, a lawyer and planter who is land rich and cash poor,
seconded the nomination.[3]

General Washington's acceptance speech was notable for its self-effacement and the fact that his false teeth made his words difficult to understand. He looks the part of a hero: a tall, heavy man, ruddy face, grave blue eyes, large hands, and the long legs of a horseman.[4] In the same State House a dozen years ago, he was appointed Commander-in-Chief of a ragtag army. Here in the same hall, the Declaration of Independence was signed by some of the same men who today listened to General Washington's grave words. A source reported the General as saying:

> It is too probable that no plan we propose will be adopted. Perhaps another dreadful conflict is to be sustained. If to please the people, we offer what we ourselves disapprove, how can we afterwards defend our work? Let us raise a standard to which the wise and the honest can repair. The event is in the hand of God.[5]

After the awe at General Washington's words had worn off, Colonel Alexander Hamilton of New York rose to nominate an official secretary for the Convention. Major William Jackson was chosen over the nephew of Dr. Franklin. A source revealed that Major Jackson won after having lobbied some of the more important delegates as early as a month ago.[6]

Major Jackson then rose to read the credentials of the seven States present: New York, New Jersey, Pennsylvania, Virginia, North Carolina, South Carolina and Delaware. It was the reading of Delaware's credentials that caused the only off-key note in an otherwise harmonious first meeting.[7]

Delaware's credentials order its delegates not to vote for any revision of the current Articles of Confederation that does not uphold the principle that each State, large and small, will have one vote and one vote only. Delaware delegate George Read wrote the credentials,[8] and insisted on the provision out of a fear that this Convention will become an instrument of the larger States to swallow up the small ones like sharks devouring minnows. Last January Mr. Read had said of the larger States: "I would trust nothing to their candor, generosity or ideas of public justice in behalf of [our] State. . . ."[9]

Four days ago, Mr. Read wrote fellow delegate John Dickinson to hurry to Philadelphia after obtaining a copy of the revolutionary plan by Virginia for reducing the power of the States.[10]

The days ahead promise not to be as harmonious as today's opening Convention session.

Saturday, May 26, 1787

If this Convention fails to create a strong national government, a group of former military officers might impose one with General George Washington as its "crowned head." The French diplomatic envoy to the 13 States has raised that frightening but implausible possibility in a confidential diplomatic dispatch to Paris, a copy of which has been obtained by this correspondent.

French envoy Louis Guillaume Otto named the Society of the Cincinnati as the organization that might carry out such a coup. The Society is made up of former military officers who served under General Washington and it is holding its biannual meeting in Philadelphia. General Washington also serves as president of the Society and has dined with its members.[1] The French diplomat points out that many of the Society members are owed money by Congress and face the prospect of not being paid under the existing Articles of Confederation and a virtually insolvent Congress. Mr. Otto went on to relate in his secret diplomatic dispatch:

> . . . they propose throwing all the States together into one mass and put at its head General Washington with all the preroga-

tives and powers of a crowned head. They even threaten to undertake such a revolution themselves with arms in hand, should they become convinced of the uselessness of the present convention.[2]

The French diplomat, however, dismisses the Society as weak, unpopular, and without the influence necessary to carry off a coup. His raising the issue, nevertheless, may reflect talk and fear among Convention delegates. It is known, for example, that Massachusetts delegate Elbridge Gerry has been a bitter critic of the Society since its founding as a fraternal organization at the formal end of the War of Independence in 1783.[3]

Mr. Gerry has held that the Society, named after the Roman General Lucius Quinctius Cincinnatus, represents the seedbed from which a domestic military aristocracy might spring. In the last few years, Mr. Gerry has helped fan public anxiety over the existence of the Society as the military arm of those who favor a new national government with power over the separate States. During the past decade, Mr. Gerry has waged a campaign against the creation of a national standing army along the lines in European nations.[4] This Convention is certain to debate the question of creating a national military force and Mr. Gerry is expected to be the leader of the opposition.[5]

General Washington is known to be highly sensitive about the Society of the Cincinnati and was reluctant to accept reelection as its president out of concern that the Society's controversial nature would be used by opponents of this Convention, like Mr. Gerry.[6] However, the Virginia delegation may be counting on the Society for support of its radical plan for a new national government. It is known, for example, that Virginia Governor Edmund Randolph, himself a former military officer, has met with Society members here in Philadelphia to sound them out on the mood of the country toward this Convention.[7]

The fact that the French monarchy has a diplomatic observer watching closely the Convention indicates that the Paris government, which poured men and money into the American Revolution, is keeping an eye on its investment.

Sunday, May 27, 1787

A source close to the Virginia delegation revealed today that a rule of absolute secrecy will govern the proceedings of the Convention being held here in Philadelphia. George Mason in a letter to his son, a copy having been obtained by this correspondent, reveals that the delegates have informally agreed to impose a public blackout on the business of the Convention while in session. Colonel Mason justifies the news blackout, in his words, to "prevent mistakes and misrepresentation until the business shall have been completed. . . ."[1]

Guards have been ordered to stand watch at the entrance to the State House to prevent spying by outsiders. Delegates are forbidden to copy from the Convention's daily records of the debates without permission.[2] A Committee on Rules, appointed at the opening session, is believed to have advanced the proposal of a pledge of secrecy. Delegates are reported to have agreed to the measure, which provides them freedom of discussion while in Convention, yet protects them from political attacks later on.[3]

The one dissenting voice is from overseas, from Thomas Jefferson, U.S. Minister to France. He is reported to have told John Adams, serving as U.S. Minister to Great Britain, that he has no doubt the proceedings here will produce measures "good & wise." He even went so far as to call this Convention "an assembly of demigods." But on the secrecy question, he was harsh and unequivocal:

> I am sorry they began their deliberations by so abominable a precedent as that of tying up the tongues of their members.

Nothing can justify this example but the innocence of their intentions & ignorance of the value of public discussions.[4]

An investigation of why the Convention is proposing secrecy shows that the last thing the authors of the gag rule want is public discussions. John Rutledge of South Carolina is reliably reported to have been the author of the secrecy proposal. He is said to have told James Wilson of Pennsylvania that if the proceedings were open and public, they would so distract and inhibit the delegates that the Convention would end in failure.[5]

Mr. Wilson reportedly went to Dr. Benjamin Franklin with Mr. Rutledge's argument. Dr. Franklin, like Mr. Wilson, dislikes the secrecy proposal but could not disagree with Mr. Rutledge's logic. Dr. Franklin is reported to have presented the secrecy question to General Washington, asking for his endorsement.

The President of the Convention said he would have to consult his Virginia colleagues. In 48 hours the General reported back to Dr. Franklin that the Virginia delegates were unanimously in favor of the secrecy rule. The secrecy rules will apparently apply not only during the proceedings, when every delegate is bound by an "oath of secrecy," but also during the lifetime of each member, so that he may not reveal what was discussed during the Convention.[6]

Dr. Franklin, this correspondent has learned, will have at least one delegate at his elbow during his public appearances outside the Convention. This is being done to remind the 81-year-old loquacious philosopher, who often gets carried away in his conversations, that he will have an oath of secrecy to uphold.[7]

Monday, May 28, 1787

Dr. Benjamin Franklin came to his first formal Convention session today in a sedan chair carried on the muscular shoulders of four convicts from the Walnut Street prison. The elderly, cheerful President of Pennsylvania finds the pain from his chronic gout and a bladder stone eased by the use of the chair, made for him in France. His mode of transportation gathers a crowd wherever he goes here in Philadelphia.[1]

Delegates watched with polite amusement as the talkative scientist-philosopher was carefully carried into the East Chamber of the State House. The first-floor room, 40 by 40 feet, has a 20-foot ceiling and high windows on both sides of the room. For warmth there are two fireplaces faced in marble.[2] Dr. Franklin was helped to a comfortable armchair at the table of the Pennsylvania delegation. Each State delegation's table is covered with a green woolen cloth topped with quill pens and ink wells. They are arranged in arcs facing the Convention President's high-backed chair on a raised dais.[3] When General Washington enters, the delegates stand as a mark of respect. Some watch in silent awe as the President of the Convention settles his large but graceful frame into the President's chair. He signals with a silent nod of his white-wigged head that the day's session should begin. Twenty-nine delegates at today's session have brought the number of States represented from seven to nine.[4]

Virginia's George Wythe, famed as a professor of law at William and Mary College, read a draft of the Convention rules prepared by the committee he heads.[5] A majority of the rules cover formal parliamentary procedures and were adopted. However, Rufus King of Massachusetts, a 32-year-old lawyer with a reputation for occasional rudeness,[6] objected to the rule allowing for any member to call for a recorded vote. Mr. King won approval for his point, stating:

> . . . as the acts of the Convention were not to bind the Constituents it was unnecessary to exhibit this evidence of the votes;

and improper as changes of opinion would be frequent in the course of the business & would fill the minutes with contradictions. [7]

Colonel George Mason of Virginia outdid Mr. King for candor, saying that recorded votes would have the effect of supplying political grapeshot to the enemies of the Convention. [8] South Carolina's Pierce Butler offered a motion to prevent absent members from publishing what they know of the proceedings. Professor Wythe's Committee on Rules was instructed to consider the issue of secrecy and to draft language to seal the lips of all the delegates. [9]

A majority of the delegates are reported grateful that the gag rule was so easily accepted. Ever since this Convention began forming, Philadelphia has been a riot of rumors. Dr. Franklin, at his home or when he travels throughout the city in his sedan chair, has been tormented with a barrage of questions from friends, associates and constituents wanting to know what this Convention plans to do. Many want reassurance that no dark plots are afoot to rob them of their liberties. [10]

Tuesday, May 29, 1787

A warning that war and anarchy confront America was issued today by the Governor of Virginia. Thirty-three-year-old Edmund Randolph outlined in a four-hour Convention speech his reasons for fearing an armed conflict unless the current Articles of Confederation are completely scrapped, this correspondent has learned. The handsome but portly six-foot Virginia Governor stated that "the confederation is incompetent to any *one* object for which it was instituted." [1]

He also charged that the Confederation has failed since 1781 to ensure against foreign invasion and has proven powerless to promote domestic unity, security and prosperity. His large brown eyes rolled and flashed as he spoke.[2] At one point he said:

> . . . let us not be affraid to view with a steady eye the perils with which we are surrounded. Look at the public countenance from New Hampshire to Georgia. Are we not on the eve of war, which is only prevented by the hopes from this convention.[3]

The Virginia Governor, descended from a landed dynastic family, allegedly said the "chief danger" the country faced was from too much democracy in some state constitutions, which placed too much power in the hands of the people, thus producing a legislative tyranny. Fresh in the minds of the delegates were outbreaks of violence over the last year in Massachusetts when debt-ridden farmers mounted an abortive siege of the State courts to prevent judicial collection of their debts.[4]

A source revealed that a letter to General Washington sent today by General Henry Knox reports that Massachusetts still seethes with hostile insurgents. The rotund former artillery officer of General Washington's army blames "the imbecilities of the State & general constitutions" for creating the mobs. "I have no hope of a free government but from the convention," General Knox writes.[5]

Governor Randolph, who helped draft Virginia's Constitution of 1776,[6] presented a 15-point plan, or "corrections," to avoid the peril of war which he predicts. It appears to be a broad blueprint for a strong central government in a republican form. It calls for national executive, legislative, and judicial branches with sweeping powers unprecedented in their scope. Such a proposed national government must be considered revolutionary.[7] The plan appears to propose sweeping away entirely the Articles of Confederation.

The Convention seems prepared to proceed on the basis of the Virginia Plan, which it has ordered printed for the delegates' consideration. Governor Randolph was careful not to claim authorship, since the 15-point proposal is reported to be by James Madison,[8] who lacks Randolph's public position and command of language. It was sound political strategy to have a State governor put forth a radical plan[9] that proposes to dissolve or dilute the power of the States.

Colonel Alexander Hamilton of New York, who has worked closely with Mr. Madison to bring this Convention into being, allegedly put today's dramatic proceedings into perspective. He said the Randolph proposals raise the question of whether the country was to have one government, or 13 separate State governments linked only by treaty for common defense and the conduct of commerce.[10]

Wednesday, May 30, 1787

A long, stony silence descended over the Convention delegates today[1] when the words "national" and "supreme" were heard, this correspondent was told. Virginia Governor Edmund Randolph proposed in a resolution to the Convention: "That a *national* Government [ought to be established] consisting of a *supreme* Legislative, Executive & Judiciary."[2]

The silence may have been less from consent to Mr. Randolph's proposal than from uncertainty and confusion over its implications.[3] George Wythe of Virginia broke the stillness, saying he presumed "from the silence of the house" that it was prepared to pass on the resolution. Pierce Butler of South Carolina said the house was not ready to vote. He asked Governor Randolph to show "that the existence of the States cannot be preserved by any other mode than a national government."[4] Governor Randolph offered this explanation of his proposal:

> It is only meant to give the national government a power to defend and protect itself. To take therefore from the respective

legislatures or States, no more soverignty than is competent to this end.[5]

What has alarmed some delegates is the fear that the proposed national government will devour and destroy the States.[6] Mr. Charles Pinckney III of South Carolina directly asked Governor Randolph whether "he meant to abolish the State Governts. altogether."[7] He replied: "only so far as the powers intended to be granted to the new government should clash with the states, when the latter was to yield." [8]

Governor Randolph appears to be proposing what has never before existed: a central national government and sovereign State governments, each with specified powers. Citizens would be expected to obey both national and State laws.[9] Stated another way, a national republican form of government, with 13 smaller republics or States as satellites.

However, two delegates questioned whether the Convention had the authority even to consider the proposal for a national government. General Charles Cotesworth Pinckney pointed out that the Convention was called for the sole purpose of revising the Articles of Confederation, not for creating a new government.[10] Elbridge Gerry of Massachusetts, a signer of both the Declaration of Independence and the Articles of Confederation, said that if the Convention had the right to approve a national government, it also had the power to "annihilate" the existing Confederation of the 13 States.[11]

Gouverneur Morris of Pennsylvania, who wears a wooden leg and a cynical expression, said that one government was better suited to prevent wars or render them less expensive or bloody than many. "We had better take a supreme government now, than a despot twenty years hence," he added.[12]

Mr. Morris spoke directly to the principal anxieties of many delegates, namely, the fear of anarchy on the one hand and of tyranny on the other. It is perhaps the primary reason why a majority today voted for the first time to consider a new national government rather than follow the Convention's original mandate to patch up the old Articles of Confederation.[13]

Thursday, May 31, 1787

The Convention today, with no debate, tentatively approved the creation of a national Legislature to consist of two branches.[1] Only Pennsylvania dissented, a source at the Convention informed this correspondent. Dr. Benjamin Franklin has long favored a single legislative branch, which is why Pennsylvania voted against the creation of a lower and an upper house.[2] The ease with which the measure passed can be explained by the fact that 11 State governments currently maintain house and senate chambers. Only Pennsylvania and Georgia have a single house. The current Continental Congress, created by the Articles of Confederation, has also operated as a single legislative body.[3]

Sharp disagreement developed, however, when the Convention took up the resolution calling for election of the first, or lower, house by the people. Roger Sherman of Connecticut was the first on his feet to object, proposing election to the lower house by the State legislatures. "The people should have as little to do as may be about the government. They want information and are constantly liable to be misled," the former shoemaker from Connecticut said.[4] Elbridge Gerry of Massachusetts agreed, saying experience in his own State has shown that politicians have misled the people. "The evils we experience flow from an excess of democracy," the New England merchant said. At the root of the evil, he added, was the dangerous belief in the "levelling spirit" of equality.[5]

Virginia's George Mason rose in rebuttal, saying that the Convention should "attend to the rights of every class of the people."[6] James Wilson of Pennsylvania, who appears owlish and scholarly behind thick spectacles, said:

> No government could long subsist without the confidence of the people. In a republican Government this confidence was peculiarly essential. . . . [it is] wrong to increase the weight of the State Legislatures by making them the electors of the national Legislature.[7]

Six States agreed, and election by the people was tentatively approved. So was a proposal giving power to the national Legislature to pass laws in all cases when the States are thought to be incompetent. Congressional veto power over all State laws was also passed without debate or dissent. The lack of debate and dissent on both questions stems from delegates' experience with the Continental Congress, which lacks the power to enforce laws.[8]

If today's session reveals one thing, it is the unanimous agreement among a majority of the delegates that the failures of the Articles of Confederation must not be repeated. Under the Articles, the individual States have encroached upon the powers of the central government, rendering it weak and ineffective.[9] Today's action giving sweeping powers to a new national government now raises the question of whether the States will agree to the sweeping radical proposals of the Virginia Plan.

As South Carolina's Pierce Butler complained today, they were "running into an extreme in taking away the powers of the States."[10]

Friday, June 1, 1787

The hated symbol of the British monarchy, King George III, surfaced today, this correspondent learned, when the Convention debated the volatile question of whether the Executive for the new national government should be single or plural.[1]

James Wilson of Pennsylvania, who was born under the British monarchy in Scotland and speaks with a thick burr, stunned delegates into silence when he proposed the national executive be a single person. Dr. Benjamin Franklin, cast in the role of Convention conciliator, urged the delegates to speak up since Mr. Wilson's proposal was of such "great importance."[2]

The pause persisted until John Rutledge of South Carolina, believed to be a secret ally of Dr. Franklin and Mr. Wilson[3], assured the silent delegates that speaking up now on the issue did not mean they could not change their minds later.[4] Mr. Rutledge declared himself in these words:

> [I am] for vesting the Executive power in a single person tho [I am] not for giving him the power of war and peace. A single man would feel the greatest responsibility and administer the public affairs best.[5]

Governor Edmund Randolph of Virginia was passionate in his opposition, saying a single Executive was "the foetus of monarchy" and urged the delegates not use the British government as its model. Three persons in the Executive, he said, would give the needed energy to act with independence.[6]

Mr. Wilson replied that the comparison with the British system was mistaken, since the 13 States were "a great confederated Republic," not a monarchy.[7] Besides, he added, the people during the American Revolution saw not the King of England as the source of tyranny but the "corrupt multitude" that composed the British Parliament.[8]

The Convention failed to resolve the issue of a single versus a plural Executive, principally because the delegates marched and counter-marched over a broad terrain of ideas without any defined direction.[9] James Madison of Virginia, who sought to provide a compass point, said that a definition of the powers of a single or a plural Executive would assist in how far "they might be safely entrusted to a single officer."[10]

Mr. Madison's use of the term "trust" is the key to understanding today's bitter debate. A single Executive strikes many delegates as a return to the broad, unlimited power used by the Royal governors when the 13 States were Colonies of England. Most of the State Constitutions, written after Independence, grant little authority to their governors and in practically all States a single Executive shares his powers with a Privy Council. State governors have their powers specifically defined to prevent a return to the unlimited powers exercised by the British Royal Governors.[11]

When Virginia's Governor Randolph proposed today a plural Executive and warned against the danger of a monarchy, he provoked in the minds of older delegates the experience of the past. If there is one consistent pattern emerging from this Convention thus far, this correspondent has learned, it is the degree to which the delegates are being guided less by theory than by practical experience.

Saturday, June 2, 1787

Concern for the corrupting influence of power on a national Executive and a proposal for sharing power dominated today's Convention debate, this correspondent has learned.

James Wilson of Pennsylvania sustained a crushing defeat when he proposed the election of a national Executive by a people's electoral college.[1] The principal reason for rejection seems to be the distrust of delegates for a process of election by the people at large which bypasses the States. Elbridge Gerry of Massachusetts pointed out that Mr. Wilson's plan of election by a people's electoral college would breed corruption and provide support for those who fear this Convention is out to strip the States of their power.[2]

Then, without further debate, the delegates tentatively approved election of a national Executive by the national Legislature for a term of seven years.[3] To guard against corruption while in office, it was decided the national Executive could be removed by impeachment. Also, to guard against corruption by being too long in office, it was agreed the Executive should be barred from serving a second seven-year term. These two safeguards clearly indicate the serious commitment Convention delegates have to an independent national Executive.[4]

Dr. Benjamin Franklin proposed that the national Executive serve without pay as a way to guard against the corrupting influences of power and money. However, most delegates opposed the proposal, concerned that only the wealthy could afford to serve without a salary. In a long speech, read to the Convention by Mr. Wilson because of Dr. Franklin's difficulty in standing, Dr. Franklin said the "love of power and the love of money . . . are two passions which have a powerful influence on the affairs of men."[5] In proposing a payless president, he may have in mind his long experience in England where British politicians line their pockets with profits from posts of honor.[6]

James Madison of Virginia made this written comment:

> No debate ensued, and the proposition was postponed for the consideration of the members. It was treated with great respect, but rather for the author of it, than from any apparent conviction of its expediency or practicability.[7]

Delaware's John Dickinson cautioned the Convention to look hard at the history of ancient republics that flourished for a moment and then vanished forever. " . . . it only proves that they were badly constituted; and that we ought to seek for every remedy for their diseases," Mr. Dickinson added.[8] The corrupting consequence of consolidating power at the center was one cause for the death of ancient republics, the Delaware scholar and writer said. He proposed to keep independent and separate the powers of each of the national Legislative, Executive and Judiciary departments.

The two chambers of the national Legislature, with considerable powers left to the separate States, Mr. Dickinson said, would prevent repeating the errors of the ancients who consolidated power instead of separating and diffusing it.[9]

The delegates do not seem to grasp that Mr. Dickinson's proposal essentially combines a strong national government with the separate States in a unique power-sharing formula. At this point, a source told this correspondent, most delegates are concerned about whether their respective States will gain or lose power, not with sharing power.[10]

Sunday, June 3, 1787

The most discussed person at this Convention is not even here. John Adams, currently the U.S. Minister to London, is apparently "exciting a good deal of attention" from many delegates with a book that he wrote and had published this spring. *A Defense of the Constitutions of the Government of the United States of America* defends a balanced form of government with three branches, a two-chamber Legislature, and a system of checks and balances. The fact that during the last few days the delegates have been debating such a system is said by some to be a testament to Mr. Adams' marked influence.[1]

Dr. Benjamin Rush, a signer of the Declaration of Independence and a famous Philadelphia physician, told a friend just yesterday that he had no doubt that the principles in Mr. Adams' book will have an influence in shaping any new national government. "Our illustrious minister in this gift to his country has done us more service than if he had obtained alliances for us with all the nations of Europe," Dr. Rush added.[2]

However, Mr. Adams has his critics. James Madison of Virginia contends that the book is hostile to republican government and favors a monarchy. Mr. Madison, in a letter to Thomas Jefferson—a copy was obtained by this correspondent—insists that Mr. Adams' book is likely to revive a desire for a British constitution. Without mentioning the points about which they may agree, Mr. Madison made these sharp observations:

> Men of learning [will] find nothing new in it. Men of taste [will] find many things to criticize. And men without either [learning or taste], not a few things, which they will not understand.[3]

If anyone could be described as the driving intellectual engine of this Convention, it is the 36-year-old scholar turned public servant, Mr. Madison. He is a small person, 5 foot 6 inches and 120 pounds, who walks with a bouncing step.[4] His blue eyes and ruddy face convey a combination of softness and strength. His hair is brushed forward over a high forehead to hide a progressive baldness.[5] The son of a wealthy Virginia planter, Mr. Madison speaks so quietly and softly at times that he is often asked to speak more loudly to be heard.[6]

Substantial evidence exists that it was Mr. Madison who drafted the plan for a new national government, which the Convention has been debating during the past week. Virginia Governor Edmund Randolph has presented what is being called the Randolph Resolutions, but the author is believed to be James Madison.[7]

During the daily Convention sessions, Mr. Madison is never still. He sits directly below the chair of the President, facing the other delegates, and with quill in hand records what is said. When he wishes to speak, which up to now has been almost daily, he rises, takes one step, turns and addresses the President of the Convention.[8]

John Adams' popular book may be a *Defense of the Constitutions*, but it appears that it is James Madison who may end up shaping a new one for the still-to-be-united States of America.

Monday, June 4, 1787

Delegates demonstrated today that experience, rather than abstract arguments, is starting to shape the character of this Convention, this correspondent has learned.

In a 7 to 3 vote (New Jersey abstained), it was firmly decided that any new national government shall have a single Executive.[1] James Wilson of Pennsylvania told the delegates in the lengthy debate that the experience of all 13 States was with a single magistrate. "The idea of three heads has taken place in none," Mr. Wilson added.[2]

Roger Sherman of Connecticut conceded such was the case. He pointed out, however, that experience has shown that a single Executive in the States could not act without a plural council. Nor did Mr. Sherman make any converts with his additional point that the hated King of Great Britain had an appointed council to advise him.[3]

The issue of experience also dominated the debate over whether the single Executive should have veto power over laws passed by the proposed national Legislature. Mr. Wilson and Colonel Alexander Hamilton of New York both proposed an absolute veto. Colonel Hamilton added that even the King of Great Britain had shown that his veto power had not been used since the Revolution.[4]

Dr. Benjamin Franklin took sharp exception. He said that it had been his experience, when he was an official of the colony of Pennsylvania, that the veto was used by the Governor to extort concessions from the State Legislature. Dr. Franklin then provided this grisly example:

> When the Indians were scalping the western people, and notice of it arrived, the concurrence of the Governor in the means of self-defence could not be got, till it was agreed that his Estate should be exempted from taxation.[5]

Also, the experience of the 13 Colonies with the abuse of the veto power by the British Royal Governors proved lasting. After independence, only three States had conferred such power on their Governors.[6] The Convention delegates today rejected the proposal for an absolute veto for the Executive. Rather, they approved a qualified veto with the provision that an Executive veto could be overturned by a two-thirds vote in both branches of the proposed national Legislature.[7]

The Convention, by approving a single national Executive with a qualified veto, hopes to check possible excesses of the national Legislature. Again, experience seems to have fashioned this decision. Many State Legislatures can pass unjust laws with impunity, unchecked in their power.[8]

Thus, the debate centered on an attempt to prevent either the Executive or the Legislature from having absolute power. The delegates hope this will prevent the abuses they have experienced under the State Legislatures, and, earlier, under the British Colonial Governors.

During today's debate over the powers of the Executive, Dr. Benjamin Franklin said he had no doubt that "The first man put at the helm will be a good one."[9] He could only be referring to General George Washington. The General was expected this afternoon to review battalions of the Philadelphia militia on the city commons. But the crush of the crowds eager to see and speak to him was so great, the military review had to be cut short.[10]

The delegates today drew on dry political experience, a sharp contrast to the emotionalism exhibited toward the hero of nearby Valley Forge.

Tuesday, June 5, 1787

Today's Convention debate illustrated the ease with which lawyers can agree one day and disagree the next, on the same issue. A count by this correspondent shows that 34 of the 55 delegates to this Convention are lawyers.[1]

In yesterday's session, the delegates agreed unanimously to create a national Judiciary consisting of one supreme court and one or more inferior courts. Apparently overnight reflection produced a fear of the consequences of power being transferred from State courts to any national tribunal.[2]

James Wilson of Pennsylvania, himself a lawyer, favors a national Judiciary over the States and the appointment of judges by the Executive.[3]

John Rutledge of South Carolina, also a lawyer and a State judge, jumped to his feet. He told the delegates that granting great power to a single person will make people think the Convention is leaning toward monarchy. Besides, Mr. Rutledge added, he favors a single supreme judicial tribunal and letting the State courts decide all cases first.[4]

Dr. Benjamin Franklin, who is not a lawyer, suggested tongue-in-cheek that the Convention consider the Scots' method of selecting judges. Lawyers always recommend the best among their ranks for judges, he said with a sly expression, "in order to get rid of him, and share his practice <among themselves>."[5]

James Madison of Virginia, while appreciating the entertainment value of Dr. Franklin's suggestion, turned serious once on his feet. Distrustful of the Legislature's appointment of judges, he was successful in getting the Convention to delete appointment by the Legislature and leave the matter of who should appoint judges for a later debate.[6]

Mr. Rutledge of South Carolina clashed with Mr. Madison on the issue of whether national inferior courts should have final authority over State courts. The South Carolina jurist said such power would be an encroachment on the States and create obstacles to adoption of the proposed system. Mr. Madison replied that:

> ... unless [national] inferior tribunals were dispersed throughout the Republic, with *final* jurisdiction in *many* cases, appeals would be multiplied to a most oppressive degree; ... A Government without a proper Executive & Judiciary would be the mere trunk of a body without arms or legs to act or move.[7]

Mr. Rutledge prevailed in having deleted the creation of inferior courts by the Executive. Refusing to concede defeat, Mr. Madison offered a resolution that granted the Congress the power to create inferior courts, and it was adopted by a sizable majority.[8]

At the end of today's session, Pierce Butler of South Carolina warned the Convention: "The people will not bear such innovations. The States will revolt at such encroachments."[9] The South Carolina planter clearly fears that State courts will become swallowed up by a new national Judiciary.

Today's session illustrated both a virtue and a vice of the pro-nationalists like Mr. Madison. The virtue is found in their energetic efforts to forge a consensus for a new national government. The vice is that the nationalists are provoking rising fears among the delegates who advocate States' rights, although a Convention majority, up to now, has gone along with the nationalists.[10]

Wednesday, June 6, 1787

In today's edition of the *Pennsylvania Packet*, delegates read a polite but pointed protest against the absolute secrecy of the Convention. The daily newspaper asked whether "it would not be dangerous" to keep closed the channel of information to the people when the Convention was meeting to decide the future "political existence and welfare of the United States."[1]

With heavy rain outside, the delegates debated behind closed doors the part the people should play in electing members to the proposed lower house in the new national Legislature. South Carolina's Charles Cotesworth Pinckney requested that delegates reconsider an earlier proposal that the States, not the people, elect the House. "If the people choose it will have a tendency to destroy the foundation of the State Governments," he said.[2]

James Wilson of Pennsylvania argued that for the government to be legitimate, it must flow from the people at large. "The Legislature ought to be the most exact transcript of the whole Society," Mr. Wilson added.[3]

Roger Sherman of Connecticut lived up to his reputation of cunning when he formulated an argument that could expose any plans of nationalists like Mr. Wilson and Mr. Madison to weaken the power of the States. If the State Governments are to be abolished, Mr. Sherman said, then election to the national Legislature should be by the people. However, if the State Governments are to be continued, then to preserve harmony with the national government the States should elect members to the lower House of the national Legislature.[4]

James Madison of Virginia quickly assured the delegates that the States were "important and necessary objects." At the same time, he added, this Convention was called because States had failed to secure private rights and justice. Then looking at Mr. Sherman, Mr. Madison asked whether republican liberty can long exist under the abuses practiced by some of the States. The remedy is the election of representatives to the lower House by the people, he said. Mr. Madison closed his lengthy speech with these words:

> It [is] incumbent on us then to try this remedy, and with that view to frame a republican system on such a scale & in such a form as will controul the evils wch [which] have been experienced.[5]

Mr. Madison was apparently pleased when the delegates voted 8 to 3 to reject election to the lower House by the State Legislatures.[6]

Mr. Sherman, although defeated, may have forced Mr. Madison to pay a price. Sources tell this correspondent that Mr. Madison came to the Convention committed to radical reduction of the States' powers, believing the States to be the source of many of the country's political ills.[7] Mr. Sherman brought the issue into the open and forced Mr. Madison to deny in public that he was privately intent on stripping the States of their power. Mr. Sherman was unintentionally aided in his efforts when George Read of Delaware bluntly said the States were useless. "A national Govt. must soon of necessity swallow all of them up," Mr. Read added.[8]

Mr. Wilson, an ally of Mr. Madison, was quick to smother the incendiary statement by insisting no incompatibility existed between the national and the State Governments, provided the latter "were restrained to certain local purposes."[9]

However, as one who knows Mr. Sherman said of him: "He is not easily managed, but if he suspects you are trying to take him in, you may as well catch an Eel by the tail."[10]

Thursday June 7, 1787

A share of Federal power was assured the separate States today when the Convention unanimously approved election to the national Senate by the State Legislatures.[1] Yesterday, the small States lost their fight against popular election to the first branch of the proposed national government. Today's vote, allowing States to elect one senator each while the first branch would be elected by the people, set the stage for a bitter struggle over the role the States should play in the new national government.[2]

The architect of today's decision is the only delegate to this Convention who participated in all phases of the American Revolution, from the Stamp Act of 1765 to the present Convention.[3] John Dickinson of Delaware, famous for his eloquent and scholarly writings, drew a parallel between the British House of Lords and the new Senate. Mr. Dickinson told the delegates that election to the Senate branch of the national Legislature by the State Legislatures would ensure men of character, rank and property, as in the British House of Lords.[4] He then lived up to his reputation for eloquence with these words:

> . . . a government thus established would harmonize the whole, and like the planetary system, the national council like the sun, would illuminate the whole—the planets revolving around it in perfect order; or like the union of several small streams, would at last form a respectable river, gently flowing to the sea.[5]

James Wilson of Pennsylvania was hard pressed to compete with such powerful eloquence. Mr. Wilson said dissensions in the new national government would occur if the House were chosen by the people and the Senate by the States.[6] The Scottish-born lawyer specifically denied Mr. Dickinson's charge that he wished to extinguish the States, or planets, instead of allowing them to move freely in their proper orbit. "The British governmt. cannot be our model. . . . Our man-

ners, our laws; ... the whole genius of the people, are
opposed to it," Mr. Wilson replied.[7]

General George Washington may have played a part in the
unanimous approval today of Mr. Dickinson's proposal for the
States to elect senators. A source close to the General reports
that in a breakfast conversation over coffee with a friend, he
asked why the friend poured his coffee in a saucer. "To cool it,"
the friend reportedly answered. General Washington is said
to have replied that the Senate was like a saucer to cool
legislation from the House.[8]

What emerged from today's debate is a novel system that
would use the Senate, elected by the States, to check any
hasty legislative initiatives by the House, elected by the people who might be stampeded by popular passions. A survey of
Convention delegates by this correspondent reveals that the
proposed use of the Senate to check the House is to guard
against what one delegate called "the turbulence and follies of
Democracy."[9]

As Mr. Dickinson told the delegates, one possible solution
to such excesses was to have the States appoint to the national
Senate candidates drawn from the ranks of wealth, prominent families, or talent. By enlarging the numbers in the
Senate, he went on, with the "wealth of the aristocracy, you
establish a balance that will check Democracy" in the House,
which is elected by the people.[10]

Friday, June 8, 1787

Small States openly revolted today over an issue that had
previously produced no disagreement among the delegates,
this correspondent was told.

On May 31 the Convention without dissent or debate authorized the proposed national Congress to veto any laws of the

13 States considered in conflict with the Constitution or with national treaties.[1]

Today, the Convention, after a debate that at times became heated, reversed itself and voted 7 to 3 against giving the new national government veto power over State laws. The eleventh State, Delaware, was divided.[2]

Gunning Bedford of Delaware, in bold but nervous tones bordering on anger,[3] may have spoken for the small States. He warned that a power to veto all State laws could become a weapon in the hands of the large States to crush the "small ones whenever they stand in the way of their ambitions or interested views."[4] Mr. Bedford complained that large States such as Virginia and Pennsylvania could combine to outvote Delaware in the national Legislature, which would give them, in his words, "enormous & monstrous influence."[5]

James Wilson of Pennsylvania insisted the Convention must decide whether the new general Government or the State Governments are to be supreme. He went on,

> We must remember the language with wh[ich] we began the Revolution, it was this, Virginia is no more, Massachusetts is no more—we are one in name, let us be one in Truth & Fact—Unless this power is vested in the Genl Govt., the States will be used by foreign powers as Engines agt[against] the Whole.[6]

Until today the issue of foreign influence had remained unspoken. However, every delegate at this Convention realizes that Great Britain and Spain intend to exploit any disunity. Both powers are convinced the 13 States will never become an effective national union capable of resisting their geographical greed and ambitions.[7]

A source close to Mr. Bedford of Delaware has informed this correspondent that he is willing to use the threat of an alliance with foreign powers if the large States persist in their demands for what he believes is a disproportionate power in the national Congress.[8]

James Madison of Virginia asked the delegates to remember that the States had violated national treaties with foreign powers and repeatedly encroached on the power of the current national Government under the existing Confederation. The proposed congressional veto of all State laws is necessary, Mr. Madison said, if the experience is not to be repeated, " . . . without this the planets [or States] will fly from their orbits," he added.[9]

The seven small and medium States combined against the three votes of the large States to defeat national veto power over State laws. (Delaware remained divided.) In doing so, the stage is now set for what one source told this correspondent is an issue that could split the Convention wide open.

George Read of Delaware on May 30 warned the delegates that unless his State was assured that each State would have an equal vote in the national Congress, it might become the duty of his delegation "to retire from the Convention."[10]

Saturday, June 9, 1787

Like a volley of sudden musket fire, a verbal war of words erupted at today's Convention over the volatile issue of how many votes each State should have in the proposed national Legislature. Until today, delegates on both sides have evaded the issue as if it were a powder barrel ready to explode.[1]

New Jersey delegate William Paterson, speaking for the small States, fired the first volley. In physical stature the smallest of the delegates, the Irish-born lawyer took calm but careful aim at his target: namely, the proposal of nationalists from the large States for proportional representation in the national Congress. The proposal, Mr. Paterson said, was "striking at the existence of the small States," by giving Virginia alone sixteen votes to New Jersey's five and Georgia's one.[2] Besides, the former New Jersey Attorney General added, delegates came to this Convention for the sole purpose of revising the Articles of Confederation. He went on in these words:

> We ought to keep within its limits, or we should be charged by our constituents with usurpation ... the people of America [are] sharpsighted and not to be deceived. ... N[ew] Jersey will never confederate on the plan before the committee. She would be swallowed up. [I would] rather submit to a monarch, to a despot, than to such a fate.[3]

Mr. Paterson's suggestion that some delegates were guilty of deception appeared to anger James Wilson of Pennsylvania. Other delegates appeared stunned as well. Mr. Paterson's words were the most heated that had been spoken up to now.[4] Mr. Wilson of Pennsylvania then added to the emotionally charged debate. He began by insisting that a majority or a minority of States might be free to go off on their own and confederate. But as for the large States, authority from the people as the principle for equality of voting meant different numbers for different representation.

Mr. Wilson, his voice rising and reverberating off the high ceiling of the hall, asked rhetorically whether New Jersey has the same right or influence in the councils as Pennsylvania. "I say no. It is unjust," Mr. Wilson thundered, adding, "I never will confederate on this plan [of State equality]. ... If no State will part with any of its sovereignty, it is in vain to talk of a national government. ..."[5]

Mr. Paterson moved to postpone the inflammatory issue in order to allow delegates a cooling-off period. No doubt exists that as delegates filed out of the State House at the end of today's stormy session, each realized a crisis has arrived.[6] Delegates seem also to realize now that their deliberations might drag on for weeks, even months.[7] Mr. Paterson's speech today represents the first open challenge to the large-State nationalists like Mr. Wilson and Mr. Madison.[8] Behind Mr. Paterson's blistering attack also lies a fundamental fact about his own State: its lack of ports and trade. Granting large States proportional voting power would mean that Virginia, Pennsylvania and Massachusetts would make small New Jersey unequal and politically weak in any territorial expansion or commercial questions arising in the proposed national Congress.[9]

Sunday, June 10, 1787

One or more delegates are alleged to have leaked secret details of this Convention to the French envoy in New York. A diplomatic dispatch written today by French Chargé d'Affaires Otto, a copy having been obtained by this correspondent, informs the Paris monarchy in accurate detail what has transpired during the last two weeks of the closed sessions.[1] The suspected source for the leak is Dr. Benjamin Franklin, who for 11 years was the U.S. envoy to Paris. However, it cannot be confirmed by this correspondent.

The possibility that certain delegates have violated their oath of secrecy has alarmed leaders of the Convention. A source close to General George Washington revealed an incident that illustrates concern over the security of the Convention debates. William Pierce of Georgia informed this correspondent that General Washington became flushed with anger when a delegate handed him a copy of the proceedings that had been dropped by one of the members. According to Mr. Pierce, the General demanded that the delegates be more careful, warning that the newspapers might publish such material and "disturb the public repose" by premature speculation.

The General then angrily threw the paper down on one of the tables saying, "I know not whose Paper it is, but there it is, let him who owns it take it." Mr. Pierce reports that

General Washington bowed, picked up his hat and left the Convention hall "with a dignity so severe that every person seemed alarmed."[2]

No delegate had the courage to pick up the copy.

The incident illustrates the overwhelming influence the General has come to have in this Convention, although he remains silent during the debates.[3] In his secret diplomatic dispatch today, the French envoy Mr. Otto forecast that the Convention will bear "the principal character traits of General Washington" of wisdom, moderation, and far-sightedness.[4]

However, at least one delegate, Luther Martin of Maryland, does not hold the General in such awe. Mr. Martin, who arrived here in Philadelphia yesterday, resents the influence General Washington and Dr. Franklin are having over the Convention. The Attorney General of Maryland made his views known in these words:

> If it was the idea of my state that whatever a Washington or Franklin approved, was to be blindly adopted, she ought to have spared herself the expence of sending any members to the Convention, or to have instructed them implicitly to follow where they [Washington & Franklin] led the way.[5]

Mr. Martin's views are not likely to go down well with his fellow Maryland delegates since a majority of them are friends of the General and approve the reform movement for a national government.[6] Mr. Martin is believed ready to join the revolt of the small States, led by William Paterson of New Jersey who is a close personal friend and college classmate of Mr. Martin's. Sources report that Mr. Paterson, Mr. Martin and delegates from Connecticut and New York may have met secretly today with the Convention in recess to plan opposition strategy to the large States.[7]

The small States have an uphill battle in opposing General Washington. His silent power on the Convention floor is matched, one source reports, by his personal encounters with delegates at social functions in the evenings after each session.[8]

Monday, June 11, 1787

Calls for coolness, conciliation and compromise did little today to move Convention delegates away from a dangerous deadlock over the number of votes each State should have in the proposed national Congress.

Roger Sherman of Connecticut, at 66 tall and lean with craggy facial features,[1] in his flat New England voice offered a compromise. He proposed that votes in the lower house be apportioned on the basis of the number of free inhabitants in the States, while in the Senate each State would have one vote. The proposal, Mr. Sherman added, was similar to the English House of Commons and House of Lords. ". . . the States would remain possessed of certain individual rights . . . otherwise a few large States will rule the rest," he said of his compromise proposal.[2]

However, delegates from the large States were in no mood for the proposal, incidentally first offered by Mr. Sherman ten years ago when the Articles of Confederation were proposed in 1777.[3] Four delegates spoke after Mr. Sherman, ignoring his proposal, each in favor of his own. It was then that James Wilson of Pennsylvania read to the Convention a lengthy speech written by Dr. Franklin. Dr. Franklin told the Convention:

> . . . we are sent here to *consult* not to *contend* with each other; and Declarations of a fixed opinion, and determined resolutions, never to change it, neither enlighten nor convince us . . . Harmony & Union are extremely necessary to give weight to our councils. . . .[4]

Despite his plea, however, by a narrow 6 to 5 vote the large States defeated Mr. Sherman's proposal for the States each to have one vote in the Senate.[5] Then by a similar one-vote margin, delegates approved proportional representation in both the House and the Senate.[6] The narrow votes seem to illustrate a deadlock between the small and the large States. Also, States with vast western lands on their borders have decided to cast their votes with the large States.[7]

James Wilson of Pennsylvania, in an apparent move to keep the smaller Southern States on the side of the large States, offered and had approved a proposal that allows States to include their slaves in computing population as a basis for representation. In April 1783 the Congress of the Confederation had adopted this measure of computation: the whole of the white population and other free citizens would be counted, with each slave measured as only three-fifths of a person.[8]

Mr. Wilson and other large State nationalists appear to have beaten back the rebellion of the small States, since they have secured tentative approval for election to both the national House and Senate in proportion to the population of the respective States. However, an informed source has told this correspondent that the rebellion of the small States may just be starting.[9]

Roger Sherman of Connecticut, the most seasoned and experienced legislator of all the delegates at this Convention, has lived by this brief motto: "When you are in a minority, talk; when you are in the majority, vote."[10]

Clearly the small States have not lost their voice just because they have lost one battle.

Tuesday, June 12, 1787

Today's Convention session resembled a ship caught in the eye of a storm; becalmed at the center while in every direction in the distance one can see the approach of angry storm clouds as the delegates chose to keep their own counsel.

The 11 States present were called on today to cast their votes on 15 different propositions,[1] the largest number of ballots cast since the Convention opened. Among other proposals, delegates approved a method of ratification of the proposed national government by State conventions, and approved the term, qualifications and eligibility to office of members of the proposed national Congress.[2] All 15 items were disposed of with such speed and general agreement that today's session gave the appearance that the momentum of the large States has not been slowed by the small States' opposition.

A clash between two delegates today suggested, however, that this Convention may sit much longer than anyone anticipates. James Madison of Virginia warned the delegates that unless a republican government is held out to the people they might, in despair, incline toward a monarchy. Elbridge Gerry of Massachusetts stiffly replied that he could not be governed by the prejudices of the people. "Perhaps a limited monarchy would be the best government, if we could organize it by creating a house of peers [Lords]; but that cannot be done," he added with an air of disappointment.[3]

At least one delegation, North Carolina, realizes that the Convention is likely to extend into July and perhaps even August. North Carolina delegate R.D. Spaight just today requested from the Governor of his State an advance on his salary by two months.[4] Also, the entire North Carolina delegation has drafted a letter to their Governor, stating in part:

> ... it is not possible for us to determine when the business before us can be finished, a very large Field presents to our

view without a single Straight or eligible Road that has been
trodden by the feet of Nations. . . . Several Members of the
Convention have their Wives here and other Gentlemen have
sent for theirs. This Seems to promise a Summer's Campaign.[5]

One delegate who recently sent for his wife is Virginia
Governor Edmund Randolph. Six days ago he wrote home
saying he expected "a very long" convention and asked his
family to make the difficult and expensive journey to Philadelphia.[6]

Delegates these last two weeks have been debating the 15
Randolph Resolutions the Governor introduced on May 29 for
a new and strong central government. As the debate has
progressed, however, Governor Randolph seems to have more
and more come to disagree with critical parts of the plan he
initially approved and introduced—but reportedly written by
James Madison.

Mr. Madison appeared stunned when Mr. Randolph suggested that preservation of the States was more important
than the Union.[7]

In today's debate, Governor Randolph must have given Mr.
Madison even greater worry when he attacked the whole idea
of participation in the new government by the people, warning about "Democratic licentiousness" and "demagogues of
the popular branch."[8]

Chosen as captain to launch proposals for the new national
ship of state, Mr. Randolph is indicating a tendency to want to
abandon ship. He may also be proving correct one observer
who has said in private that Mr. Randolph suffers from only
one flaw: " . . . an instability of conduct and opinion resulting
not from moral but [from] intellectual causes."[9]

Wednesday, June 13, 1787

The Convention of 11 States reached a crossroads today when
the Virginia Plan for a new national government, debated
item by item and modified by resolutions over the last two
weeks, was read in its entirety to delegates.[1] The original 15
resolutions submitted by Virginia Governor Edmund Randolph have now been enlarged to 19 items, which differ in a
large degree from the Articles of Confederation now in existence.[2]

A source close to the Convention told this correspondent
that the delegates have come a long way in a short time in
forging a consensus for a new national government.[3] The
Virginia delegation, and particularly James Madison, is
reported pleased at what appears to be a general endorsement of the 19 Resolutions read to the delegates today. The
Virginia Plan is reported to be a more comprehensive
endorsement of the nationalist proposals than either Mr.
Madison or James Wilson of Pennsylvania had expected two,
even three, weeks ago when the Convention began.[4]

However, an informed source cautioned that the Virginia
Plan remains only a roadmap for the delegates; there are
political signposts that the Convention may still have a difficult journey ahead.[5] Mr. Madison may have given an indication that the consensus of the delegates is as thin as egg shells
that could crack under pressure. The floor leader for the
nationalists reported today that, rather than call for a vote on
his 19-point plan now before the Convention, he has postponed it until tomorrow, as Mr. Madison put it, "to give an
opportunity for other plans to be proposed."[6]

What he meant by "other plans" was not made clear. But
unconfirmed reports circulating around the State House indicate that the small States may be on the verge of putting forth
their own set of proposals as a rival to the Virginia Plan. A
reliable source has told this correspondent that the small
States have secretly met over the last few days and drafted a

series of resolutions that they plan to present to the Convention.[7] The leader of this group of small States is believed to be William Paterson of New Jersey. Mr. Paterson four days ago shattered the calm of the Convention with a series of verbal broadsides against the Virginia Plan. Here in part is what he told the stunned delegates:

> . . . the basis of our present authority is founded on a revision of the articles of the present confederation, and to alter or amend them in such parts where they may appear defective. Can we on this ground form a national government? I fancy not. . . .
>
> We are met here as the deputies of 13 independent, sovereign states, for federal purposes. Can we consolidate their sovereignty and form one nation, and annihilate the sovereignties of our states who have sent us here for other purposes? . . . I will never consent to the present system, and I shall make all the interest against it in the state which I represent that I can. Myself or my state will never submit to tyranny or despotism.[8]

The passionate opposition of Mr. Paterson is explained by a source who knows him well. While Mr. Madison and Mr. Wilson have built their political reputations in the Continental Congress, Mr. Paterson's entire career has been in the service of his State. When he was New Jersey attorney general, for example, he was reported to have expended great effort to reinforce the people's faith in local government. Seen from his viewpoint, the Virginia Resolutions would write New Jersey out of existence and with it his life's work. Mr. Paterson is known to believe that rapid changes in society and government present a threat to stability and order.[9]

Thursday, June 14, 1787

William Paterson of New Jersey turned up the political heat inside the Convention hall today, matching the growing hot weather outside the State House here in Philadelphia.

The diminutive Mr. Paterson was first on his feet today, proposing and receiving postponement of a vote on the Virginia Plan for a new national government. Mr. Paterson told the delegates that New Jersey and other small States wanted time to study the 19-point proposal of the large State nationalists and to put forth a plan "materially different from the system now under consideration."[1]

The large States have dominated the debate, and now it is the turn of the small States to present a counterproposal, being increasingly unhappy with the implications of the Virginia Plan. Virginia's Edmund Randolph immediately seconded the motion and the Convention unanimously concurred, for the large States do not intend to ram through a plan, and the Convention rules calling for a debate will be followed.

A source close to the Convention has concluded that today's development means that every delegate here is aware that a new chapter may have opened in the deliberations of this political conclave.[2] The proposed national government put forth by the nationalist large States has filled the small States with fear, some reported "aghast" at the powers that advocates such as Mr. Madison would confer on a national government.[3] Delegates from New Jersey, Connecticut, New York and Maryland oppose the new national government because it is a radical, if not revolutionary, departure from the current Articles of Confederation. Other States, such as Delaware, oppose the new government unless it guarantees the principle of equal representation of the States in the proposed national Congress.[4]

John Dickinson of Delaware castigated Mr. Madison for misjudging the mood of the small States in these words:

You see the consequence of pushing things too far. Some of the members from the small States wish for two branches in the General Legislature, and are friends to a good National Government; but we would sooner submit to a foreign power, than submit to be deprived of an equality of suffrage, in both branches of the legislature, and thereby be thrown under the domination of the large States.[5]

There is an irony in Mr. Dickinson's angry words. Only twelve days ago he is reliably reported to have told Dr. Benjamin Rush, a prominent Philadelphia physician, that the Convention delegates "are all *united* in their objects and he expects they will be equally united in the means of attaining them."[6]

Mr. Madison also appears guilty of over-optimism. In a letter written eight days ago to Thomas Jefferson in Paris, a copy having been obtained by this correspondent, Mr. Madison said: ". . . it is possible that caprice if no other motive may yet produce a unanimity of the States in this experiment."[7]

This Convention has now agreed to consider not one but two plans for a new national government. But a third plan put forth by South Carolina's Charles Pinckney III was presented over two weeks ago and has been ignored by the Convention. The unanimous agreement of the delegates today to consider a plan by Mr. Paterson has reportedly made Mr. Pinckney upset with everyone, whether from a small or a large State.[8]

Friday, June 15, 1787

New Jersey delegate William Paterson placed before the Convention today a nine-point proposal that would revise the existing Articles of Confederation.[1] The proposal serves as an alternative to the Virginia Plan which would sweep the

Articles into the ashbin of history. "No government could be energetic on paper only, which was no more than straw," Mr. Paterson said of both plans.[2]

Viewed side by side, the plans are sharp if not stark in contrast. John Lansing of New York told the delegates today that Mr. Paterson's plan preserves the existing federal government of the States, while the plan presented by Mr. Randolph is a national government that would destroy the States. He later went on to draw a comparison between the two plans in terms of political power:

> ... the plan of Mr. R.[andolph] in short absorbs all power except what may be exercised in the little local matters of the States. ... N. York would never have concurred in sending deputies to the convention, if she had supposed the deliberations were to turn on a consolidation of the States, and a National Government.[3]

Alexander Hamilton of New York, who has been at odds with fellow New York delegates Mr. Lansing and Robert Yates ever since the Convention got under way, said he does not favor either the New Jersey Plan or the Virginia Plan.[4] In taking such a position, Colonel Hamilton, who helped engineer this Convention into existence, has placed himself in the position of a political orphan; he is now an outsider who had hoped to influence the Convention at large.[5]

The nine-point proposal presented today by Mr. Paterson is reported by a source as not of his own creation. Rather, the New Jersey Plan, as it is now being termed, is believed to be the creation of a committee of delegates from several States.[6] Observers believe the plan suffers from several critical flaws: too little, too late, too feeble and too contradicting.

Supporters of the New Jersey Plan are united only by their opposition to the Virginia Plan put forth by the large States.[7] Advocates of the Virginia Plan have also had the strategic advantage of time for preparation and plotting for strategy before introducing it. A source close to the Convention told this correspondent that had the New Jersey and the Virginia Plans been introduced together, the sharp contrasts might have forced the delegates to choose the New Jersey proposal. The large States have dominated the debates during the last three weeks, during which time the delegates have become accustomed to the revolutionary proposals for a new national government.[8]

It is reliably reported that Mr. Paterson is privately convinced that his nine-point plan has little chance of being adopted. It is understood that his strategy is to use the proposal as leverage to force the large States to give ground and concede equality of representation for the States.[9]

William Pierce of Georgia has said that while Mr. Paterson's five-foot-two frame does not convey any great talents, he chooses the "time and manner of engaging in a debate, and never speaks but when he understands his subject well."[10]

Saturday, June 16, 1787

Verbal thunderbolts electrified the Convention today when the debate between the small and the large States was directly and dramatically joined over the New Jersey and the Virginia Plans.[1]

William Paterson of New Jersey made two essential points to the delegates. First, the New Jersey Plan "sustains the sovereignty of the respective States" while the Virginia Plan destroys it. Second, his proposal reforms the Articles of Confederation in accord with the original mandate given the Convention delegates and favored by the people.

"... If the confederacy [is] radically wrong, let us return to our States, and obtain larger powers, not assume them of ourselves," Mr. Paterson said of those delegates who have proposed going beyond reform of the Articles to creating a new national government.[2]

James Wilson of Pennsylvania rose to his feet in rebuttal, subjecting both plans to a point-by-point comparison. As to the assertion that the Convention lacks the power to do anything but reform the Articles, the owlish-appearing Pennsylvanian said the delegates are authorized "to conclude nothing" but are at liberty "to propose anything."[3] Mr. Wilson also aimed a verbal arrow at the Achilles' heel of the New Jersey Plan, pointing out that it cannot be approved unless Rhode Island, absent from the start of this Convention, gives its assent.[4] (The Articles of Confederation require that any changes must be approved by all 13 States.)

Mr. Wilson then went on to make this point:

> . . . the people expect relief from their present embarrassed situation and look up for it to this national convention; and it follows that they expect a *national government*, and therefore the plan for Virginia has preference to the other. . . .[5]

John Lansing of New York, a 33-year-old lawyer and experienced State legislator,[6] argued that great changes can only be introduced gradually. Otherwise, Mr. Lansing said, the people will become confused and uncertain with the Virginia Plan, which is not only "novel" but without parallel. "The States will never sacrifice their essential rights to a national government," he grimly warned.[7]

Virginia Governor Edmund Randolph had his own dark warnings to offer. If the New Jersey Plan were adopted, he said, it would repeat "the imbecility of the existing confederacy" when the States encroached on the national Congress and left the country exposed to foreign intrigue. The Virginia Governor added that France remains unpaid for its support as do American officers and soldiers who fought for independence. This debt is a matter of gratitude and honor, and the bravery of the American troops is degraded by the weakness of the government, he suggested. "When the salvation of the

Republic [is] at stake, it would be treason to our trust, not to propose what we found necessary," Governor Randolph said, his words rolling over the Convention like thunder.[8]

Today's stormy and electrically charged debate was made supremely ironic by what today's *Gazetteer* reported. Apparently some delegates fear that the people would despair if they knew the degree of disagreement among the delegates and they leaked to the *Gazetteer* a fabrication. For the *Gazetteer* reported: "We hear that the greatest unanimity subsists in the Councils of the Federal Convention."[9]

Sunday, June 17, 1787

Convention President George Washington is reliably reported to be increasingly dismayed and even disgusted over the deadlock that has developed in the last two weeks between the small and the large States.[1] It is not clear whether his attendance today at church and an eight-mile carriage ride into the country to have dinner with friends did anything to abate his anger and frustration.[2]

Colonel Alexander Hamilton of New York, a former military aide to the General, is reported to be similarly frustrated. This correspondent has been told that Colonel Hamilton believes that the New Jersey and Virginia Plans now before the Convention, in recess today, are far too timid. Sources here say that Colonel Hamilton has prepared his own plan and may offer it as early as tomorrow.[3]

The handsome New York political leader has been one of the major forces that has brought this Convention into being. However, he is reported to have been frustrated by fellow New York delegates John Lansing and Robert Yates. Both have generally sided with the small States, ensuring that Colonel Hamilton's vote in the Convention would not count on crucial issues.[4] Compounding Colonel Hamilton's political problems is the fact that both Mr. Lansing and Mr. Yates are close personal friends and political allies of New York Governor George Clinton. He sent both delegates here to do nothing more than revise the Articles of Confederation.[5]

Colonel Hamilton has made it clear in the few times he has spoken that he favors scrapping the Articles. His personality and approach may be a contributing factor to his isolated role at this Convention. "He has a little too much ambition and too little prudence," the French diplomatic envoy in New York is reported to have written recently of Colonel Hamilton.[6]

Georgia delegate William Pierce is slightly more polite:

> Colonel Hamilton is deservedly celebrated for his talents. He is a practitioner of the Law, and reputed to be a finished Scholar. ... He is about 33 years old, of small stature, and lean. His manners are tinctured with stiffness, and sometimes with a degree of vanity that is highly disagreeable.[7]

It is believed to be Colonel Hamilton's vanity that has caused a temporary rupture in his relationship with General Washington. However, the General himself is not the easiest person to know, as illustrated by an incident revealed to this correspondent that took place at a social affair.

Pennsylvania delegate Gouverneur Morris, who wears a wooden leg and has a reputation for boldness, was certain he had the best of an argument with Colonel Hamilton. Thinking he had broken through the famous frosty reserve of General Washington, since they were close friends, he slapped the General on his back in front of a group of dinner guests, exclaiming, "Ain't I right, General?" regarding his discussion with Colonel Hamilton. Mr. Morris later reported: "The [General] did not speak, but the majesty of the American people was before me. Oh, his look! How I wished the floor would open and I could descend to the cellar! ... my eye would never quail before any other mortal."[8]

Monday, June 18, 1787

The Philadelphia State House today was the scene of one of the most puzzling performances by a delegate since this Convention opened three weeks ago.[1]

Colonel Alexander Hamilton of New York effectively committed political suicide today when during a four-hour speech he put forth an 11-point proposal so radical that it was received with silence rather than rebuttal. The cool reception of both small and large States to his proposals was a contrast to the fearfully hot weather outside.[2] The lengthy speech by the handsome and impeccably dressed New York delegate, who has married into a wealthy family, proved to be such a disturbing surprise to the delegates that it was neither referred to a committee nor seconded by any delegate for later Convention debate.[3]

Colonel Hamilton's speech was without a doubt the product of extensive preparation and deliberation.[4] After a lengthy historical and philosophical explanation why the country needs a powerful central government, Colonel Hamilton said he is opposed to both plans now before the Convention.[5] In their place he proposed: a two-house Congress to pass all laws; a Senate and president elected for life; and that Governors of the States, appointed by a national government, have veto power over their respective State laws.[6] He then told the delegates:

> I confess that this plan and that from Virginia are very remote from the idea of the people. Perhaps the Jersey plan is nearest their expectation. But the people are gradually ripening in their opinions of government—they begin to be tired of an excess of democracy—and what even is the Virginia plan, but *pork still, with a little change of the sauce.*[7]

James Madison of Virginia is reliably reported by one delegate as saying that he did not relish Colonel Hamilton's gastronomical metaphor and was planning a verbal vindication of the Virginia Plan.[8]

The cynical Gouverneur Morris of Pennsylvania is reported to have said that Colonel Hamilton's speech was one of the most able and impressive he had ever heard.[9]

Dr. William Samuel Johnson of Connecticut, who has been silent so far, may have summarized the impact of Colonel Hamilton on the delegates. Dr. Johnson said: ". . . he has been praised by every body, he has been supported by none."[10]

For just what reasons the large and small States interrupted their heated debate over the New Jersey and Virginia Plans and gave the entire day over to Colonel Hamilton, remains a mystery. What he hoped to accomplish also remains a political puzzle. One observer close to the Convention told this correspondent that the delegates may have wanted a chance to catch their breath, thus the reason for giving over the floor to the New York delegate. But certainly Colonel Hamilton's speech and his proposals rank as an "unreal interlude" in the struggle for power between the small and the large States.[11]

For example, Colonel Hamilton won few friends today when he told the delegates that the British government "was the best in the world" and he doubted "any thing short of it would do in America."[12]

Tuesday, June 19, 1787

The obituary of the Articles of Confederation may have been agreed upon today by a majority of States at this Convention.

Virginia's James Madison, in a long and what one observer maintains was a masterly speech,[1] subjected the New Jersey Plan of the small States to a point-by-point verbal demolition. Using the deaths of the ancient confederacies as his anvil and the perceived failures of the current Articles as his hammer, Mr. Madison pounded away at the New Jersey proposals for reforming the current Confederation of 13 States. The concept of confederacies, Mr. Madison said, "was the cobweb wch[which] could entangle the weak" and could become "the sport of the strong."[2] He then went on to say:

> It is evident, if we do not *radically* depart from a federal plan [of States], we shall share the fate of ancient and modern confederacies. The amphictyonic [ancient Greek] council, like the American congress, had the power of judging in the *last resort* in war and peace. . . . what was its fate or continuance? Philip of Macedon, with little difficulty, destroyed every appearance of it.[3]

At the conclusion of Mr. Madison's speech, Rufus King of Massachusetts proposed that the New Jersey Plan be buried and the Virginia Plan for a new national government become the sole concern of the Convention.[4] Seven States agreed, three opposed, with one State (Maryland) divided. The failure of the supporters of the New Jersey Plan to rise in rebuttal to Mr. Madison today was a mute tribute to the effective death blow he delivered to their hopes.[5] In killing the New Jersey Plan, delegates on both sides have also acknowledged that the Articles of Confederation is a dead letter document.[6]

However, the small States have indicated they are far from defeated. A source has told this correspondent that the small States believe that while they do not have the strength to prevail, neither do the large ones have the votes to pass the Virginia Plan as currently constituted.[7] John Lansing of New York, an ardent supporter of the small States, is reported to have said after today's defeat that the strategy now is for the States' rights group to gain enough strength to deadlock the Convention in order to wrest a compromise from the nationalists.[8]

James Wilson of Pennsylvania went out of his way to assure the delegates that it was not desirable to destroy the State

Governments. Mr. Wilson also seems to have suggested a partnership between the States and the proposed national government by his historical references. "In all extensive empires a subdivision of power is necessary," Mr. Wilson said, adding that "Persia, Turkey and Rome, under its emperors, are examples in point."[9]

Mr. Wilson also said, borrowing a sea phrase, he was "for taking a new departure, and I wish to consider in what direction we sail, and what may be the end of our voyage."[10]

Mr. Wilson may have been expressing out loud what many delegates have been thinking. This Convention has been in session for almost four weeks and some delegates are beginning to wonder whether they are aboard a ship that has charted a course in circles.

Wednesday, June 20, 1787

A growing concern is coursing through this Convention that a dangerous impasse is developing that, if not broken by compromise, could lead to the break up of this political conclave.[1]

Connecticut's Oliver Ellsworth, a 37-year-old State Superior Court judge,[2] issued a warning during today's session. Mr. Ellsworth said it would be "highly dangerous" not to consider the Articles of Confederation still in effect, and insisted that any plan sent to the States must be as proposed amendments to the Articles.[3] Mr. Ellsworth appeared unmoved by the defeat yesterday of the New Jersey Plan, that scuttled any hope of the small States that this Convention would settle for amending the Articles.

In an apparent effort to soften the blow of yesterday's defeat, the Convention today agreed to a motion by Mr. Ellsworth that the word "national" be dropped from the Virginia Plan. In its place, "the United States" is to be used to describe the proposed national government.[4] The words "united States" appear in the Articles of Confederation, but the change in the Virginia Plan does nothing to alter the national nature of that proposal, which is opposed by Mr. Ellsworth and others.[5] The change is a compromise in style, not in substance.

Roger Sherman of Connecticut suggested a way out of the current impasse when he renewed his proposal that representation in the proposed national Congress be split. The House would have proportional representation as demanded by the nationalists, while in the Senate the States would have an equal vote. Then alluding to the equality of votes in the Continental Congress, Mr. Sherman went on to point out that during the War of Independence the single branch Continental Congress carried the States through the conflict. He noted:

> ... we were crowned with success. We closed the war, performing all the functions of a good government, by making a beneficial peace. But the great difficulty now is, how shall we pay the public debt incurred during that war. The unwillingness of the states to comply with the requisitions of congress, has embarrassed us greatly.[6]

James Wilson of Pennsylvania rejected Mr. Sherman's argument, insisting that it was not the Continental Congress that carried the country to success during the war, but other causes. Mr. Wilson then skillfully drew silent General George Washington into the debate. "That powers were wanting, you, Mr. President, must have felt," Mr. Wilson said, turning to the General.[7] Every delegate is aware of the endless frustrations General Washington endured at the hands of the feeble and quarrelsome Continental Congress during the War of Independence.[8]

Colonel George Mason of Virginia sought to calm the political passions of both sides with words counseling conciliation. "If we mean the good of the whole, . . . our good sense upon reflection, will prevent us from spreading our discontent further," he said.[9] Nevertheless, Colonel Mason demonstrated some discontent of his own that may have disturbed his fellow Virginia delegates. He was worried, he said, that too much power was being proposed for the new national government. "I will never consent to destroy state governments," he warned.[10]

Thursday, June 21, 1787

The tone and tenor of delegate debate today underwent a sharp swing from confrontation to conciliation, as both sides agreed to disagree with polite reason rather than inflammatory rhetoric.[1]

The highly respected lawyer and religious leader, Connecticut delegate William Samuel Johnson, asked the delegates whether it were not possible for the Convention to harmonize the individuality of the States with the goals and objectives of the proposed national government.[2] Dr. Johnson said the question was whether the advocates of the national government could demonstrate that "individuality of the States would not be endangered" without giving them an equal vote in the national congress by which to defend themselves.[3]

James Wilson of Pennsylvania, who went out of his way to express his respect for Dr. Johnson, then turned the argument on its head. "How can the national government be secured against the states? Some regulation is necessary,"[4] he said. By defining and designating the powers of each, he added, no danger would come to States' rights. Besides, the Scottish-born lawyer went on, under the Virginia Plan, as it now stood, the States had the right to appoint representatives to the national Senate, providing "an opportunity of defending their rights."[5]

James Madison of Virginia pointedly asked whether the State governments ever encroached on the corporate rights of their citizens. He insisted that the relationship between the States and the national government would be similar to that of States with their cities. He then went on to say:

> I could have wished that the gentleman from Connecticut had more accurately marked his objections to the Virginia plan. I apprehended the greatest danger is from the encroachment of the states on the national government— This apprehension is justly founded on the experience of the ancient confederacies, and our own is a proof of it.[6]

It is significant that both Mr. Wilson and Mr. Madison chose to confront the Connecticut delegation directly. That small State has come to play a leading role in the Convention, principally because of the brilliance of its three delegates. Dr. William Samuel Johnson, Oliver Ellsworth and Roger Sherman all favor a balance between the rights of the States and the need for a new national government with prescribed powers. Connecticut has come to command the leadership role of New England, formerly held by Massachusetts in earlier congresses.[7]

The strategy of the small States, presumably devised by Connecticut, is to contest every element of the Virginia Plan in an effort to modify its impact. Today, for example, this correspondent has learned, the Convention voted to reduce the term of office for House members from three to two years. And the Senate term was reduced from seven to six years.[8] This was clearly a defeat for Mr. Madison who favored a nine-year term. He argued for longer terms for two reasons: the time elected lawmakers would need to learn the craft of government, and the great distances they have to travel from their States.[9]

Several factors contributing to the ineffectiveness of the Continental Congress are the great distances State representatives must travel, and the snail's pace of transmitting written communications to their respective Governors and Legislatures.[10]

Friday, June 22, 1787

Alarm spread through the ranks of the large States today when it was proposed that the members of the national congress be paid for their services by their respective States.

Oliver Ellsworth of Connecticut made the potentially explosive suggestion when the Convention took up the question of whether elected national lawmakers should receive "fixed stipends to be paid out of the Nationl Treasury."[1] Judge Ellsworth insisted that the style of living and incomes were different in each State. Since the number of lawmakers in the national Congress would be determined by population, he added, the small States would have less of a financial burden than the larger ones.[2] The point was a sharp reminder to the nationalists of the intense opposition the small States have for the makeup of both houses of Congress on the basis of population. The proposal appears to be a political device to unnerve the nationalists and seems to have succeeded, this correspondent has learned.

Virginia Governor Edmund Randolph insisted in intense language that salaries should be paid out of the National Treasury. "If the states were to pay the members of the Natl. [national] Legislature, a dependence would be created that would vitiate the whole System," Governor Randolph said.[3] James Wilson of Pennsylvania and James Madison of Virginia both agreed, insisting that if the States held the exclusive power to pay elected lawmakers, the national Legislature would be thrown entirely "into the hands of the States" and "ruin the fabric"[4] of the entire Virginia Plan for a national government. Colonel Alexander Hamilton of New York added to the verbal volley of the nationalist opposition:

> A state government will ever be the rival power of the general government. It is therefore highly improper that the state legislatures should be the paymasters of the members of the national government. All political bodies love power, and it will often be improperly attained.[5]

Judge Ellsworth answered that his State did not trust the proposed general government and the extensive powers it may assume. The States would not adopt such a government, he warned. ". . . let it ever be remembered, that without their approbation your government is nothing more than a rope of sand," he added with a ringing defiance.[6]

Mr. Wilson was equally defiant, suggesting that it would not be the State Legislatures that would decide the fate of a national government, but the State ratifying conventions composed of the people.[7] However, when the delegates voted as to whether salaries should be paid out of the National Treasury, the proposal was defeated five States to four, with two divided.[8] The splintered close vote indicates that the small States have developed a determined and united strategy against the large States.[9]

As this correspondent reported yesterday, the author of the small States strategy appears to be Roger Sherman of Connecticut, with the help of his two fellow delegates. Each appears to be taking turns contesting specific points of the Virginia Plan. Mr. Wilson of Pennsylvania and Mr. Madison of Virginia, for all their scholarly learning, appear to be having difficulty matching the self-educated Mr. Sherman's talent for tying up the Convention with talk.

Saturday, June 23, 1787

Convention debate today picked up where the delegates had left off yesterday, moving in circles over how to prevent corruption of the proposed national Congress. The issue was confronted as though wrestling with drifting heat waves.

Yesterday Colonel Alexander Hamilton of New York took exception with those delegates who held up the British parliamentary system as an example of corruption. Their example contained a few truths and much falsehood. He said, corruption is inherent in man, not in institutions, adding,

> One great error is that we suppose mankind more honest than they are. Our prevailing passions are ambition and interest; and it will ever be the duty of a wise government to avail itself of those passions, in order to make them subservient to the public good. . . .[1]

During today's session, the corruption issue was again taken up in debate, after the large States lost the vote barring State officeholders from seeking national office.[2]

James Madison then proposed that national legislators be prohibited from accepting federal offices for a year after their term expired,[3] thus avoiding to a large extent venality and use of friendships within the Congress.[4] Major Pierce Butler of South Carolina insisted that even this proposal did not go far enough. The corrupt conduct of King George III, he said, involved bribing his opponents with pensions and appointments to the House of Lords in order to remove them from the House of Commons. It is unwise to entrust persons with power, for abuse operates to the advantage of those entrusted with it, the Southern planter added.[5]

Elbridge Gerry of Massachusetts believes that officeholders might well be influenced by the Executive and look up to him for appointments.[6]

Colonel Mason of Virginia cited the "shameful" practice in his own State of appointments by the Legislature. Efforts at checking such corruption, he went on, proved to be no check at all. "If we do not provide against corruption, our government will soon be at an end," the 61-year-old statesman said.[7]

Mr. Madison pointed out that reluctance of the best citizens of his native Virginia to serve in public office allowed men of unfit character to rise to power.[8] "My wish is that the national legislature be as uncorrupt as possible," Mr. Madison stated.[9] When the vote was taken, Mr. Madison's proposal for a year's compensation after an expired term suffered a crushing 8 to 2 defeat, with one State divided.[10]

Rufus King of Massachusetts, clearly irritated at the dead end nature of the debate, insisted that too much was being made of the corruption issue and the Convention was running the risk of doing more harm than good. "We refine . . . too much—nor is it possible that we can eradicate the evil," he claimed.[11]

Today's debate clearly illustrates a division between those delegates who believe that corruption is inherent in man and those who believe it can be managed or curbed by government law. Such a debate has been going on among philosophers in England and France for decades. Nevertheless, the delegates are influenced by the ideas of public talents and virtue based on classical principles.[12]

Sunday, June 24, 1787

After 25 separate sessions, some lasting up to six hours, a few delegates are beginning to express the belief that this Convention is approaching a deadlock. Yesterday's session, devoted to preventing corruption in the national Legislature, was, in the final analysis, an evasion of the central issue deadlocking the delegates: namely, equal versus proportional representation in the proposed national Legislature.

This correspondent has been informed by one observer that
frustration has grown so great some delegates are privately
talking of quitting and going home.[1] Several, for reasons of
health, family and business, have already departed. Rufus
King of Massachusetts has, in the last week, expressed irritation that the New Hampshire delegation has failed to take its
seat at the Convention.[2] Unlike Rhode Island, which has flatly
refused to attend, New Hampshire has failed to send its
delegates because it could not, or would not, pay travel
expenses.[3] It is a critical question what effect two additional
States at this Convention might have on the current deadlock
between the large and small States.

The Convention was in recess today, providing delegates
some relief from the spell of hot, muggy weather that hangs
over Philadelphia like a stifling blanket. The weather has
added to general delegate discontent.[4] To make matters
worse, the windows of the State House during the current
heat wave are shut to safeguard the secrecy of the debates
and to keep out the flies and noise. Northern delegates swel-
ter and suffer in their woolen suits. Only the Southern delegates, in their lighter clothing, are dressed to endure the
lifeless air inside the State House.[5] Early during the Convention, the rumbling of carts on Chestnut Street proved to be so
distracting to the delegates, earth was ordered spread on the
cobblestone streets to muffle the sound.[6]

When the debates resume tomorrow, South Carolina's
Charles Pinckney III is expected to deliver a major speech.
An advance text obtained by this correspondent reveals that
one of the Convention's youngest delegates will argue that the
Convention must cease trying to frame a national government
on the British model. Mr. Pinckney will argue instead that
the Convention must create a new national government
uniquely American:

> . . . we cannot draw any useful lessons from the examples of
> any of the European states or kingdoms; much less can Great

Britain afford us any striking institution, which can be adapted to our own situation—unless we indeed intend to establish an hereditary executive, or one for life.[7]

Ever since this Convention began, the youthful and ambitious Mr. Pinckney has struggled without much success to get his fellow delegates to take him seriously. One observer believes that his speech is likely to suffer the same fate, although he may cause some to think more about what it means to be Americans instead of former subjects of Great Britain.[8]

Observers who have read Mr. Pinckney's speech are somewhat puzzled by one of his statements. As a large plantation owner with hundreds of slaves, he insists in his speech: "I lay it therefore down as a settled principle, that equality of condition is a leading axiom in our government."[9]

Monday, June 25, 1787

The large States of Virginia, Pennsylvania and Massachusetts were charged today with proposing a single national government although these largest States have proved "Worst Governed."[1]

Oliver Ellsworth of Connecticut was the small States' point man today, delivering up that indictment at today's Convention session as delegates vainly sought to wrestle with the question of composition of a national Senate.

James Wilson of Pennsylvania had provoked Mr. Ellsworth by opposing election by the State Legislatures. Mr. Wilson insists that individuals in the national government will lay aside their State connections and act for the general good of the whole. "We must forget our local habits and attachments. The general government should not depend on the state governments," Mr. Wilson added.[2]

His motion to reverse an earlier vote for election of the Senate by the State Legislatures, and have elections by the people of the *United States*, did not even summon a second.[3]

Judge Ellsworth, in replying to Mr. Wilson, said that every state has its particular views and prejudices. Without their cooperation, he went on, it would be impossible to support a national republican government over so vast a geographical area as America. Virginia has been obliged to concede her inability to extend her government to the Kentucky territory. Massachusetts cannot keep the peace 100 miles from her own capital, Judge Ellsworth added, referring to the violent disorders over the last ten months that have troubled many delegates. He then went on:

> If the principles & materials of our Govt. are not adequate to the extent of these single States; how can it be imagined that they can support a single Govt. throughout U. States. The only chance of supporting a Genl. Govt. lies in engrafting it on that of the individual States.[4]

James Madison of Virginia sought to postpone the issue but was defeated. The Convention then went on to reaffirm by 9 to 2 election of the Senate by the State Legislatures.[5] Mr. Madison and Mr. Wilson may now realize that election of the Senate by the States is a stepping stone for equal State representation,[6] as demanded by the small States.

Underlying today's debates is the unresolved question of whether the Senate is to be based on proportional or equal representation.

Mr. Wilson appealed to the delegates to realize that their labors were like laying the foundation of a building "which is to last for ages, and in which millions are interested."[7] However, while the Pennsylvania lawyer has his eye on the future, a majority of the delegates are concerned about the past and present political relationships among the separate States. Mr. Wilson's arguing for the surrender of such relationships, in the name of the common good, is viewed as both unrealistic and impractical.

Judge Ellsworth may have dealt the most telling blow to Mr. Wilson's argument today when he implied that election by the people at large is a "perfect *utopian* scheme," when what are needed are wisdom and firmness.[8]

Tuesday, June 26, 1787

Concern over political conflicts between the wealthy and the poor surfaced for the first time today, raising the question of whether disagreements about the proposed national government are more social than political.

A majority of State delegates today approved a six-year term for members of the proposed national Senate, a third subject to rotation every two years.[1] Earlier, the Convention set 30 as a minimum age requirement for serving in the Senate[2] and age 25 for House members, and a two-year term for the House.[3]

James Madison of Virginia argued unsuccessfully for a nine-year Senate term in today's debate. A longer term in the Senate, composed of the higher classes appointed by the State Legislatures, Mr. Madison insisted, would act as a check against power sliding into the hands of the poor represented in the lower House and who may err from popular passions of the moment. The danger of a conflict of different interests between economic classes in the future was clearly possible, he warned. "In framing a system which we wish to last for ages, we shd[should] not lose sight of the changes which ages will produce," he added.[4]

The scholarly son of a wealthy Virginia planter was answered by a former poor shoemaker. The self-educated

Roger Sherman of Connecticut said he favored four- or six-year terms, in order to preserve good behavior. "A bad government is worse for being long," said Mr. Sherman.[5]

Colonel Alexander Hamilton of New York suggested that the disorders of democracy made real the dangers of political conflicts between the rich and the poor. He went on:

> ... if we incline too much to democracy, we shall soon shoot into a monarchy. The difference of property is already great amongst us. Commerce and industry will still increase the disparity. Your government must meet this state of things, or combinations will in process of time, undermine your system. ... [6]

One observer of this Convention believes the arguments of Mr. Sherman and Elbridge Gerry, both from New England, defeated the nine-year Senate term favored by Mr. Hamilton and Mr. Madison.[7] "Demagogues are the great pests of our government, and have occasioned most of our distresses," noted Mr. Gerry, the successful Massachusetts merchant.[8]

Today's debate brought into the open a largely concealed dimension of the struggle this correspondent has noted at the Convention. The fear Mr. Madison, Mr. Hamilton and a few others have of the poor gaining a political upperhand is apparently behind their original demand that the separate States be subordinated to a national government erected in their place. Almost all delegates fear an excess of popular democracy and favor an enlightened elected elite.

Mr. Sherman and Mr. Gerry, both self-made men, disagree with elitist rule, however benign. Not only do they see it as contrary to the American Revolution that overthrew British elitist rule, but it is a repudiation of the principles of the Declaration of Independence that led to the creation of the individual 13 States.[9]

Wednesday, June 27, 1787

Dismay, disgust and despair overwhelmed the Convention today after Luther Martin of Maryland exhausted himself and the delegates in a three-hour heated harangue on States' rights.[1]

According to one delegate friendly to his cause, he "exhausted the politeness of the Convention" by a speech calculated to induce sleep.[2] The 39-year-old Maryland State attorney general, careless in both dress and speech, chose the hottest day since the Convention began to lecture the delegates on the rights of free men and of free States.[3] At least two delegates reported that Mr. Martin's speech wandered so it was difficult to follow, let alone record.[4] Several observers suggested to this correspondent that Mr. Martin has a drinking problem, in an era of heavy drinking men. One, however, maintains that "his mighty drinking" problem does not affect his performance as a lawyer and that his memory is phenomenal.[5]

The Maryland attorney general told the delegates that it was the duty of any general government to protect the State governments and its powers ought to be kept within narrow limits. He said:

> We are proceeding in forming this government as if there were no state governments at all. . . . the corner-stone of a federal government is *equality* of votes. States may surrender this right; but if they do, their liberties are lost.[6]

Mr. Martin, drunk or sober, has stated finally the central issue that has caused the delegates to reach their current impasse. Since June 11, when the Convention voted to have the proposed national House and Senate seats determined by population, the Southern States have demanded that each State have one equal vote in the Senate.[7] Mr. Martin said today what others from the small States have been saying for almost two weeks. Namely, a national House and Senate based on population would give Virginia, Pennsylvania and Massachusetts combined political power to outvote the less populous ten smaller States. "I would not trust a government organized upon the reported plan, for all the slaves of Carolina or the horses and oxen of Massachusetts," Mr. Martin declared.[8]

The hostile reception Mr. Martin received from both sides may be due less to what he said than to the inflammatory method he used to make his case. William Pierce of Georgia reported that the Maryland attorney general has a great deal of information, but a bad delivery combined with a wordy speaking style. ". . . he never speaks without tiring the patience of all who hear him," according to Mr. Pierce.[9]

The most hostile reaction to Mr. Martin came from his small State ally, Oliver Ellsworth of Connecticut. He, along with Roger Sherman, has been working quietly and patiently these past two weeks with a skillful strategy of pressure to effect a compromise with the large States. Mr. Martin's performance in behalf of the small States may have harmed their cause and reinforced the view held by large State delegates like General Washington that advocates of States' rights are demagogues.

Thursday, June 28, 1787

Debate grew so stormy today that 81-year-old Dr. Benjamin Franklin proposed that henceforth the Convention open each session with prayers. Dr. Franklin made his proposal after a day marked by dramatic clashes and tedious talk.

Luther Martin of Maryland for a second straight day rubbed raw the nerves of the delegates with his defense of the Confederation.[1] "Is the old confederation dissolved, because some of the states wish a new confederation?" he asked.[2]

A sigh of relief swept the Convention when Mr. Martin sat down. However, the mood of the nationalists turned angry after John Lansing of New York proposed that State representation in the House be equal—as specified in the Articles of Confederation—and not, as the Convention had voted earlier, by State population. James Madison of Virginia and James Wilson of Pennsylvania could barely contain their despair as each rose in rebuttal. They cited again the failures of ancient confederacies and of the current one governing the 13 States. Mr. Madison insisted that differences of the large States in manners, religion and economies would prevent them from combining against the small.[3] However, Roger Sherman of Connecticut remained an unyielding Yankee. Under proportional representation in the national Congress, he said, four States would govern nine. "As they will have the purse, they may raise troops, and can also make a king when they please," Mr. Sherman added.[4]

Mr. Madison shot back: "There is a danger in the idea of the gentleman from Connecticut. Unjust representation will ever produce it. . . . The counties in Virginia are exceedingly disproportionate, and yet the smaller has an equal vote with the greater, and no inconvenience arises."[5]

It was here that Dr. Franklin made his proposal that each session open with prayers, reminding the delegates that prayers opened each session of the Continental Congress in this very State House during the War with Great Britain. Those prayers were graciously answered, he said in a low, soft and hesitant voice. Directing his words towards General Washington, Convention President,[6] Dr. Franklin noted the small progress made by the Convention, and then went on:

> I have lived, Sir, a long time, and the longer I live, the more convincing proofs I see of this truth—*that God governs in the affairs of men.* And if a sparrow cannot fall to the ground without his notice, is it probable that an empire can rise without his aid? . . . without his concurring aid we shall succeed

in this political building no better than the Builders of
Babel. . . .[7]

The proposal for prayers was not adopted, for two reasons.
First, the Convention has no funds, as North Carolina's cler-
gyman delegate Hugh Williamson bluntly pointed out.[8] Second, Colonel Alexander Hamilton of New York observed that
approving prayers this late in the Convention would "lead the
public to believe that the embarrassments and dissensions
within the convention had suggested this measure."[9]

Little doubt exists that Dr. Franklin's proposal had a sober-
ing impact on the contentious delegates. He reminded them
that their failure might force mankind to despair of establishing government by human wisdom and thus leave the ordeal
to "chance, war and conquest."[10]

Friday, June 29, 1787

A dark cloud of despair settled over the Convention today, as
one by one delegates who took the floor openly expressed
their fears of what the Convention's failure might mean for
the future of the country.[1] Dr. Benjamin Franklin's rejected
proposal yesterday for prayers tempered the heat of the delegates but did little to move them out of the torrid desert of
their debate.

Dr. William Samuel Johnson of Connecticut opened today's
session by counseling compromise. Once again he proposed on
behalf of his State that the House in the national government
be elected by the people and the Senate by the States. A
general government cannot be formed "on any other ground,"
the respected 60-year-old Connecticut lawyer said, obviously
weary with the endless, bitter debate. He added that "A state
exists as a political society . . . and the interests of the states
must be armed with some power of self-defence."[2]

James Madison's reply was like a pistol shot. The States are not sovereign, he insisted, and should be placed under control of the general government to the degree at least that they were during the rule of Great Britain.[3] The States must renounce the "unjust" principle of equality of voting, Mr. Madison went on, or run the risk of adopting the political evils that had resulted in the Old World.[4] "If the States have equal influence and votes in the Senate, we are in the utmost Danger," the normally soft-spoken Virginia scholar retorted.[5]

Colonel Alexander Hamilton of New York insisted that the Convention deadlock was over not the principle of State liberties, but that of political power. He joined Mr. Madison in warning against the dangers of domestic dissolution, adding that only foreign nations can benefit from any future alliance with breakaway States. He then went on to warn:

> Unless your government is respectable, foreigners will invade your rights; . . . even to observe neutrality you must have a strong government.—I confess our present situation is critical. We have just finished a war which has established our independency, and loaded us with a heavy debt.[6]

Elbridge Gerry of Massachusetts insisted that the current Confederation is dissolving and the fate of the Union will be decided by the Convention. "Instead of coming here like a band of brothers . . . we seem to have brought with us the spirit of political negotiators," the sparrow-sized Mr. Gerry observed in a rebuke to both sides.[7]

When today's debate was done, a Convention majority turned down equality of voting in the national Legislature as demanded by the small States. Thus, two weeks of often bitter debate had not changed a single vote as the large States rejected compromise.[8] Oliver Ellsworth of Connecticut told the weary delegates he did not despair and still hoped for a solution, for " . . . if no compromise should take place, our meeting would not only be in vain but worse than in vain."[9]

Saturday, June 30, 1787

Emotionally charged verbal grapeshot exploded between the large and small State delegates today on the question of equal or proportional representation in the proposed national Senate. There is a possibility that the Convention could break up in bitter and angry failure.

James Wilson of Pennsylvania may have primed today's explosion by suggesting that the small States, by their position, were abandoning the country. He said he would deplore such a development, but remains unyielding. If a minority will not join with a majority on just and proper principles, let a separation take place, he suggested. "Can we forget for whom we are forming a Government?" the portly Pennsylvania lawyer asked. "Is it for *men*, or for the imaginary beings called *States*?"[1]

Connecticut's Oliver Ellsworth fired back in rebuttal that it was untrue that a minority will rule the majority if the States were given equal votes in the proposed national Senate. The power is given to the few to save them from being destroyed by the many. "We are running from one extreme to another." Mr. Ellsworth went on. "We are razing the foundations of the building. When we need only repair the roof."[2]

James Madison of Virginia, in a rare display of debater's distemper, served up what amounted to personal insult. The generally low-key scholar accused Connecticut of not shouldering its fair share of the burden during the War of Independence.[3] Mr. Ellsworth was immediately on his feet. Turning to General George Washington in the President's chair, he asked for confirmation that such a charge was untrue. The General chose silence rather than take sides. The Connecticut delegate said of his State, "The muster-rolls will show that she had more troops in the field than even the state of Virginia."[4]

The most explosive outburst of today's session came from Delaware's Gunning Bedford. In a slashing attack on the motives of the large States, the corpulent Delaware lawyer was as blunt as he was blistering with these words:

I do not, Gentlemen, trust you. If you possess the power, the abuse of it could not be checked; and what then would prevent you from exercising it to our destruction? . . . Sooner than be ruined, there are *foreign powers who will take us by the hand.*[5]

Rufus King of Massachusetts angrily rebuked Mr. Bedford for his outburst. However, the fear of separate States forming an alliance with a foreign power has been on every delegate's mind. Mr. Bedford bluntly brought the issue into the open.[6]

Today's session marked a perilous peak. The Convention began five weeks ago with calm, dignified debate and has moved relentlessly toward personal passions and State loyalties.[7] Tempers on all sides have been rubbed raw by today's explosive session.[8] Observers believe that only two things can save the Convention from collapse: a compromise plan acceptable to both sides; or, someone changing his stand.[9]

One thing has become apparent: the Convention must alter its current course or face shipwreck.

Sunday, July 1, 1787

Convention delegates were in recess today, allowing a cooling off period after yesterday's emotionally charged confrontation between the large and the small States.[1] The session was so stormy that after adjournment Colonel George Mason of Virginia told a friend the fate of the Convention is likely to be decided in the next few days.[2]

General George Washington, in private, blames the current perilous Convention impasse on what he calls "demagogues" championing States' rights. In a letter written to a friend today—a copy was obtained by this correspondent—the President of the Convention vented his anger at the small States. He charges them with holding to narrow State concerns while the whole of the country is in crisis. Nevertheless, the hero of the War of Independence, who endured many a crisis himself, is taking a positive view, despite the current Convention deadlock. Hoping that "justice" will prevail in the end, General Washington in his letter today went on:

> Happy indeed would it be if the Convention shall be able to recommend such a firm and permanent Government for this Union . . . every body wishes—every body expects something from the Convention—but what will be the final result of its deliberations, the book of fate must disclose. . . .[3]

General Washington is known to have been distressed that Colonel Alexander Hamilton of New York left Philadelphia yesterday.[4] Observers are divided in their opinion why Colonel Hamilton chose to leave a Convention he worked so hard to bring into being, and at the very moment of its most critical crisis. One observer told this correspondent that Colonel Hamilton chose to leave because of his lack of influence and the belief that he was wasting his time.[5] Another observer has taken at face value Colonel Hamilton's explanation that he has neglected his legal practice and his family in New York. He has promised to return in ten or twelve days. However, a close personal friend, Georgia delegate Major William Pierce, has challenged one of Colonel Hamilton's clients to a duel over an affair of honor. His efforts to prevent bloodshed between the two may keep him away from the Convention longer than he anticipates, according to this observer.[6]

Colonel Hamilton is known to have been frustrated in recent weeks by his two fellow New York delegates who have opposed him by voting with the small States. An unconfirmed report circulating here in Philadelphia says that John Lansing and Robert Yates may walk out of the Convention in the hope of breaking it up, rather than see a national government established.[7] A less drastic step by the small States surfaced at yesterday's stormy session. It was proposed and quickly rejected that General Washington, as President of the Convention, write a letter to the governor of New Hampshire demanding immediate attendance of that State's delegation.[8] Political infighting and lack of money for travel have kept the New Hampshire delegates home.

Just about all the delegates understand that if New Hampshire and Rhode Island had been present in the last few weeks, the current deadlock would have been broken in favor of the small States and the Convention would have reached its ultimate decision much earlier.[9]

Monday, July 2, 1787

This Convention stood dangerously poised today astride a great fissure of disagreement that split it right down the middle when the 11 States cast their votes for or against equality of voting in the proposed national Senate.[1]

Five small States voted for the measure proposed earlier by Oliver Ellsworth of Connecticut, and five States voted no. The 11th State, Georgia, was divided because Major William Pierce was in New York preparing to fight a duel, and William Few was attending sessions of the Continental Congress.[2] Georgia's two remaining delegates at the session today split their vote. Abraham Baldwin, formerly of Connecticut, voted for equality of representation in support of the small States out of the belief that if the measure failed they would walk out of the Convention.[3]

Maryland would also have been divided, rather than casting its vote with the small States, had delegate Daniel of St. Thomas Jenifer arrived for the day's session before the vote took place. His out-of-breath and apologetic late arrival prompted Rufus King of Massachusetts to demand the vote be taken again. This is clearly against Convention rules.[4] The 5 to 5 deadlock vote stood for no decision, to the despair of some and to the relief of others.[5]

South Carolina's Charles Cotesworth Pinckney suggested the formation of a committee composed of one delegate from each State to work out a compromise. Roger Sherman of Connecticut summed up the stalemate by saying that the Convention had come to a full stop. "It seems we have got to a point, that we cannot move one way or the other. Such a committee is necessary to set us right," he added.[6]

James Madison of Virginia was disturbed by the proposal and told the Convention:

> I have observed that committees only delay business; and if you appoint one from each state, we shall have in it the whole force of state prejudices. The motion of the gentleman from South Carolina can be as well decided here as in committee.[7]

Mr. Madison's worst fears were confirmed when the Convention voted to create the committee. The eleven delegates elected clearly demonstrate that it has been "loaded" in favor of the compromises supported by the small States, to the dismay of Mr. Madison and James Wilson of Pennsylvania. One observer points out that stacking the committee was the work of cooler heads. The large States could have won today by the thin vote of one, but only at the price of small State hostility to the overall plan for a new national government.[8] A majority of delegates now know the small States will not surrender. They also know that despite his unpopularity, Luther Martin of Maryland is correct when he concludes that the Convention is on "the verge of dissolution, scarce held together by the strength of a hair."[9]

A sigh of relief swept through the Convention when the delegates voted to adjourn to celebrate the Fourth of July holiday. As they filed out of the State House today, perhaps the warning of Elbridge Gerry of Massachusetts haunted their thoughts: "Something must be done, or we shall disappoint not only America, but the whole world."[10]

Tuesday, July 3, 1787

Playing the part of Constitutional carpenter, Dr. Benjamin Franklin proposed, and the Grand Committee of 11 States tentatively approved today, a compromise to break the bitter deadlock between the small and the large States.[1] The Grand Committee—composed of one delegate from each State—was elected yesterday and met today while the Convention is in recess to prepare for the Independence holiday.

The 81-year-old Dr. Franklin proposed the compromise in these words:

> If a proportional representation takes place, the small States contend that their liberties will be in danger. If an equality of votes is to be put in its place, the large States say their money will be in danger. When a broad table is to be made, and the edges ⟨of planks do not fit⟩ the artist takes a little from both, and makes a good joint.[2]

Dr. Franklin's compromise is not new, except for one key provision. Essentially it is the same proposal put forth repeatedly by Connecticut. The Committee agreed that the makeup of the lower house would be based on population, and in the upper house each State would have an equal vote. However, in return for this concession to the small States, the lower house would be vested with exclusive power over originating taxes and appropriations.[3]

The compromise hammered out today is regarded as a victory by the small States, who fear domination by the large States of Virginia, Pennsylvania and Massachusetts.[4] Thus, it is expected that when the Committee report is debated in full Convention James Madison of Virginia and James Wilson of Pennsylvania are likely to voice vigorous objections. Pennsylvania's Gouverneur Morris is also expected to attack today's Grand Committee's compromise.

Mr. Morris, who has been absent from the Convention almost a month on business matters, was quoted by one observer as saying that everyone, including General Washington, is despondent in the belief that the Convention is about to dissolve into failure.[5]

General Washington went for a horseback ride today and later sat for his portrait by the artist Charles Willson Peale.[6] One observer reports that while Mr. Peale and his sons worked at easel and sketch pads, with the smell of linseed oil and paint pigments mixing with the hot summer air, the General had time to mull over in his mind the crisis confronting the Convention.[7]

General Washington's despair may have been deepened by the departure four days ago of Colonel Alexander Hamilton. "I am sorry you went away—I wish you were back," he is reported to have written to his former military aide.[8] The General has looked on Colonel Hamilton almost as an adopted son. This correspondent has learned that Colonel Hamilton, in a letter today to General Washington, expressed the view that a golden opportunity may be lost to rescue the country from its current crisis if the Convention fails.[9]

General Washington may be wounded by such words. Here he sits in Philadelphia, beset by crisis, while Colonel Hamilton has departed the political battlefield. The General may wonder whether such conduct in 1776 would have allowed the 13 States to celebrate tomorrow the 11th anniversary of the Declaration of Independence.

Wednesday, July 4, 1787

Philadelphia worked itself into a state of patriotic exhaustion today in celebrating the 11th anniversary of the Declaration of Independence. Pealing church bells, 13-gun artillery salutes, and marching fife-and-drum bands gave residents reason to retire to the city taverns and drink 13 toasts to the future health of the still-to-be *united* States of America.[1]

Toasts were also offered to "The Grand Convention" and its delegates, "May they form a Constitution for an eternal Republic," some toasters said with slurred speech.[2] After a parade to the State House, where the Declaration was first proclaimed in 1776, General George Washington led most Convention delegates to the Reformed Calvinist Lutheran Church. Sitting silently and solemnly in the packed church, General Washington heard James Campbell preach a sermon aimed, in part, at the Convention delegates.

"Methinks, I already see the stately fabric of a free and vigorous Government rising out of the wisdom of the Foederal Convention," said Mr. Campbell.[3]

General Washington and other delegates must have been relieved that no hint of the crisis facing the Convention had leaked out to the public and the press. Both continue to expect great things of the Grand Convention, blissfully ignorant of the bitter and stormy debates of the last few weeks.

Today's July 4 celebration, here in Philadelphia and elsewhere, has been the occasion for countless public speeches extolling in extravagant terms the Declaration of Independence and the American Revolution. Philadelphia physician and a signer of the document, Dr. Benjamin Rush offered a detailed assessment of the events since 1776. He then went on:

> There is nothing more common than to confound the terms of the *American revolution* with those of *the late American war*. The American war is over: but this is far from being the case with the American revolution. On the contrary, nothing but the first act of the great drama is closed.[4]

However, Dr. Rush's view—that this Convention is the continuation of what was begun with the Declaration 11 years ago—is contradicted by two other signers. During the last five weeks, delegates Roger Sherman of Connecticut and Elbridge Gerry of Massachusetts have argued that the Convention was only authorized to revise the existing Articles of Confederation. Both Mr. Sherman and Mr. Gerry signed the Articles and both are convinced the States they represent are the political expression of the Declaration.[5] The proposed national government now being debated at this Convention and favored by Dr. Rush, is viewed by States' rights delegates like Mr. Sherman and Mr. Gerry as a departure from the Declaration that created the States and the Articles of Confederation.[6]

It is on this fundamental issue of taking power away from the States and giving it to a new and powerful central government that this Convention now finds itself foundering in a sea of angry and bitter debate. But to most Americans caught up in today's July 4 celebrations, their freedom is a seamless fabric. The events of 1776 and 1787 are, for them, from the same bolt of patriotic cloth. As the *Pennsylvania Gazette* wrote in the form of a toast today: "The members of the present Convention—may they do as much towards the support of our independence as their virtuous President did towards its establishment."[7]

Thursday, July 5, 1787

Grim images of the gallows, the sword, and a civil war hung over today's Convention session as one set of delegates called for compromise while another set scorned the word as a surrender to injustice.

Elbridge Gerry of Massachusetts today submitted to the

full Convention the proposed compromise hammered out by the Grand Committee of 11 States over the July 4 holiday recess. The compromise contains three elements: one representative for every 40,000 inhabitants in the proposed House; the lower chamber would have the power to originate money bills without alteration by the proposed Senate; and in the upper house each State would have an equal vote.[1] "If we do not come to some agreement among ourselves some foreign sword will probably do the work for us," Mr. Gerry warned as he argued for compromise.[2]

James Madison of Virginia and James Wilson of Pennsylvania made no attempt to conceal their scorn for the proposed compromise. Sourly, Mr. Madison suggested that the power to originate money bills was no concession at all.[3] If seven States in the upper house favored a money bill, he pointed out, they could get members from the same States in the lower house to originate it. He added: "It [is] in vain to purchase concord in the Convention on terms which would perpetuate discord among [our] Constituents."[4]

Gouverneur Morris of Pennsylvania, with verbal rapier strokes, cut away at the proposed compromise. The country must be united by persuasion or the sword will do it, the wealthy delegate with a wooden leg said, while remaining seated. If the States had equal votes in the Senate, he predicted, the horrors of civil war would be followed by the Gallows & Halter and finish what the sword had started. How far foreign powers would take part in the horrors he foresaw, he could not say. But, he grimly went on, of one thing he was certain, State attachments and loyalty were poison for the country. "We cannot annihilate; but we may perhaps take out the teeth of the serpents," he said of the States.[5]

William Paterson of New Jersey complained that images of the sword and the gallows were the product of Mr. Morris's calculation rather than his conviction. The diminutive judge from New Jersey also complained that Mr. Madison and Mr. Morris were abusing the small States.[6]

Colonel George Mason of Virginia sought to purge today's bitter debate with sweet reason:

> There must be some accommodation . . . or we shall make little further progress in the work. . . . I will bury my bones in this city rather than expose my country to the consequences of a dissolution of the convention without anything being done.[7]

General George Washington may have been moved by Colonel Mason's words of warning. An observer has informed this correspondent that despite Mr. Madison's bitter opposition to the clause concerning money bills, the General is prepared to support it.[8]

If this proves to be true, General Washington may turn out to be a silent force that saves this Convention from itself.

Friday, July 6, 1787

The large States unleashed today a divide-and-conquer offensive against the compromise plan favored by the small States, but were frustrated by the political fox of this Convention: Dr. Benjamin Franklin.

Dr. Franklin, a master at political maneuvering, issued a warning when James Madison of Virginia and Mr. Wilson of Pennsylvania sought to take up separately the second and third proposals of his compromise plan: namely, the right of the lower house to originate money bills and one vote for each State in the upper house. These proposals, Dr. Franklin said, must be taken together and not separately.[1]

Frustrated that their divide-and-conquer strategy had been exposed, large State delegates took aim at the power of the lower house to originate money bills. The small States argued that this was a concession to the large States.

Mr. Wilson bitterly assailed the proposal, insisting it was

no concession at all by the small States; "... it would be found to be a trifle light as air," the Pennsylvanian Scotsman added[2]—his burr magnifying his tone of contempt. Gouverneur Morris growled that the exclusive power to originate money bills in the lower house would deprive the country of the services of the upper house. He then went on:

It will be a dangerous source of disputes between the two Houses.... Suppose an enemy at the door, and money instantly & absolutely necessary for repelling him, may not the popular branch avail itself of this duress, to extort concessions from the Senate destructive of the Constitution itself....[3]

Refusing to be frightened by such rhetoric, five States against three, with three divided, voted to retain the money bill section as part of the compromise report.[4] Exclusive power over money bills in the lower house defeats the plan of the nationalists for the Senate to act as a brake on the lower branch of the legislature.

Today's defeat illustrates that the tide has turned against the nationalists, who now find themselves swimming against it.[5] Today's vote also appears to indicate that the currents for compromise at this Convention are growing stronger with each session.[6]

Perhaps a stronger tide against the nationalists is tradition. At least seven of the 13 State governments give their lower houses the exclusive power to originate money bills as a means of keeping close watch on how the people's money is spent by their representatives.[7] Dr. Franklin used that argument today when he said: "... it was always of importance that the people should know who had disposed of their money, & how it had been disposed of, [this is best attained] if money affairs [are] confined to the immediate representatives of the people."[8]

Colonel Mason spoke today for the moderates in the large States, if not for the whole Convention, when he urged "that

some points must be yielded for the sake of accommodation."[9]
His remarks were clearly aimed at Mr. Wilson and Mr. Morris
of Pennsylvania and Mr. Madison of Virginia. In the early
stages of the Convention, these three nationalists led the
drive for accommodation only now to be its major foes.

Saturday, July 7, 1787

Weariness and the hot summer weather appeared to overwhelm Convention delegates as they staggered and stumbled
through today's session like a band of exhausted sleepwalkers.

However, a majority of States did give their tentative
approval today to a compromise report calling for each State
to have one vote in the proposed Senate. "This is the critical
question," Elbridge Gerry of Massachusetts said.[1]

Roger Sherman of Connecticut, in supporting equality of
voting in the Senate, demonstrated none of his usual talent
for driving directly to the heart of an issue. Instead, he
seemed to wander in his remarks—his words weighed down
with weariness as he warned that *without* equality of voting
in the Senate the proposed national government would be
"feebler than it has ever yet been."[2]

But James Madison of Virginia said that *with* equality of
voting in the Senate the new government would be "rendered
as impotent and as short lived as the old."[3] Mr. Madison has
stubbornly refused to concede defeat on this issue, despite
that in today's voting six States to three, with two divided,
tentatively approved equality of voting in the Senate. The
vote clearly unsettled an otherwise steady Mr. Madison.[4]

William Paterson of New Jersey demonstrated the same
unyielding quality today. The New Jersey jurist said that if
equality of voting in the Senate were not acceptable to the
large States, then perhaps "we had better divide & lose no

longer Time."[5] One observer believes that this challenge to
the Convention is a deliberate tactic by the small States to
convince the large ones of their firmness on the issue of
equality of voting.[6]

The weary disagreement inside the State House is a sharp
contrast to how the public and the press perceive the debates.
The deadlocked delegates read in today's *Pennsylvania
Packet*:

> So great is the unanimity we hear that prevails in the Conven-
> tion upon all great federal subjects, that it has been proposed
> to call the room in which they assemble Unanimity Hall.[7]

The cynical and worldly Gouverneur Morris of Pennsylvania must have found this statement particularly humorous.
This correspondent has learned that in today's secret session,
Mr. Morris made no effort to be conciliatory toward the
States' rights delegates. Bluntly he told the Convention it was
one of the great misfortunes that the country as a whole had
been sacrificed to local views. Suppose the States should give
themselves up to foreign influence, he went on, suggesting
that if all the State constitutions were "thrown into the fire,
and all their demagogues into the ocean," perhaps America
would be happier.[8]

Mr. Morris's lengthy speech was the only one during today's
session that contained any energy. With good reason, for he
has been absent for a month. He is fresh and full of fire while
his fellow delegates are weary of the war of words that does
not seem to have any end in sight.

Sunday, July 8, 1787

The New York delegation is reliably reported ready to return home, leaving only 10 States at this bitterly deadlocked Convention that, according to one delegate, is "on the verge of dissolution, scarce held together by the strength of a hair."[1]

Robert Yates and John Lansing are expected to leave Philadelphia after the July 10 session. Both have been increasingly dissatisfied with the proposed new government and particularly the sweeping powers it may assume.[2]

New York's third delegate, Colonel Alexander Hamilton, left at the end of June, also disappointed at the direction of a convention he had played a prominent part in engineering into existence. Colonel Hamilton's poor performance here is a puzzle to some observers.[3] The New York lawyer and legislator has privately charged that Judge Yates' and Mr. Lansing's decision to desert the Convention is on the direct instructions of New York Governor George Clinton, a bitter political enemy of Colonel Hamilton.[4]

Judge Yates and Mr. Lansing, in a letter to the New York Governor (a copy having been obtained by this correspondent), spelled out their public reasons for leaving the Convention. One reason concerns their original instructions contained in their credentials, which specifically mandate them to do no more than amend the current Articles of Confederation. Yet the Convention in the last few weeks has cast aside the Articles in favor of a new and powerful central government. Judge Yates, also speaking for Mr. Lansing, said in his letter:

> ... We have the strongest apprehensions, that a government so organized, as that recommended by the convention, cannot afford that security to equal and permanent liberty, which we wished to make an invariable object of our pursuit.[5]

Observers are divided as to the real reason for their departure. One suggests that the goal of their departure is to cripple the Convention, causing a permanent deadlock and its eventual dissolution.[6] Another asserts that their departure is for the purpose of returning to New York for court sessions. Judge Yates sits on the New York bench and Mr. Lansing is an attorney and mayor of Albany.[7] Colonel Hamilton also gave as a reason for leaving, the neglect of his legal practice.

Colonel George Mason of Virginia has revealed, however, that when the three New York delegates were present at the Convention, their disagreements were so fundamental that he cannot recall "*one single instance*" when they voted together. Colonel Mason also maintains that Colonel Hamilton became so frustrated at the deadlock within the New York delegation that it contributed to his own departure.[8]

New York, with 340,000 inhabitants, is the fifth most populous State. It is doubtful that departure of the New York delegates will lead to the breakup of the Convention. Most delegates have accepted their pending departure for reasons of business at home and not an implied censure of the Convention.[9]

The larger question, however, is what New York will do when it is asked to ratify the work of this Convention, which Judge Yates and Mr. Lansing have consistently opposed.

Monday, July 9, 1787

A political chess game was played out at today's session with slaves as pawns, injecting an explosive new element into a convention already on the edge of exhaustion and the brink of breakup.[1]

Gouverneur Morris of Pennsylvania presented a Committee of Five report proposing that the lower house be temporarily composed of 56 members. The national legislature would also be given the power to regulate the number of representatives from each State based on wealth and population. The proposal clearly favored the wealthier Southern States.[2] When challenged, Mr. Morris admitted the report lacked firm figures for computing State inhabitants, including slaves. "The Report is little more than a guess," Mr. Morris conceded.[3] However, he sought to assure wary delegates that the report was designed to avoid the danger that new States formed in the West would eventually outvote the Atlantic States and dominate the new national government.[4]

Sensing that counting slaves was a power play to inflate representation in favor of the large States, William Paterson of New Jersey protested the rule of wealth and population as too vague. Slaves were property, Mr. Paterson insisted, without liberty, without the means of acquiring property, and subject to the will of their masters who could vote while slaves could not. The proposal would further encourage the slave trade since the slave-holding South would have incentive to increase their representation, the New Jersey Attorney General argued. Besides, he demanded, since slaves are not represented in the States why should they now be counted in the national government? He then went on to ask:

> What is the true principle of Representation? It is an expedient by which an assembly of certain individ[ua]ls, chosen by the people is substituted in place of the inconvenient meeting of the people themselves. If such a meeting of the people was actually to take place, would the slaves vote? they would not. Why then shd [should] they be represented.[5]

James Madison of Virginia turned the argument on Mr. Paterson, rather than answer it. He reminded Mr. Paterson that his statement on representation "must for ever silence the pretensions of the small States to an equality of votes with the large ones."[6] Mr. Madison proposed that the lower house be represented according to the States' free inhabitants, while the upper house, conceived as the guardian of property, be represented according to all white and black inhabitants.[7]

One observer believes that Mr. Madison's proposal is really aimed at defeating the entire compromise now before the Convention, but it is likely to fail.[8]

Although at least 30 delegates at this Convention own slaves, every State but South Carolina has now banned their importation.[9] Seven out of the 13 States either have outlawed the institution or are in the process of doing so. Virginia delegates like George Washington, Edmund Randolph and George Mason have called for its abolition in their State.[10]

"Every master of slaves is born a petty tyrant," Colonel Mason states. "They bring the judgment of heaven on a Country."[11]

Tuesday, July 10, 1787

In a private display of anger and despair at the chaotic direction of this Convention, General George Washington revealed today in a letter to a former military aide (a copy having been obtained by this correspondent) that his patience and innate optimism have deserted him.[1]

Writing to Colonel Alexander Hamilton in New York, the hero of Valley Forge confessed that the current Convention deadlock gives little grounds for hope that a new national government can be formed. General Washington went on to give this gloomy outlook:

> In a word, I *almost* despair of seeing a favourable issue to the proceedings of the Convention, and do therefore repent having had any agency in the business.

> The men who oppose a strong & energetic government are, in my opinion, narrow minded politicians, or are under the influence of local views.[2]

However, General Washington indicated in his letter to Colonel Hamilton that the current deadlock would not dis-. courage renewed effort until a new constitution is signed. One observer points out that the General's letter was partly a rebuke to Colonel Hamilton for leaving the Convention at the peak of the current crisis and partly a plea that he return to Philadelphia from New York.[3]

A former French officer who has observed General Washington as he has left the Convention during the past few days reports: "The look on his face reminded me of its expression during the terrible months we were in Valley Forge Camp."[4]

Today's session provides an illustration of why the General is gloomy. Reliable sources report that Rufus King of Massachusetts submitted yet another committee report that assigns a specific number of representatives to each State.[5] At once a scuffle of arguments erupted over how many representatives each State should receive in the proposed congress.[6] South Carolina's delegation objected to the report on the grounds that the numbers favor the North and would adversely affect the State's lifeblood: which is exports.[7] An effort to take away one representative from New Hampshire and to increase numbers for the Carolinas and Georgia was defeated 7 to 4 by the States.[8]

James Madison of Virginia proposed that the number of representatives be doubled, making the districts smaller. It was voted down as too expensive.[9] Next, Edmund Randolph of Virginia proposed that the national legislature cause a census to be taken to determine wealth and population of the States as the basis for deciding representation.[10] That proposal was postponed after Gouverneur Morris of Pennsylvania predicted it would place shackles on the legislature and, as their population grew, the Western States would attain power over the Atlantic States.[11]

The final frustration for General Washington may have been the next to the last motion of today's session. The Committee of Eleven, to which was referred the report of the

Committee of Five on the subject of representation, was requested to furnish the Convention with the principles upon which it assigned a specific number of representatives from each State. The motion lost 10 to 1.

The only unanimous vote of today's session was to adjourn.[12]

Wednesday, July 11, 1787

Conflict at this Convention shifted from large States versus small States to a sectional clash between the North and South, leaving today's session in a confused shambles over the decision what part black slaves should play in representation.[1] Delegates began by considering Governor Edmund Randolph's proposal for a periodic census as a method to determine representation based on population and wealth. Hugh Williamson of North Carolina proposed that any census be based on all free white inhabitants and three-fifths "of those of other descriptions."[2] South Carolina's delegates immediately demanded that blacks be counted "*equally* with the whites"[3]—the word "slave" a taboo term among some delegates. "The people of Pena. [Pennsylvania] would revolt at the idea of being put on a footing with slaves," Gouverneur Morris indignantly replied.[4] Besides, he added, a census would give power to new Western States to ruin interests of the Atlantic States. The best course was to fix no rule, but leave the issue to the people's representatives—namely, Congress.

James Madison of Virginia is reported to believe that Mr. Morris's motive for omitting slaves from the proposed census and leaving to Congress the power to deal with the West, is a political ploy to protect the commercial interests of the seaboard States.[5] Mr. Madison said that he was a little surprised to hear Mr. Morris express such confidence in Congress. Particularly since he had spoken in the past of the "political depravity of men" in power.

Mr. Madison then went on to criticize Mr. Morris:

> ... But his reasoning [is] not only inconsistent with his former reasoning, but with itself. at the same time that he recommended this implicit confidence to the Southern States in the Northern Majority, he was still more zealous in exhorting all to a jealousy of a Western majority. To reconcile the gentln. [gentleman] with himself it must be imagined that he determine[s] the human character by the points of the compass.[6]

A census every 15 years was tentatively approved. However, to the proposal that slaves be counted as three-fifths of a white free inhabitant, James Wilson of Pennsylvania objected. If slaves are property, he asked, why should not other property become part of the computation?[7] Gouverneur Morris said he was reduced to the dilemma of doing injustice to the Southern States or to human nature. He chose to do injustice to the South. He went on to predict that the Southern States would never confederate without their slaves.[8] Mr. Morris may have put his finger on a political reality, despite his strong opposition to slavery.

This reality may have been at work today after the Convention voted 6 to 4 to reject counting slaves as a fraction of whites. Without debate or explanation, the Convention voted unanimously to reject the entire compromise proposal debated over the last week. The delegates, as a result, now find themselves having not advanced a single step.[9]

Thursday, July 12, 1787

A Convention majority voted today to sanction the Southern States' slave doctrine, namely that a black slave is both property and three-fifths of a free white person when computing political representation.[1]

Gouverneur Morris of Pennsylvania paved the way for today's compromise action, clearly the product of a prearranged agreement. Mr. Morris proposed that representation be tied to taxation. Pierce Butler of South Carolina, without hesitation, said there was "justice" in Mr. Morris's proposal. One observer believes his move was designed to quiet the fears of Southerners over the future of the slave issue.[2]

General Charles Cotesworth Pinckney added he "likes the idea," agreeing with Mr. Morris that taxation should be restricted to *direct* taxes and the Legislature be restrained from taxing exports. As a South Carolinian whose exports depend on the labor of blacks, he wanted any agreement on the representation ratio fixed and "the execution of it enforced by the Constitution."[3]

North Carolina's William Davie cast a chill over the humid Convention hall when he said some delegates wanted to deprive the Southern States of any share of representation for their blacks. The North Carolina lawyer and planter warned that his State would never confederate on any terms that did not include defining blacks as three-fifths of whites. "If the Eastern States meant therefore to exclude them all together the business was at an end," he bluntly added.[4]

Rufus King of Massachusetts was the only delegate who spoke up against the threat of a Southern walkout. Warning that a union without justice could not last long, Mr. King said it was shortsighted not to realize the Southern States are more numerous than the North and that the South will use the threat of a walkout to awe justice. He went on with these words:

If they threaten to separate now in case injury shall be done them, will their threats be less urgent or effectual, when force shall back their demands. Even in the intervening period there will be no point of time at which they will not be able to say, do us justice or we will separate.[5]

Then, by a vote of 6 to 2, with two States divided, delegates approved representation and direct taxation based on a State's free white population and three-fifths of its slave population. Mr. King is reported to have voted against the proposal. One observer points out that, although disapproving of slavery, he may believe the compromise is necessary as the only practical way of securing sectional agreement.[6]

Later the Massachusetts lawyer noted that the three-fifths ratio in counting slaves was included in the current Articles of Confederation by the Continental Congress in April 1783.[7]

The key players in today's session included not only Mr. Morris of Pennsylvania but also the three delegates from Connecticut. Although Oliver Ellsworth and Dr. William Johnson offered compromise proposals that failed to be adopted, Connecticut's Roger Sherman is reported by one observer to have struck a bargain with South Carolina's John Rutledge on the slave issue over a private dinner at the Indian Queen Inn two weeks ago.[8] If this is true, it means that the important players at this Convention are not always those who have given the longest and most frequent speeches.

Friday, July 13, 1787

Wealth as the basis for representation was unanimously rejected today by a Convention composed of a majority of wealthy delegates.[1]

Virginia Governor Edmund Randolph opened today's session by proposing that the word "wealth" be deleted from a July 9 resolution approving population and wealth as the basis for representation.[2] Immediately, Gouverneur Morris of Pennsylvania objected. Rising population in the South and the growth of new States in the West, he argued, would overwhelm the Northern and Middle States and bring on a war with Imperial Spain for control of the Mississippi. Mr. Morris, clearly threatening to side with the small States, then warned that some Northern States, to protect themselves against Virginia and other large Southern States, might be forced to vote for the "vicious principle of equality" in the Senate.[3]

His threat is an indication that a few large States are weakening in their opposition to the small States' demand for equality of voting in the Senate, which has deadlocked the Convention.[4] Mr. Morris's threat also confirms that the divisions have shifted from small versus large States to a struggle between Northern and Southern States.[5]

One observer believes that a speech by James Wilson of Pennsylvania today effectively rebutted Mr. Morris and produced the unanimous Convention vote (Maryland was divided) to strike wealth as the basis of representation.[6] The Scottish-born lawyer squinted through his rounded spectacles at the Convention and said he did not harbor the same fears as his fellow Pennsylvanian Mr. Morris. The majority should rule, he said, and to fear the growth of population is to commit the same fatal error of the British—who feared population growth in their Colonies only to end up losing them. Mr. Wilson then went on:

> [I] . . . could not agree that property was the sole or the primary object of Governt. & Society. The cultivation & improvement of the human mind was the most noble object. With respect to this object, as well as to other *personal* rights, numbers were surely the natural & precise measure of Representation. . . .[7]

Concern about the future role of new States in the West was given perhaps historic significance by news today from New York. Sources have informed this correspondent that the Continental Congress in New York has approved what is termed the Northwest Ordinance of 1787. The act arranges for admission of new States in the West on the basis of equality with the existing 13 States, provides for a Bill of Rights, and prohibits slavery.[8] Eight States approved the measure, ironically four of them from the slave-holding South.[9]

The Northwest Ordinance, which prohibits slavery, is a contrast to the debate here in Philadelphia about whether slaves should be considered property or a fraction of free whites when computing representation in the new Legislature. But as South Carolina's Pierce Butler told the delegates today: "The security the Southn. States want is that their negroes may not be taken from them which some gentlemen within or without . . . have a very good mind to do."[10]

Saturday, July 14, 1787

The large States unleashed a desperate last-ditch effort today to block State equality of voting in the proposed Senate.[1]

Luther Martin of Maryland set the stage for today's critical struggle. Impatient at the long delays and deadlock, he proposed that the compromise containing equality of voting in the Senate be dealt with by the entire Convention.[2] Roger Sherman of Connecticut, apparently anticipating such a maneuver by the large States, warned the delegates that the "conciliatory plan" had to be considered as a whole since a great deal of time had been spent on it. ". . . if any part should now be altered, it would be necessary to go over the whole ground [of representation] again," the unyielding Yankee warned.[3]

James Wilson of Pennsylvania, in a transparent effort to use talk as a delaying tactic, insisted that equality of votes was of such critical importance that "every opportunity ought to be allowed, for discussing and collecting the mind of the Convention on it."[4]

Mr. Martin, ignoring the month of deadlocked debate, bluntly suggested that if no accommodation were possible, the small and large States should dissolve into two confederacies "if they desired it."[5]

Charles Pinckney III of South Carolina then made his move. The planter proposed a Senate composed of 36 seats, each State to have a number proportionate to its population.[6] Mr. Wilson seconded the large State proposal, to the surprise of no one. And also to the surprise of no one, James Madison of Virginia called the proposal "a reasonable compromise."[7]

One observer points out that Mr. Pinckney had made a similar proposal for the Senate back in June, but Mr. Madison and Mr. Wilson were so certain then of large State success for proportional representation they had refused to give it their support.[8] Now in desperation, Mr. Madison sought today to frighten the Southern slave-holding States with the danger of domination by Northern States if they did not vote for the 36 seats in the Senate:

> ... The real difference of interests lay, not between the large & small, but between N. [Northern] & Southn States. The institution of slavery & its consequences form the line of discrimination. There [are] 5 States on the South, 8 on the Northern side of this line.[9]

Nevertheless, Mr. Pinckney's proposal was defeated, 6 States to 4. Mr. Madison and Mr. Wilson did succeed in delaying a full Convention vote on the entire compromise. At the same time, the biggest problem the large States now face is the danger of division within their own ranks. Massachusetts, for example, appears splintered. Elbridge Gerry argued for accommodation; his fellow delegate Rufus King favored standing firm against equality in the Senate. Caleb Strong was worried that without accommodation "the union itself must be dissolved."[10]

It is the fear of Convention dissolution, if the current deadlock continues, that benefits the small States. A month ago, Mr. Madison and Mr. Wilson, as leaders of the large States, were confident they would carry the Convention with them. Now they have been forced to adopt the strategy of their adversary Roger Sherman, who believes that when you are in the majority, vote, and when in a minority, talk.

Sunday, July 15, 1787

Informed sources report that when the Convention reconvenes tomorrow, a key vote will be taken that could decide the fate of this political conclave that has thus far met in 49 sessions and voted on 155 separate propositions.[1]

Rufus King of Massachusetts is reported to have confided in a private memorandum written today that he was mortified at the outcome of yesterday's vote.[2] The Convention yesterday refused to approve a proposal that would have made seats in the Senate proportionate to the population of each State. Mr. King has stubbornly argued that he favors "the doing of nothing" rather than grant an equal vote to all States. "It would be better ... to submit to a little more confusion & convulsion than to submit to such an evil," he angrily stated in his letter.[3]

However, General George Washington is reported by one source as saying that a compromise is mandatory. This same source also says that during the last few days a group of unnamed delegates has met privately. General Washington may have attended the secret meeting that agreed to accept a

compromise proposal fostered by Dr. Benjamin Franklin.[4]
His compromise is expected to be put to a vote at tomorrow's
Convention session.

Five days ago General Washington in a private letter
angrily lashed out at delegates whom he called "narrow-
minded politicians." He said he regretted having anything to
do with this Convention.[5] Today, his gloomy outlook is gone.
The General dined at the lavish home of his host, Robert
Morris and remained indoors all day.[6] His complete change of
attitude from five days ago is indicated in the letter General
Washington wrote today to his nephew, George Augustine
Washington, at his Mount Vernon plantation. The letter, a
copy having been obtained by this correspondent, provides
specific instructions for painting and plastering a room of the
main Mount Vernon home. He also instructed his nephew on
the planting of crops:

> I would have you, as soon as possible, begin to Sow Wheat in
> Corn ground. I do not think that Corn receives any benefit
> from working after it begins to Tassle and Shoot, but sure I
> am, that nine years out of ten, early sown Wheat will be
> best. . . .[7]

General Washington would not have turned his attention to
problems of his plantation if he were not confident that delegates had reached a compromise and would cease sowing the
seeds of angry discord. This sudden change may have something to do with change in the weather. Two days ago a cold
front blew in from the Northwest, pushing the oppressive
heat and humidity of recent weeks out of Philadelphia. The
skies over the city are a clear blue and a sharp snap is in the
air.[8] The climatic change is reported to have a tonic effect on
most delegates. For the first time in weeks they can sleep
soundly at night and enjoy themselves during the day's
recess. Even the swarms of mosquitoes have fled with the
heat and humidity.[9]

Tomorrow's Convention session should reveal whether the

change in physical climate will have made a change in the Convention's political climate.

Monday, July 16, 1787

A single State saved this Convention today from the reefs of political shipwreck.

By a 5 to 4 vote, with one State divided, delegates gave final approval today to a bitterly debated compromise plan. The compromise gives each State an equal vote in the proposed Senate and proportional representation in the proposed House of Representatives. Until today's vote, the Convention has been like a boat floating motionless in midstream, its strongest oarsmen on both sides pulling toward opposite shores.[1]

Today's vote signals a victory for the small States. If the compromise had been defeated, most observers believe that the small State delegates would have walked out and gone home for good.[2] North Carolina's vote for the compromise spelled the difference between victory and defeat—between permanent dissolution of this Convention and its continuance. Massachusetts, as the divided large State, was neutralized, thus sinking for good the hopes of large State leaders who worked to defeat equality of voting in the Senate.[3] James Madison of Virginia is reported in a state of shock over the vote, scornfully believing that today's Convention vote was a surrender rather than a compromise.[4]

Virginia Governor Edmund Randolph inflamed emotions on both sides at today's session. He proposed that the Convention adjourn so "the large States might consider the steps proper to be taken in the present solemn crisis, . . . and that the small States might also deliberate on the means of conciliation."[5]

Quick as a hunting hound after a hare, William Paterson of New Jersey made a statement that stunned the entire Convention:

> . . . that it [is] high time for the Convention to adjourn, that the rule of secrecy ought to be rescinded, and that our Constituents should be consulted. No conciliation could be admissible on the part of the smaller States on any other ground than that of an equality of votes in the 2d. [second] branch. . . .[6]

Governor Randolph nervously protested he was misunderstood; he did not mean permanent adjournment, but only until tomorrow so another compromise plan he had drafted could be studied. Shrewdly and to the point, John Rutledge of South Carolina said that all the large States had to do "was to decide whether they would yield or not. . . ."[7]

With these words, the Convention voted to adjourn until tomorrow. One observer believes that Mr. Paterson's challenge to adjourn and to end the secrecy rule was a final counterattack to prevent the large States from browbeating the smaller States into giving up the victory they had won today. Every delegate knows that had they rescinded the secrecy rule and agreed to consult their constituents back home, the Convention would be shattered into so many pieces that they would be impossible to put back together.[8]

As Delaware's silent delegate Jacob Broom told the Convention today: "Such a measure . . . would be fatal."[9]

Tuesday, July 17, 1787

After weeks of bitter debate, deadlock and the danger of dissolution, today's Convention delegates demonstrated a movement toward a consensus on the formation of a new national government.[1]

A majority voted today to give the proposed new congress sweeping powers to legislate in cases affecting the general welfare and in those to which the States are separately incompetent. "This is a formidable idea. It involves the power of violating all the laws and constitutions of the States," Virginia Governor Edmund Randolph said with obvious alarm at the sweeping nature of the proposal.[2]

It is significant that the small States voted for this sweeping grant of power. Until now, the small States had opposed the proposed new national government as contained in the Virginia Plan. Having secured yesterday an equality of voting in the Senate, the small States joined hands today with their former opponents to grant the new congress powers to permit it to function as a national political force.[3]

Prior to today's formal Convention session, the large States held a crisis caucus in a vain effort to agree on some common policy after yesterday's defeat at the hands of the small States.[4] "The time was wasted in vague conversation . . . , without any specific proposition or agreement," James Madison of Virginia bitterly reported later.[5] Mr. Madison suffered another defeat today when the Convention by a wide margin refused to endorse his proposal that the national government have the power to veto all State laws. He made his case with these words:

> The necessity of a general Govt. proceeds from the propensity of the States to pursue their particular interests in opposition to the general interest. This propensity will continue to disturb the system, unless effectually controuled. . . .[6]

While rejecting Mr. Madison's arguments, the Convention unanimously agreed that all laws and treaties passed and ratified by the national legislature "shall be the supreme law of the respective States." One observer points out that this proposal by Luther Martin of Maryland was a consolation prize to Mr. Madison and a means to soothe his wounded pride.[7]

In today's session, delegates also turned their attention to the national Executive of the new government, voting that it be single rather than plural as some delegates have previously demanded. It is expected that in the days ahead the question of the powers and term of the national Executive will be debated extensively.

Today's session clearly illustrates two things. First, a profound change has taken place, with delegates moving toward conciliation and consensus on the form and powers of the proposed national government.[8] Second, the form of new government that seems to be emerging is neither national nor federal, but a compound of both. Until now such a power-sharing arrangement between the States and a national government was believed politically impossible.[9]

Wednesday, July 18, 1787

Like a team of horses in harness and finding their stride, delegates quickened the pace of their deliberations today and decided provisions for the Judicial branch of the new national government.

The Convention without debate today unanimously agreed to the establishment of a Supreme Court. And without dissent, the powers granted to the high court are far more sweeping than had been recommended earlier.[1] The new Congress was also granted power to create lower courts.[2]

However, as in previous sessions, delegate disagreement surfaced over why the existing State courts could not perform the function of the proposed national inferior courts and thus prevent expensive duplication.[3] Pierce Butler of South Carolina raised this point. Luther Martin, Maryland's Attorney General, insisted that inferior federal tribunals sitting in the States will create jealousies and jurisdictional disputes.

". . . the Courts of the States can not be trusted with the administration of the National laws," Virginia Governor Edmund Randolph bluntly insisted.[4] Enlarging on this essential point, Nathaniel Gorham of Massachusetts told the delegates:

> There are in the States already (federal) Courts with jurisdiction for trial of piracies &c. committed on the Seas. no complaints have been made by the States or the Courts of the States. Inferior tribunals are essential to render the authority of the Natl. Legislature effectual.[5]

Mr. Gorham also raised a critical point when the delegates debated the method of appointing judges. In the Virginia Plan, it had been proposed that Congress appoint judges, similar to the practice of 10 States which give governors power of judicial appointment.[6] Mr. Gorham pointed out that experience in Massachusetts for 140 years is that the governor appoints judges with the advice and consent of the second branch. He proposed the individual national Executive be given the power to appoint judges with the advice and consent of the national Senate.[7] The proposal lost by a divided 4 to 4 vote, with one State absent. However, the proposal is expected to come before the Convention again.

The ease with which delegates have agreed on the formation of the national judiciary is in sharp contrast to the time and energy devoted thus far to the legislative and executive branches of the proposed national government. One observer attributes this disparity to the belief of most delegates that the Judiciary is the least powerful and active branch of government. Besides, this observer adds, the delegates are in general agreement on the principles that should be embodied in forming the Judiciary. One such principle is that the Judiciary should be independent.[8]

This was illustrated in today's session when Colonel George Mason of Virginia objected to the Executive appointing judges who might later be faced with trying an Executive in an impeachment trial. "If the Judges were to form a tribunal for that purpose, they surely ought not to be appointed by the Executive," Colonel Mason said.[9]

Thursday, July 19, 1787

The past and the future collided today to frustrate efforts of Convention delegates to decide the issue of the Executive—method of appointment, term of office, and eligibility for re-election.[1]

Gouverneur Morris of Pennsylvania in a lengthy speech today argued for popular election of a single powerful Executive. The vast geography of the country, he reminded the delegates, requires a chief Executive with power to pervade every part of it. Election by the Legislature will make him a prisoner of a powerful and wealthy class who could impose a legislative tyranny. "One great object of the Executive is to controul the Legislature," Mr. Morris added.[2]

Virginia Governor Edmund Randolph argued for election by the national Legislature with the provision that the Executive be barred from seeking re-election. "If he ought to be independent, he should not be left under a temptation to court a re-appointment," Governor Randolph said.[3]

Rufus King of Massachusetts said he did not like the idea of one term and proposed instead that electors chosen by the people should choose a single Executive. William Paterson of New Jersey said the States should choose the electors.[4] James Madison of Virginia then raised the most critical issue of today's debate:

> If it be a fundamental principle of free Govt. that the Legislative, Executive & Judiciary powers should be *separately* exercised; it is equally so that they be *independently* exercised.

There is the same & perhaps greater reason why the Executive shd [should] be independent of the Legislature, than why the Judiciary should: A coalition of the two former powers would be more immediately & certainly dangerous to public liberty.[5]

Ignoring Mr. Madison's arguments, a Convention majority voted that the Executive would be chosen by electors, appointed by State Legislatures, and his term would be six years. Governor Randolph is reported to be dismayed at this development. The Convention had earlier agreed on election of the Executive by Congress, as contained in the original Resolutions sponsored by Governor Randolph.

One observer points out that today's development illustrates to Governor Randolph how the original proposals in the Virginia Plan are being bent out of shape.[6]

Today's confusing and contradictory action can be explained in historical and generational terms. Those delegates who favor making the Executive dependent on either the national or State Legislatures came to political maturity prior to 1776. They remember the tyranny of the powerful single Executive, either in the Colonies or under the Stuart kings of Great Britain. Those who favor an independent powerful Executive are younger and do not draw on the same experience; they rely more on theory and ideology than on history.[7]

It is this conflict between the experience of the past and a faith in the future that must be reconciled if a national Executive is to be created.

Friday, July 20, 1787

With the history of powerful and unaccountable executive power in mind,[1] a majority of eight States today approved impeachment of the proposed national chief executive if convicted of "malpractice or neglect of duty."[2]

The impeachment issue produced a spirited series of statements after South Carolina's Charles Pinckney and Gouverneur Morris of Pennsylvania proposed exempting the national Executive from impeachment. "If he be not impeachable whilst in office, he will spare no effort or means whatever to get himself re-elected," replied North Carolina's William Davie.[3]

Mr. Morris insisted that the right of impeachment would render an Executive impotent and "dependent on those who are to impeach."[4] Colonel George Mason of Virginia pointed out in reply that the delegates had debated with difficulty as to the method of choosing the Executive. He disliked the system approved yesterday of electors choosing the Executive, Colonel Mason added, principally because of the danger that the electors could be corrupted by the candidates. He then went on:

> No point is of more importance than that the right of impeachment should be continued. Shall any man be above Justice? . . . Shall the man who has practised corruption & by that means procured his appointment in the first instance, be suffered to escape punishment, by repeating his guilt?[5]

Dr. Benjamin Franklin pointed out that the alternative to impeachment in the past, when a chief magistrate made himself obnoxious, was assassination. " . . . he was not only deprived of his life but of the opportunity of vindicating his character," the 81-year-old Dr. Franklin noted.[6]

Mr. Pinckney, defending his proposal in the face of overwhelming opposition, argued that the Executive's independence would be destroyed since impeachment could become a political weapon in the hands of the legislators. "A good magistrate will not fear them. A bad one ought to be kept in fear of them," Elbridge Gerry of Massachusetts sharply replied.[7]

Rufus King, replying to his colleague, wondered if the three great departments of the proposed government would remain separate and independent if one had the power of impeachment. If judges, he added, are subject to impeachment and hold office "during good behaviour" perhaps the same standard should apply to the Executive. "But under no circumstances ought he to be impeachable by the Legislature," Mr. King insisted.[8]

Just before the issue was put to a vote, Mr. Morris did something out of character. He told the Convention that the arguments presented had forced him to change his opinion. Citing the corrupt practice of bribing the crowned heads of Europe, he was for impeachment of an Executive. Besides, he asked, might not a future chief Executive be bought by a greater interest and betray his trust?

". . . no one would say that we ought to expose ourselves to the danger of seeing the first Magistrate in foreign pay without being able to guard against it by displacing him," Mr. Morris added in an ominous punctuation to today's session.[9]

Saturday, July 21, 1787

Fearing a coalition of political power, the Convention for a third time refused to approve today a fusion of veto power of the national Judiciary and Executive as a means to checkmate the power of the Legislature.[1]

James Wilson of Pennsylvania told the Convention that such Revisionary power was needed. The power of Judges to rule only when a law was unconstitutional did not go far enough. Unjust, unwise, dangerous and destructive laws passed by the Legislature would be beyond the power of Judges. "Let them have a share in the Revisionary Power," the Pennsylvania lawyer argued and their opinions will counteract "the improper views of the Legislature."[2]

Nathaniel Gorham of Massachusetts said there was a presumption in the proposal that judges possessed the knowledge to pass on public policy. Let the Executive call on judges for their opinions, he said, but don't give them statutory power.[3] Oliver Ellsworth turned the argument around. Judges, the Connecticut lawyer said, had more wisdom, firmness and accurate knowledge of the law "which the Executive can not be expected always to possess."[4]

James Madison of Virginia, the author of the proposal to unite the Judiciary with the Executive in a Council of Revision,[5] argued the measure would arm the two branches against the encroachment of the Legislative branch. "Experience in all the States had evinced a powerful tendency in the Legislature to absorb all power into its vortex," Mr. Madison added.[6]

Elbridge Gerry of Massachusetts expressed irritation that this matter had been debated and defeated, only to be revived. The proposal was an improper power coalition between the Judiciary and Executive, setting them up as guardians of the people's liberty, which is a function of the Legislature. "It was making Statesmen of Judges," the Massachusetts merchant added.[7]

At least five delegates argued that in England judges sat in Parliament and gave their opinions against legislation before it was passed.[8] Luther Martin, Maryland's Attorney General, turned the debate back to the domestic impact of the proposal. It was a dangerous innovation to combine the Judiciary with the Executive thus granting judges a double veto power. He continued:

A knowledge of mankind, and of Legislative affairs cannot be presumed to belong in a higher degree to the Judges than to

the Legislature. . . . It is necessary that the Supreme Judiciary should have the confidence of the people. This will soon be
lost, if they are employed in the task of remonstrating agst
[against] popular measures of the Legislature.[9]

Mr. Madison's proposal was defeated, as was his move to
give the Executive the power to appoint judges subject to
confirmation by the Senate. Fearful of an extension of Executive power, the Convention voted to uphold appointment of
judges by the Senate.[10]

However, in a unanimous vote, the Convention approved
the power of an Executive veto with the provision that it could
be overturned by a two-thirds vote in the House and the
Senate.

Today's debate and votes clearly illustrate that a Convention majority fears all forms of power concentration.

Sunday, July 22, 1787

A North Carolina delegate revealed today that in the next few
days the Convention will appoint a committee to begin drafting a document containing the outline of a new national government.

Hugh Williamson made the disclosure today in a letter
written to a James Iredell, a friend and prominent North
Carolina lawyer.[1] Mr. Williamson, a 48-year-old preacher-
physician,[2] made the disclosure in direct violation of the
secrecy rule that has sealed the lips of most Convention delegates since mid-May. This correspondent has obtained a copy
of Mr. Williamson's letter, in which he noted:

> After much labor the Convention have nearly agreed on the
> principles and outline of a system. . . . This system we expect
> will, in three or four days, be referred to a small committee, to

be properly dressed; and if we like it when clothed and equipped, we shall submit it to Congress, and advise them to recommend it to the hospitable reception of the States.[3]

Dr. Benjamin Franklin, in a letter written today to the naval hero of the American Revolution, John Paul Jones, revealed less, but he did confirm the Convention has made progress in framing a new national government. " . . . the Convention goes on well and . . . there is hope of a great Good to result from their Counsels," Dr. Franklin told Captain Jones.[4]

Mr. Williamson also disclosed that the two delegates from New Hampshire have finally arrived here in Philadelphia. New Hampshire had refused to pay the travel expenses of John Langdon and Nicholas Gilman. Mr. Langdon, after almost two months, decided to pay out of his own pocket the cost of attending this Convention rather than have New Hampshire remain unrepresented.[5] Mr. Langdon, 46 years old, is a wealthy merchant who built ships for the new American navy during the War of Independence. He is currently speaker of the New Hampshire Legislature.[6] Mr. Gilman is 32, a merchant, and a veteran of General Washington's army.[7]

With the Convention in recess today, General Washington left Philadelphia at 5:00 A.M. with four other delegates and visited the country home of his former military quartermaster, General Thomas Mifflin. One source says the trip was made to inspect vineyards and beehives and to have dinner with General Mifflin.[8]

In 1777, General Mifflin was involved during the darkest days of the War of Independence in a political plot to remove General Washington as military commander for alleged incompetence.[9] Today's meeting was reported by one observer as burying the last bitter memories of what has come to be called the "Conway Cabal"[10]— so named for one of the ringleaders. The Conway Cabal included Dr. Benjamin Rush, the prominent Philadelphia physician and a signer of the Declaration of Independence.[11] Now Dr. Rush, like many in this city, takes it for granted that General Washington will be unanimously selected as the first chief executive of any new national government.[12] Ironically, General Washington's quiet, behind-the-scenes influence on the Convention has done much to shape the very office everyone assumes he will be the first to occupy.[13]

Monday, July 23, 1787

A majority of States today renounced a role in ratifying any new national constitution, turning the task over to State conventions elected by the people. During the last eleven years a majority of the State Legislatures was the sole instrument for ratifying constitutions and in only two States was approval of the people sought.[1]

Oliver Ellsworth of Connecticut tried to head off today's precedent-shattering decision by proposing that the question of ratification be referred directly to the States. ". . . a new sett of ideas seemed to have crept in since the articles of Confederation were established," Mr. Ellsworth observed. "Conventions of the people, or with power derived expressly from the people, were not then thought of."[2]

Colonel George Mason of Virginia said the power of the people to ratify a new national constitution was the most important of all the resolutions to come before this Convention. The State Legislatures have no power to ratify, only the people have, Colonel Mason insisted. He went on:

> . . . this doctrine should be cherished as the basis of free Government . . . In some of the States the Govts. were ⟨not⟩ derived from the clear & undisputed authority of the people. This was the case in Virginia. Some of the best & wisest citizens consid-

ered the Constitution as established by an assumed authority. A National Constitution derived from such a source would be exposed to the severest criticisms.[3]

Virginia Governor Edmund Randolph warned delegates that ratification by the State governments will turn the fate of the new constitution over to demagogues who will lose political power in the States under the new national government.[4] Elbridge Gerry of Massachusetts insisted that the people were incompetent and could not agree on anything. If any changes are to be made in the Articles of Confederation, he added, they require approval of all the State Legislatures.[5]

James Madison replied that just as it was better to call this Convention rather than look to the old Congress of the Confederation for a new constitution, so it was better to look to State ratifying conventions, not to State Legislatures.[6]

When the vote was taken, all the States but Delaware voted for State ratifying conventions. Thus was decided the much debated issue whether this Convention was amending the Articles of Confederation, or acting in a revolutionary way by establishing its authority in the people. It is the people who will accept or reject what has been done by the delegates.[7]

Today's decision came none too soon. Two days ago the Philadelphia newspapers for the first time began reporting there was vigorous opposition by New York's State Government to a new constitution.[8]

Delegates gave unanimous approval today to a proposal to form a Committee of Detail to begin drafting a document.[9] However, an ominous hush fell over the Convention Hall when South Carolina's Charles Cotesworth Pinckney warned that his State would vote against any final document if no security were provided for the Southern States against the emancipation of their slaves and taxes on State exports.[10]

Every delegate dreads facing these issues, knowing the Convention could be confronted with another crisis of dissolution.

Tuesday, July 24, 1787

The shaping of a draft constitution was placed today in the hands of five delegates, elected as a Committee of Detail to draw up a document "comformable to the Resolutions passed by the Convention."[1]

The Committee of Detail reflects the sectional composition of this Convention: two from the North, one from the Middle States, and two from the South.[2] John Rutledge of South Carolina was the unanimious choice of the Convention as committee chairman. The 47-year-old lawyer and jurist is described as the "foremost statesman" south of Virginia.[3] According to one observer, Mr. Rutledge is a practical politician yet holds a vision for both the present and the future.[4]

His selection today as chairman of the committee that will draft the new constitution comes only one day after his South Carolina colleague, Charles Cotesworth Pinckney, issued an ominous warning. He told the Convention yesterday that his State would vote against any report of the Committee of Detail if it did not contain security for the Southern States against emancipation of their slaves and taxes on State exports.[5]

The ease with which delegates elected the Committee of Detail is in sharp contrast to the struggle they had in deciding the mode of election of a national Executive. The debate became so complex and confusing that Elbridge Gerry of Massachusetts suggested the issue be turned over to the newly elected Committee of Detail. "Perhaps they will be able to hit on something that may unite the various opinions which have been thrown out," observed the frustrated Mr. Gerry.[6]

Gouverneur Morris of Pennsylvania summarized the conflict at today's Convention session:

> ... if a good organization of the Execu[tive] should not be provided [I doubt] whether we should not have something worse than a limited Monarchy. ... It is ⟨the⟩ most difficult of all rightly to balance the Executive. Make him too weak: the

Legislature will usurp his powers; Make him too strong: he will usurp on the Legislature.[7]

A Convention majority did change its mind today and tentatively restored the right of the national Congress to elect the Executive, rather than the State Legislatures via a system of electors. James Wilson of Pennsylvania suggested that fifteen members of Congress elect the Executive by a lottery. "We ought to be governed by reason, not by chance," snorted Rufus King of Massachusetts, suggesting in turn that the entire issue be postponed.[8] So it was, the delegates were exhausted by today's session of chasing the Executive and getting nowhere.

Despite today's stalemate, delegates are reported impatient to begin soon a 10-day recess so the Committee of Detail can get on with its mandate to hammer out a working document.

Reports are that General George Washington is confident the Convention will succeed at what it set out to achieve. Apparently his mind is at ease, for he wrote a long letter today to his nephew George Augustine Washington, instructing him what crops needed special attention at Mount Vernon.[9]

Wednesday, July 25, 1787

Fear that a future national Executive might fall under foreign influence contributed to the delegates' failure at the Convention today to agree on how the Executive should be elected.

James Madison of Virginia, in a lengthy speech, sought to resolve the stalemate and failed.[1] Mr. Madison issued a grim warning that the ministers of foreign powers would make use of every opportunity to intrigue and meddle in the election of a national Executive. A system of electors chosen by the people, he argued, was one way to minimize the danger. He pressed his argument further:

> Limited as the powers of the Executive are, it will be an object of great moment with the great rival powers of Europe who have American possessions, to have at the head of our Governmt. a man attached to their respective politics & interests. No pains, nor perhaps expence, will be spared, to gain from the Legislature an appointmt. favorable to their wishes.[2]

Colonel George Mason of Virginia said that while he concurred there was a "great danger of foreign influence," he favored election of the Executive by the national Legislature.[3] Pierce Butler of South Carolina said the two great evils of cabal at home and of influence from abroad could not be avoided if Colonel Mason's proposal were adopted. He favored election of the national Executive by electors chosen by the States. " . . . the Govt. should not be made so complex & unwieldy as to disgust the States," the South Carolinian warned. "This would be the case if the election shd [should] be referred to the people."[4]

Gouverneur Morris of Pennsylvania said election by the people was the best mode to avoid past evils. Elbridge Gerry of Massachusetts replied that the idea of popular election of the Executive was "radically vicious" and the ignorance of the people would provide a small group of men the means to manipulate the election by "throwing such a power into their hands."[5]

Fear of foreign influence has concerned not just Convention delegates. Just today, John Jay, the Foreign Secretary of the Confederation, wrote a letter from New York to Convention President George Washington—a copy was obtained by this correspondent. Secretary Jay urged the Convention to provide that foreigners not be allowed to serve in the new national government. He also urged that the Convention "declare expresly that the Command in chief of the american army shall not be given to, nor devolve on, any but a natural *born* Citizen."[6]

Every Convention delegate fears any future moves by European powers, specifically in the vast unsettled wilderness to the West. It is an issue that has surfaced in Convention debates and is likely to produce bitter delegate disputes in future sessions. Potential profits from Western land speculation and the politics of population growth provide an explosive combination at this Convention.

Just this week the French envoy in New York is reported to have told his superiors, in a secret diplomatic dispatch to Paris, that the Western wilderness "contains enough land to pay the whole domestic debt of the United States."[7]

Thursday, July 26, 1787

A collective sigh of relief swept over the Convention Hall today as delegates unanimously voted a 10-day recess to give the five-man Committee of Detail time to draft a constitution.[1]

The move to recess came after a majority of States approved a single national Executive for a term of seven years, but he is barred from seeking re-election. No less than seven different plans had been proposed for electing the Executive since June 1. Ironically, the proposal approved today is the exact plan submitted to delegates in the original Randolph Resolutions when the Convention first convened two months ago.[2]

Colonel George Mason of Virginia insisted that re-election of the national Executive be prohibited. Preservation of rights of the people, he added, forms the "pole star of his political conduct" and he should at a fixed period return to the mass [public life] in order to feel and respect those rights as the "very palladium of Civil liberty."[3]

Dr. Benjamin Franklin agreed, saying that apparently

some thought that returning the magistrate to the mass of the people was degrading. He said:

> In free Governments the rulers are the servants, and the people their superiors & sovereigns. For the former [the rulers] therefore to return among the latter [the people] was not to *degrade* but to *promote* them— and it would be imposing an unreasonable burden on them to keep them always in a State of servitude, and not allow them to become again one of the Masters.[4]

Colonel Mason's view prevailed: the Executive shall be barred from seeking re-election. The Virginia statesman, however, did not prevail with his proposal that persons with unsettled accounts, or being indebted to the government, be barred from election to the national Legislature.

Gouverneur Morris of Pennsylvania was quick to protest. Few owed money to the government, he argued, while many had unsettled accounts with the government. Mr. Morris then asked: "What will be done with those patriotic Citizens who have lent money, or services or property to their Country, without having been yet able to obtain a liquidation of their claims? Are they to be excluded?"[5]

This correspondent has learned that at least thirty delegates to this Convention currently hold certificates of the public debt.[6] The principal reason this Convention was called was to deal with the collapse of public credit.[7] Nine to two States voted down Colonel Mason's proposal to exclude persons with unsettled accounts or those indebted to the government.

James Wilson of Pennsylvania said that in the future the public safety may depend on voluntary aids of private individuals, as it had in the past. He sounded the high note of the day: "We should consider that we are providing a Constitution for future generations, and not merely for the peculiar circumstances of the moment."[8]

Today's Convention session marked a milestone down a

twisting and often difficult road for the delegates. What has been spun out over the last two months has been a set of new and even revolutionary general principles. The task ahead is to take the threads of such general principles and weave them into a full constitutional fabric.[9]

Friday, July 27, 1787

The Committee of Detail, charged with drafting a new constitution, held its first session today at the State House here in Philadelphia. Its chairman gave a dramatic indication of the course he intends to chart.

John Rutledge of South Carolina is reported to have opened today's session by pulling from his pocket a copy of a constitution drawn up in 1520 by five Iroquois Indian nations and reading it aloud. The four other committee members listened in silence as the South Carolinian softly read in part from the 267-year-old document: "We, the people, to form a union, to establish peace, equity and order. . . ."[1]

With these words, Mr. Rutledge indicated that while Convention delegates in their debates referred to contemporary Europe and reached back to the ancient empires of Rome and Greece, in drafting the document, the committee must realize they are of this soil and none other.[2]

South Carolina's Charles Pinckney III, one of the youngest delegates at the Convention, had sounded a similar theme last month when he told the delegates that some had unwisely considered themselves inhabitants of an old country, rather than of a new one. He then said:

> The people of this country are not only very different from the inhabitants of any State we are acquainted with in the modern world; but I assert that their situation is distinct from either the people of Greece or Rome, or of any State we are

acquainted with among the antients [ancients] . . . can the military habits & manners of Sparta be resembled to our habits & manners?[3]

Mr. Pinckney had labored for months over his own detailed plan for a new national government and had submitted it at the start of the Convention.[4] Although the delegates chose to ignore his proposal, they did refer it and a plan of New Jersey's William Paterson to the Committee of Detail.[5]

It is reliably reported that Mr. Rutledge is prepared to use as the basis for drafting a constitutional document, both the Pinckney and Paterson proposals, as well as the Randolph Resolutions debated during the last two months. He is expected to draw also on the existing Articles of Confederation and the Constitutions of the 13 States.[6] In addition, he has the assistance of his four committee colleagues: James Wilson of Pennsylvania, a lawyer; Nathaniel Gorham of Massachusetts, a merchant; Oliver Ellsworth of Connecticut, a judge and experienced legislator; and Edmund Randolph of Virginia, that State's governor.

A clue to John Rutledge's character may be gleaned from the fact that during the War of Independence he headed the government in South Carolina and was affectionately referred to as "Dictator John."[7] However, a few days before he was unanimously elected Chairman of the Committee of Detail, he told his fellow delegates: "As we are laying the foundation for a great empire we ought to take a permanent view of the subject and not look at the present moment only."[8]

Saturday, July 28, 1787

The three-act comic opera "Powers of Enchantment" played in Philadelphia today,[1] providing some delegates a cultural diversion from the politics of the Convention.

After the Convention recessed for 10 days, delegates who live within one or two days' travel headed home by horseback or coach to attend neglected business and to refresh lagging spirits. Delegates who live at greater distances are passing the time in the city by a variety of diversions. One observer reports that some delegates are giving advice to the Committee of Detail, now at work drafting a constitution since the Convention recessed two days ago.[2]

James Madison is presumed to be in contact with two members of the Committee of Detail: James Wilson of Pennsylvania and Edmund Randolph of Virginia. He is also believed to be working on the extensive notes he has taken during the Convention debates of the last two months.[3] Mr. Madison was hard pressed to explain in a letter written to his father today why he could not reveal details of the Convention sessions because of the rule of secrecy.[4] The older Mr. Madison, in Virginia, is reported to have written to his son that if he could not tell what was discussed in the Convention, might he not tell what was *not* discussed.[5]

It is a surprise to some that so few have violated the secrecy rule. Almost nothing of substance about the Convention proceedings has appeared in the press. The exception—besides this correspondent—is today's *Pennsylvania Herald*, which reveals that a Committee of Detail has been appointed to draft a new constitution. The *Herald* was gushing today in its praise of the Convention—assuring its readers that a plan for a new government would emerge from the Convention because the delegates were "distinguished for their wisdom and patriotism."[6]

However, sources reveal that Maryland delegate Luther Martin privately is acid in his assessment of many of his colleagues. Besides sneering at General George Washington and Dr. Benjamin Franklin, the Maryland Attorney General has been furious about the Convention's rule of secrecy. The day before the Convention recessed, he was defeated in an effort to have delegates take copies of the Convention Resolutions to study over the recess in order to make suggestions upon reconvening.[7] His anger was evident, as he said:

> ... the *same spirit* which caused *our doors to be shut,* our *proceedings* to be *kept secret,—our journals to be locked up,* and *every avenue, as far as possible, to be shut* to *public information,* prevailed also in this case; ... [8]

Behind Mr. Martin's angry words is a political reality. He opposes a new national government and has worked to defeat or weaken all proposals that place in peril the power of the individual States. Mr. Martin knows that the secrecy rule favors supporters of the proposed national government and works against his dedicated efforts to expose what he perceives as an effort to enslave the States.

Sworn to secrecy and thus prevented from using allies in the press, Mr. Martin is angry because nothing but gushing praise about the Convention appears in the Philadelphia papers.

Sunday, July 29, 1787

The Committee of Detail is reliably reported today to have settled on a series of steps for drafting a new constitution to meet its August 6 deadline. The Convention imposed the deadline, but otherwise gave the Committee no specific instructions.

A source close to the drafting Committee states that Chairman John Rutledge of South Carolina feels he and his four colleagues are free to make significant contributions of their own.[1] Nonetheless, the Committee intends to incorporate elements of the resolutions that were hammered out during two months of Convention debate.[2]

Three members of the Committee reportedly have assumed the major task of drafting the document. Governor Edmund Randolph of Virginia is writing the first draft, following closely the delegates' resolutions hammered out in debate in 59 separate sessions. The Randolph draft is then to be discussed with his four colleagues, with Mr. Rutledge and James Wilson of Pennsylvania making deletions and revisions.[3] Governor Randolph describes the overall approach to the draft constitution:

1. To insert essential principles only, lest the operations of government should be clogged by rendering those provisions permanent and unalterable, which ought to be accomodated to times and events.   and

2. To use simple and precise language, and general propositions, according to the example of the (several) constitutions of the several states.[4]

It is reliably reported that Committee members seem to be relying for guidance more on the New York State Constitution of 1777 than on the 12 others. The Committee is also reported to be making extensive use of the existing Articles of Confederation.[5] This is a surprise to some observers since the Articles underwent a severe verbal battering in the Convention debates. They have been blamed for many of the political and economic problems that the Convention was convened to resolve.

Besides agreeing on a division of tasks for drafting the document, the Committee of Detail appears to have agreed on new names for elements of the new national government.

The national Legislature is to be called simply "Congress." The first branch is to be known as "The House of Representa-

tives" and the second branch simply "The Senate." The
Supreme Judicial Tribunal is to be called "The Supreme
Court." The national Executive is "President of the United
States of America" and addressed as "His Excellency."[6]

The five members of the Committee of Detail have been
working night and day since the Convention recessed three
days ago. Some of their sessions have been held at the Philadelphia State House, where the full Convention has been
meeting. Other sessions have been at the private home of
committee member James Wilson of Pennsylvania. Still
others have been held at the Indian Queen Inn where many of
the Convention delegates are staying.[7]

One source maintains that while the Committee clearly
represents the will of the entire Convention, it is the Chairman, John Rutledge of South Carolina, who is shaping the
draft document's content and character.[8]

Monday, July 30, 1787

Convention leaders are reported alarmed at rumors that a
"Philadelphia plot" is maturing to make King George's second
son America's first elected monarch.[1]

Delegates have reported receiving letters demanding to
know if the rumors are true, that they are considering a king
to head the new national government.[2] The source of the
rumor has been traced to Connecticut and a printed circular
suggesting that the States are so incompetent to govern
themselves the second son of King George should be sum-
moned.[3] One observer points out that two months of secret
Convention sessions, combined with leaks to the press that a
strong government is being formed, have given substance to
the circular's assertions.[4]

During Convention sessions, this correspondent has

learned, the subject of an elected monarch came up during debates about the election of a President and his powers in a new national government. Hugh Williamson of North Carolina, for example, opposed a single person as President and favored a three-man national Executive. A single President, he warned on July 25, would eventually end as an elected king:

> He will spare no pains to keep himself in for life, and will then lay a train for succession of his children. It [is] pretty certain ... we should at some time or other have a King; but [I wish] no precaution to be omitted that might postpone the event as long as possible. ... [5]

Early during the Convention, delegates such as Governor Edmund Randolph and George Mason, both of Virginia, voiced vigorous opposition to a single person as Executive. Bluntly, Governor Randolph told the delegates on June 1 that the country had no cause to copy the British system. The proposal for a single person as Executive, he warned, was nothing but "the foetus of monarchy."[6]

Governor Randolph, as a member of the Committee of Detail, is reported to have placed in the draft constitution severe limits on the President's authority. However, this correspondent has learned that Committee Chairman John Rutledge of South Carolina has overruled Governor Randolph and is providing substantial powers for the President in time of war.[7] This may provoke some heated debate when the Convention reconvenes on August 6. The office of President is foreign to most delegates and does not exist under the current Articles of Confederation.[8]

Delegates' fears about the President have been eased considerably by the widespread assumption that the first person to occupy the office will be General George Washington. While Convention leaders consider what to do about the rumors that they intend to create a king, General Washington has reportedly gone trout fishing in the vicinity of Valley

Forge.[9] The trip to fish peacefully and quietly on a warm summer day provides a rude contrast for the General.

Only 10 years ago—amid the deep snows of winter—he and his ragged army at Valley Forge wondered whether the War of Independence would end with their hanging as traitors to the King.

Tuesday, July 31, 1787

General George Washington made a solitary, poignant pilgrimage to Valley Forge today and reported finding his winter military camp of 1777 in ruins and reclaimed by the wilderness.[1]

On the way back from the scene of the blackest moment in his military career, the General stopped to talk to some local farmers who gave him useful information for planting buckwheat at his Mount Vernon plantation. He had never seen Valley Forge in the summer and was reported to have inspected the ruins on horseback. He confided none of his innermost emotions to his trout-fishing companion, Gouverneur Morris of Pennsylvania,[2] although his thoughts and emotions must have been of that winter a decade ago. Philadelphia was in the hands of the enemy, his army was near naked and starving, and a plot was maturing to remove him as military commander of the army.[3] Now, only 10 years later, he is peacefully fishing for trout on this hot summer day and waiting as President of the Convention to find out what final form the new national government might take.

William Pierce of Georgia offered this assessment after weeks of watching General Washington silently preside over the Convention debates:

> Having conducted these states to independence and peace, he now appears to assist in framing a Government. . . . he may be

said to be the deliverer of his Country; —like Peter the great he appears as the politician and the States-man; and like Cincinnatus he returned to his farm perfectly contented with being only a plain Citizen ... and now only seeks for the approbation of his Country-men by being virtuous and useful.[4]

The noted French author Hector Joan de Crèvcccœur four days ago wrote from New York to a friend in Paris expressing astonishment that General Washington would come out of retirement to expose his reputation to a Second American Revolution by serving as President of the Convention.

The author of the best-selling book, *Letters of an American Farmer*, has returned to America after a two-year absence. In that time, he reports, great changes have taken place. The Spanish have closed the Mississippi to American navigation and the British have increased their forces in Canada. The people, he adds, look to General Washington and the Convention to solve these and other political and economic problems with a new national government.[5]

James Monroe, writing from Fredericksburg, Virginia, to Thomas Jefferson in Paris, also looks to the General and the Convention. He said in his July 27 letter to the American Minister to France, "I trust that the presence of Gen. Washington will have great weight in the body itself ... and that the signature of his name to whatever act shall be the result of their deliberations will secure its passage thro [throughout] the Union."[6]

With all eyes and expectations turned toward Philadelphia and General Washington, his decision to go trout fishing provided a period of relaxation and reflection on how far the country has come in 10 short years.

Wednesday, August 1, 1787

A civil war of words exploded in the open today, forecasting a bitter public struggle, in print and among various political factions, over the proposed new constitution.

The *Pennsylvania Herald* in today's edition attacked New York Governor George Clinton for his criticism of the Convention and its goal of a new national government. The *Herald* said:

> A gentleman from New York informs us that the anti-foederal disposition of a great officer of that State has seriously alarmed the citizens. . . . At this critical moment, men who have an influence upon society should be cautious what opinions they entertain and what sentiments they deliver—[1]

The "gentleman from New York" the *Herald* cited as its source is believed to be Colonel Alexander Hamilton, a bitter political enemy of New York Governor Clinton. Colonel Hamilton left the Convention as a delegate from New York over a month ago. One observer believes that rather than return to the Convention, as he promised General Washington, he has stayed in New York to counter Governor Clinton's criticism of the Convention.[2]

Such criticism began after New York delegates Robert Yates and John Lansing left Philadelphia on July 10 for good. Both reported to Governor Clinton that the Convention had gone beyond its original instructions to revise the Articles of Confederation and was planning a despotic government.[3]

An unsigned letter in a New York newspaper, on July 21, attacked Governor Clinton for prejudicing the country against the work of the Convention before it was even complete. The letter, allegedly written by Colonel Hamilton, amounted to a declaration of war and over the last 10 days supporters of Governor Clinton and of Colonel Hamilton have been drawn into a civil war of words waged in the New York and Philadelphia newspapers.[4] The *Pennsylvania Herald*'s charges today are the latest, but probably not the last.

The French envoy to New York has apparently taken sides in this public battle. He is reported to have written to Paris in a July 25 secret diplomatic dispatch that there had not been "the slightest provocation" for the attack on Governor Clinton.[5]

True or not, Colonel Hamilton's alleged letter, according to one observer, has shattered the atmosphere of approval in New York that had extended to the Philadelphia Convention. What had once been silent disapproval by Governor Clinton and his followers has now exploded into a bitter public partisan dispute over the Convention and the proposed new constitution.[6]

Colonel Hamilton's decision to provoke a public debate—and observers agree that the letter was his[7]—before the Convention has even completed its work is baffling. Particularly since General Washington specifically wrote Colonel Hamilton, saying he wished Colonel Hamilton had not left Philadelphia, and missed him.

There is an irony in Colonel Hamilton's actions. As a lawyer for Georgia delegate William Pierce, he managed to settle peacefully, after returning to New York, an affair of honor that nearly ended in a duel for Mr. Pierce.[8] At the same time, within days of his successful role as a mediator, he has started a partisan political duel in the public arena that may go beyond the Convention.

Thursday, August 2, 1787

The Committee of Detail is reported today to have included in its draft of a new constitution a provision that would make future American presidents virtual military dictators in time of war.[1]

Committee Chairman John Rutledge is said to be the author of the provision, which was not granted by the full Convention in its weeks of debate on the powers of the President. Such a provision was also not contained in the initial draft constitution prepared by Committee member Governor Edmund Randolph of Virginia. Mr. Rutledge is reported to have crossed out limited authority over the militia, contained in Governor Randolph's draft, and written in complete military authority for the President in time of war.

One observer believes the former Governor of South Carolina based this on his own experience during the War of Independence when he had the responsibility of defending his State militarily, but lacked full authority to do so.[2]

The issue of the role of the military is certain to arise when the Convention reconvenes from its current 10-day recess. The most likely delegate to raise objections is Elbridge Gerry of Massachusetts. During the July 25 session, this correspondent has learned, Mr. Gerry warned the Convention that a danger of manipulation of free elections existed from the Society of the Cincinnati, which is composed of retired military officers who served under General Washington.[3]

Just today a friend of Mr. Gerry's accused the Society and the Convention of conspiring to create a standing army for the purpose of imposing a military and political aristocracy on the country. Mrs. Mercy Warren says in a letter today that the fruits of freedom won in the American Revolution are imperiled by ambitious men with a passion for power rather than liberty. She writes:

It is difficult to calculate the consequences of current appearances; the spirit of intrigue is matured in this country. . . . A sample of this truth may be exhibited in the future establishments of America, and the systems of policy that may be adopted by the busy genius's now plodding over untrodden ground, and who are more engaged in the fabrication of a strong Government than attentive to the ease, freedom and equal rights of man.[4]

Although Mrs. Warren is a woman, and cannot vote, her views carry considerable influence beyond her native New England. Besides being the sister of famed Revolutionary orator James Otis, she is a writer of some renown, and the first historian of the American Revolution. Mrs. Warren is admired and her opinions are held in high regard by almost all of the American Revolutionary leaders, including John Adams, Thomas Jefferson and General George Washington.[5] Her critical views of this Convention count.

She is highly critical, however, of General Washington for leaving retirement and accepting the role of President of the Convention. Mrs. Warren fears his prestige will allow his former officers to impose a military aristocracy on the country at the expense of personal freedom. She also accuses General Washington of restlessness in retirement and missing the applause of the public, unable to "become a calm and disinterested spectator on the transactions of statesmen and politicians. . . ."[6]

Friday, August 3, 1787

The American Minister to France proposed today that the Convention in its draft constitution deal with the chaotic commercial relations of the 13 States and find a formula to pay off the Confederacy's $100 million debt.[1]

Thomas Jefferson wrote today in a letter to Virginia Governor Edmund Randolph that the States' commercial relations should be regulated by Congress as a means to pay off their debts. "A delinquent State makes itself a party against the rest of the Confederacy," Mr. Jefferson adds.[2] The debt of the current American Confederation has been a source of acute embarrassment to Mr. Jefferson ever since he took up his diplomatic post in Paris.[3]

America owes millions to the French monarchy for the military and financial support it gave the breakaway British Colonies during the War of Independence. One observer believes that the current financial crisis facing France can be traced, in part, to the money, men and war materials the Americans received throughout most of their war.[4] The financial crisis facing France is also reported so serious that one observer in France said that riots have broken out with mobs shouting revolutionary slogans and hanging government ministers in effigy. He also discloses that a feeling is growing in France that the country is on the eve of a "great revolution in the government . . . and a strong leaven of liberty, [is] increasing every hour since the American Revolution."[5]

Mr. Jefferson, the author of the Declaration of Independence, has received reports in Paris that the Convention in Philadelphia is seriously considering a monarchy. He expresses his displeasure at the reports:

> I am astonished at some people's considering a kingly Government as a refuge. . . . Send them to Europe to see something of the trappings of monarchy, and I will undertake that every man shall go back thoroughly cured.[6]

While approving of the Convention, Mr. Jefferson has been critical of its rule of secrecy. The most direct contribution he has made to the Convention was the books that he sent to James Madison of Virginia. Mr. Madison has referred to them extensively during Convention sessions in arguing against confederacies as being inherently weak.[7]

Since Mr. Jefferson went to Paris to replace Dr. Benjamin Franklin as U.S. Minister to France, he has been busy seeking treaties of commerce and loans from France and other European countries. He is also working to convince Europe that the still-to-be united States can be trusted to meet their obligations and pay their debts.[8]

It is for this reason that Mr. Jefferson wrote to Virginia Governor Randolph today, urging the Convention to devise some formula for the States to pay their debts. He has lobbied Convention delegates and friends since the Convention began to give the new government the powers necessary to deal with the problems of commerce and finance.

It is doubtful, however, that Mr. Jefferson fully understands in Paris that what has been happening here in Philadelphia is a revolution in government far greater than the new one he anticipates or the one he helped precipitate 11 years ago.

Saturday, August 4, 1787

The Committee of Detail has completed drafting a new constitution today and ordered a Philadelphia printer to strike off copies for members of the Convention, according to Maryland delegate James McHenry.[1]

Mr. McHenry is a former secretary to General George Washington, but because of family illness he has been absent from nearly all of the sessions of this Convention.[2] Nonetheless the Maryland physician has apparently managed to review the draft constitution and study the broad powers granted the proposed new national government.[3] Those powers are apparently not to his liking. Mr. McHenry is reported to have convened a meeting of the Maryland delegation today to discuss a strategy of opposition when the full Convention reconvenes in two days. Only two of the other four

Maryland delegates disagreed with Mr. McHenry. He proposes merely to amend the Articles of Confederation, rather than allow the Convention to adopt a new constitution.[4]

This correspondent has learned this of the Maryland delegates:

> "Finding that we could come to no conclusions," Mr. McHenry later said, "I recommended meeting again to-morrow, for unless we could appear in the convention with some degree of unanimity it would be unnecessary to remain in it, sacrificing time and money without being able to render any service. . . ."[5]

Behind the threat to walk out of the Convention at this late date is a concern about the power of the new Congress to regulate commerce among the States and what impact this would have on Maryland. Mr. McHenry believes that unless the draft constitution is changed on the issue of regulating commerce among the States, the Maryland delegation should withhold its approval. It is likely that the delegates may become locked in bitter debate on the regulation of commerce, particularly since that power also includes the regulation of slavery.[6]

The fact that the Committee of Detail is ready with the draft constitution two days ahead of its deadline is attributed to the skill of Chairman John Rutledge. Only eight intensive day-and-night sessions were required to draft the document. It is said to consist of 23 articles divided into 41 sections and that it steers a middle course between two extremes.[7]

Philadelphia printers Dunlap and Claypoole are reported to have printed only 60 copies of the document, consisting of seven numbered pages with broad margins for delegates' notes as they debate the entire document.[8]

It is unlikely that the Maryland delegation will succeed in having the Committee of Detail postpone its report so the Articles of Confederation can be reconsidered. Maryland's proposal indicates that advocates of a new national government still face opposition and that plans for a new constitution are far from secure.[9] It may also mean that this Convention still has many stormy sessions ahead.

New Hampshire Delegate Nicholas Gilman is reported to have stated five days ago that it was his belief the work of the Convention might not be completed until September.[10]

Sunday, August 5, 1787

General George Washington, rested and relaxed after several days of trout fishing, arrived back in Philadelphia today and prepared himself as President of the Constitutional Convention for its reconvening tomorrow after a 10-day recess.[1]

The Convention will formally receive tomorrow the draft of a new constitution drawn up over the last 10 days by a five-member Committee of Detail. Some delegates may find it is different from what they expected.[2] For example, the powers of Congress and the Executive are closely specified and limited with an eye toward checks and balances between the two branches. However, the Judicial branch has been given final authority and power to overturn the work of the two other branches of the new national government. This is believed to be the work of Committee Chairman John Rutledge of South Carolina. He is reported to have said when serving in his native State's Assembly: "Give us good judges and we will have good rule."[3]

Some observers are surprised the Committee of Detail took only eight days to complete its work of drafting the 23 articles of the complex document. It is reported that the Committee constructed the document from diverse sources. Among them: the Convention resolutions approved by the delegates; two plans rejected by the Convention; the Articles of Confederation; and the separate State constitutions. The

Committee also drew on an August 1781 report to the Continental Congress authored by Edmund Randolph of Virginia and Oliver Ellsworth of Connecticut, both members of the Committee of Detail. Nearly two dozen recommendations in their six-year-old report were inserted into the draft document.[4]

Weaving all of these elements into one coherent constitutional fabric fell to James Wilson of Pennsylvania.[5] Georgia Delegate William Pierce says this of the Scottish-born lawyer:

> Government seems to have been his peculiar Study, all the political institutions of the World he knows in detail, and can trace the causes and effects of every revolution from the earliest stages of the Greecian commonwealth down to the present time. No man is more clear, copious, and comprehensive than Mr. Wilson. . . .[6]

The work of the Committee of Detail was the second phase of this Convention. The first was the delegate debates during the last two months over whether a new national government was necessary, and if so, its general form. Tomorrow begins phase three, when the delegates will debate line by line the Committee of Detail's draft document of the proposed new constitution to replace the Articles of Confederation.

One observer believes that the clash and conflict ahead will be between sectional economic and political interests. It is expected that delegates will haggle and trade with each other to minimize the impact of the new government on their individual State interests.[7] The Maryland delegation illustrated this when they met yesterday in caucus to consider the impact of the new constitution on Maryland's commerce.

Thus, the coming Convention sessions will be a struggle between the general interest of the 13 States and their special interests.

Monday, August 6, 1787

In a moment of high drama, delegates watched with anticipation today as John Rutledge of South Carolina, Chairman of the Committee of Detail, approached the table of Convention Secretary William Jackson and delivered a draft of the new constitution.[1]

The hall of the State House was hushed as the 3,500-word document was slowly and clearly read aloud by Secretary Jackson, his voice echoing off the hall's high ceiling. The preamble to the proposed constitution begins with these words:

> We the people of the States of New Hampshire, Massachusetts, Rhode-Island and Providence Plantations, Connecticut, New-York, New-Jersey, Pennsylvania, Delaware, Maryland, Virginia, North-Carolina, South-Carolina, and Georgia do ordain, declare, and establish the following Constitution for the Government of Ourselves and our Posterity.[2]

The preamble may have startled some delegates into the realization that the *people* and not the States are to be the architects of the new government.[3] However, the wording is almost the exact language used in the preamble of Massachusetts' first constitution.[4]

Whether by accident or design, the Committee of Detail by borrowing so much from the States has disarmed critics of the new national government who claim it will destroy the States. Borrowing so heavily from past political experience also allows the proposed government to appear less revolutionary and conveys a sense of continuity.

Article I of the document, borrowed from the Articles of Confederation, apparently achieves the sense of continuity by declaring that the style of the "Government shall be, 'The United States of America.' "[5]

The name appears intended to express the concept of unity within the diversity of the 13 States.[6]

Besides declaring that the new government shall consist of supreme Legislative, Executive and Judicial powers, the draft constitution contains prohibitions on the powers of the States. The States are prohibited, for instance, from making treaties with foreign nations, from coining money, from emitting bills of credit or making anything but gold and silver a tender in payment of debts, and from imposing taxes on foreign imports. While the Articles of Confederation limits the power of the States, the proposed national government radically reduces the power of the States even further.[7]

At the same time, the draft document ensures that the Southern slave-holding States, like South Carolina, will be protected. Buried in the section dealing with the powers of the Legislature, the document specifically prohibits the national Congress from imposing taxes on or interfering with the transportation of the slave trade.[8] The clause is clearly a response to the threat of South Carolina on July 23 that if it did not have protection for its slaves, it would not agree to the plan for a new national government.[9] It is this issue, along with the regulation of commerce, that is likely to produce heated Convention conflict.

Apparently the sweeping nature of the draft constitution moved some delegates to suggest a two-day recess to provide time to study the document.[10] The move was voted down and the Convention will meet tomorrow morning to begin what promises to be the major ordeal of constructing a government.

Tuesday, August 7, 1787

Convention delegates collectively gritted their teeth today and began to debate item by item, line by line, and word by word, the 23 articles and 41 sections of the draft constitution.[1]

The delegates unanimously approved the preamble and Articles I and II, which name the new government "The United States of America" and create the Legislative, Executive and Judicial branches.

Sharp disagreement surfaced over the provision proposing that any free person may vote without qualification. At present, no citizen in the 13 States may vote unless he owns property (land) or pays taxes.[2]

Gouverneur Morris of Pennsylvania proposed that voting be limited to freeholders (that is, farmers who own property). James Wilson objected, saying those not owning property yet qualified to vote for State Legislators would be barred from voting for members of the national Congress. Oliver Ellsworth of Connecticut, who with Mr. Wilson on the Committee of Detail helped draft the provision for voting rights without property ownership, warned the Convention: "The people will not readily subscribe to the Natl. Constitution, if it should subject them to be disfranchised."[3]

Mr. Morris brushed aside all arguments and bluntly said he had learned not to be a dupe of the words "taxation & Representation":

> ... give the votes to people who have no property, and they will sell them to the rich who will be able to buy them. We should not confine our attention to the present moment. The time is not distant when this Country will abound with mechanics & manufacturers who will receive their bread from their employers. ... The ignorant & the dependent can be as little trusted with the public interest.[4]

Dr. Benjamin Franklin, in a weak voice, offered the strongest reply to Mr. Morris. The 81-year-old philosopher and diplomat said that it was the common people who helped win the American War of Independence. The character of the American common man could be seen, Dr. Franklin said, in the conduct of American seamen when captured by the British and thrown into prison. Most refused to accept bribes and service on British Ships-of-the-Line in exchange for release from prison, while captured English seamen preferred service on American ships to prison. "This difference of behavior," Dr. Franklin argued, "arises from the operation of freedom in America. . . ."[5]

When the issue was put to a vote, Mr. Morris's proposal was defeated; only Delaware favors limiting voting to freeholders.[6]

General Washington's neutrality as President of the Convention is to be tested for the first time as the Convention proceeds with debating the proposed constitution. Delegates refused to commit the entire draft of the proposed constitution to a second committee for review and revision. In the past, major questions were dealt with in this manner, freeing General Washington from becoming directly involved in the debates. Now, as presiding officer, General Washington must rule on endless motions in the debates.[7]

A new heat wave hit Philadelphia today. With the windows of the State House closed, and the rise of delegates' temperatures during their debates, the atmosphere indoors may exceed the torrid summer weather outdoors.[8]

Wednesday, August 8, 1787

The first skirmish regarding the new constitution occurred in the Convention today over the volatile issue of computing slaves in the rule of representation, only to have both sides beat a hasty retreat.[1]

The explosive issue suddenly surfaced after delegates had resolved one other thorny issue. The Convention decided to leave voter qualification to the States because delegates could not devise a uniform rule consistent with varying, conflicting qualification codes in the 13 States.[2]

Rufus King of Massachusetts fired the first verbal broadside at the Committee of Detail's recommendation that a slave be computed as three-fifths of a person when counting population as a basis for deciding the number of representatives in Congress. "The people of the N⟨orthern⟩ States could never be reconciled ⟨to it⟩," thundered the Massachusetts lawyer. "No candid man could undertake to justify it to them."[3] Mr. King was saying, in effect, the draft constitution proposed to sanction the slave trade.[4]

Roger Sherman of Connecticut, in reply, said he regarded the slave trade as a wicked injustice but the matter had been settled by the Convention "after much difficulty & deliberation."[5] What Mr. Sherman did not say was that he and John Rutledge of South Carolina had privately settled the matter over dinner at the Indian Queen Inn in late June. Mr. Rutledge promised to support Connecticut's Western land claims against Pennsylvania if Mr. Sherman would support South Carolina on the slave trade issue.[6]

Gouverneur Morris of Pennsylvania is probably aware of the deal, and was unusually moralistic for so worldly a political cynic. He told the Convention that slavery was a curse of heaven on the States where it prevailed, adding:

> Domestic slavery is the most prominent feature in the aristocratic countenance of the proposed Constitution . . . . [I] would sooner submit [myself] to a tax for paying for all the Negroes in U. States. than saddle posterity with such a Constitution.[7]

Charles Pinckney replied that slavery was a Southern issue and there were other sectional problems: such as New England's fight over fishing rights with Great Britain and the development of Western lands, which were more burdensome to the United States than slavery. James Wilson, to the relief of most delegates, insisted the passionate debate was premature. However, the sparks generated by the issue may be a forecast of the fire to come.[8]

When today's session was at an end, the issue was left in limbo rather than rub raw the emotions of delegates faced with a long list of items to consider. Today's session demonstrates that the Convention is beginning to display sectional divisions. One is how to calculate slaves in the ratio for population representation in the House of Representatives. Another is that the Northern shipping States might want to impose restrictions on Southern exporting States that demand unrestricted commerce.[9] This particular issue appears to be hidden behind Northern denunciation of slavery and the South's defense of the institution.

These issues could well determine the character of future legislation affecting the commerce of both North and South.

Thursday, August 9, 1787

The fear of national Representatives and Senators being turned into tools of foreign powers led the Convention today into a spirited debate on the number of years a foreign-born person must reside in the country before being eligible for election to Congress.

The issue surfaced in yesterday's session when Colonel George Mason of Virginia suggested that seven years residency be required before a foreign-born could serve in Congress. If the term were less, Colonel Mason warned, a rich foreign nation like Great Britain might "send over her tools who might bribe their way into the Legislature for insidious purposes."[1] The Convention agreed to seven years yesterday.

Then today, Gouverneur Morris of Pennsylvania insisted

on a 14-year residency requirement. Charles Pinckney of South Carolina proposed a 10-year residency for Senators, because they would be involved in treaty making and foreign affairs.[2] After all, the South Carolinian remarked, ancient Athens "made it death for any stranger to intrude his voice into their legislative proceedings."[3]

James Madison of Virginia objected to a long term, saying it would taint the proposed constitution as ill liberal. He went on:

> ... it will discourage the most desirable class of people from emigrating to the U.S. Should the proposed Constitution have the intended effect of giving stability & reputation to our Govts. great numbers of respectable Europeans; men who love liberty and wish to partake its blessings, will be ready to transfer their fortunes hither.[4]

Major Pierce Butler of South Carolina, born in Ireland and a former officer in the British army,[5] said he was for a long residency requirement. Major Butler added that the British were strict on the subject of foreign-born serving in their government. Foreign habits, opinions and attachments, he went on, made him "an improper agent in public affairs."[6] James Wilson of Pennsylvania, born in Scotland, disagreed. With his pronounced burr growing thicker with his emotions,[7] he related how his foreign birth made him the object of "degrading discrimination" in the legal profession.[8]

Gouverneur Morris of Pennsylvania said the question was not one of feelings but one of reason. "We should not be polite at the expense of prudence," he said. ". . . The men who can shake off their attachments to their own Country can never love any other."[9]

Dr. Benjamin Franklin, the most experienced of the delegates in foreign affairs, reminded the delegates that the country has many friends in Europe, many who fought in the recent War of Independence. "Even in the country with which we have been lately at war," Dr. Franklin noted, "we have now & had during the war, a great many friends not only among the people at large but in both Houses of Parliament."[10]

The thought remained unspoken, but as many delegates voted for a nine-year residency, rather than 15 years, they may have been thinking of America's foreign debt and the need for expanded foreign trade.

Friday, August 10, 1787

Rejecting long established practices in a majority of States, the Convention today approved citizenship, age and residency as the only three qualifications for election to the House and the Senate.

Charles Pinckney of South Carolina sought to have property qualifications accepted, insisting it would ensure independence. "It was prudent when such great powers were to be trusted to connect the tie of property with that of reputation," the youthful and wealthy South Carolina delegate said.[1] John Rutledge concurred with his colleague, explaining that members of the Committee of Detail had recommended no qualifications because they could not agree among themselves.[2]

Dr. Benjamin Franklin, the oldest delegate, was credited by one observer with scuttling the property qualification.[3] Still seated in his chair because of gout and a painful bladder stone, the 81-year-old diplomat said he disliked everything that debased the spirit of the common people. Some of the greatest rogues he was ever acquainted with, Dr. Franklin said, were the richest rogues. He then said:

> We should remember the character which the Scripture requires in Rulers, that they should be men hating covetousness—This Constitution will be much read and attended to in Europe, and if it should betray a great partiality to the rich—

[it] will not only hurt us in the esteem of the most liberal and enlightened men there, but discourage the common people from removing to this Country.[4]

James Madison of Virginia reported that Mr. Pinckney's motion to include property as a qualification for election to Congress was defeated by "so general a *no*" that a roll call vote was not recorded.[5]

Mr. Madison then proceeded to attack the proposal for leaving all qualifications for election to Congress itself. If a future Congress could decide qualifications for both electors and the elected, Mr. Madison said, "it [the Congress] can by degrees subvert the Constitution." The British Parliament had the power over both electors and elected and it was a lesson worthy of the delegates' attention, he noted. "They had made the changes in both cases subservient to their views, or to the views of political or Religious parties," Mr. Madison added.[6]

With 11 States in attendance, the delegates have turned their backs on the long-standing traditions in the separate States of requiring not only religious and residential qualifications, but also property ownership. The Convention has voted only that the qualifications for office be citizenship, residency of nine years, and age—30 for the Senate, and 25 for the House.[7]

Colonel George Mason had successfully argued that the opinions of anyone below age 25 were certain to be crude and erroneous. It may be true, he said, that the Continental Congress proved in the past to be a good school for the young, but let them in the future, "bear the expence of their own education."[8]

Saturday, August 11, 1787

Delegates sworn to Convention secrecy found themselves in the paradoxical position today of insisting that the public had a right to know what the future national Congress was doing in its sessions.

The issue arose at today's session when the Convention took up the section in the draft constitution requiring that the House and the Senate each keep a journal of their proceedings. James Madison of Virginia and John Rutledge of South Carolina proposed that each house "from time to time" publish a journal, except the Senate may at the same time be a judge of whether secrecy is required when it is not acting in its Legislative capacity.[1]

The words of the proposal had hardly died away when every State but Virginia voiced vigorous objections. Of particular concern was the implication that the Senate might act in some capacity other than Legislative. James Wilson of Pennsylvania may have spoken for many delegates when he said:

> The people have a right to know what their Agents are doing or have done, and it should not be in the option of the Legislature to conceal their proceedings. Besides . . . it would furnish the adversaries of the reform with a pretext by which weak & suspicious minds may be easily misled.[2]

All agreed that each house shall keep a journal of its legislative proceedings and shall publish it from time to time.[3] But the phrase, "except such parts thereof in [the Senate's] Judgment require secrecy," passed by a narrow 6 to 4 vote with one State divided.[4]

The Articles of Confederation requires monthly publication of the proceedings of the Continental Congress in New York except when they relate to treaties, alliances and military operations.[5] No delegate commented on the irony of today's decision requiring public disclosure of future Congresses while the windows of the Convention Hall are shut and an armed sentry is posted below to prevent any outsiders from overhearing the Convention debates.[6] One source reports, moreover, that leaders of this Convention are planning to prevent publication of their own proceedings, with the consent of General Washington. This source also reports that publication of the Convention debates would provide opponents in the States ammunition to shoot down ratification of the proposed constitution.[7]

The most powerful foe of this Convention from the very start has been Patrick Henry of Virginia. If he had agreed to serve as a delegate, he would have ranked next to General Washington in influence and standing. Mr. Henry's absence has caused considerable concern among delegates.[8]

Opposition to a new constitution exploded two weeks ago in the New York newspapers, pitting Delegate Colonel Alexander Hamilton against the State's popular Governor, George Clinton.[9] And three days ago opposition to the work of the Convention appeared in Pennsylvania.[10] Most Convention delegates are concerned that even before their work is completed, mounting opposition in a handful of States could undo months of labor. North Carolina's Richard Spaight is reported to have told a close personal friend in a letter this week that it is "in the powers of one or two States" to defeat the proposed new constitution and prevent a binding and permanent union.[11]

Sunday, August 12, 1787

A deep division is reported to have developed in the Virginia delegation during the last few weeks, foreshadowing serious trouble in that key State for the new constitution when it faces ratification.

Rumors are circulating in Virginia that delegates Colonel George Mason and Governor Edmund Randolph have increasingly dissented from decisions of a Convention majority.[1] Governor Randolph is said by one observer to be deeply disturbed at Convention implementation of the original Virginia Plan, which he introduced as the Randolph Resolutions.[2]

Governor Randolph is equally unhappy about the action taken by the Convention on August 8. On that day, seven States, including Virginia, voted to kill the provision granting the House exclusive power to originate money bills.[3] Governor Randolph sat through that session four days ago smoldering with anger and saying nothing. Colonel Mason, speaking for the two of them, said that striking out that section was to unhinge the compromise that had saved the Convention from dissolution. If the House does not have exclusive power over the national purse, he added, the Convention was opening the way for government by aristocracy. Colonel Mason then went on, speaking for Governor Randolph as well:

> ". . . [My] idea of an Aristocracy was that it was the governt. of the few over the many. An aristocratic body, like the screw in mechanics, workig. its way by slow degrees, and holding fast whatever it gains, should ever be suspected of an encroaching tendency—The purse strings should never be put into its hands."[4]

Colonel Mason and Governor Randolph fear that the Convention will eventually grant the Senate power over the public purse—and with equal representation for each State, the Senate does not represent the people, they feel. There is now such a serious division between the two delegates and James Madison that Mr. Madison is deeply worried it will deadlock the Convention. In an effort to prevent this, he has urged Virginia delegate and physician Dr. James McClurg to return to Philadelphia.[5] Dr. McClurg left during the last week of July with the intention of not returning. In an August 5 letter replying to Mr. Madison—a copy was obtained by this correspondent—Dr. McClurg flatly rejected the idea of returning, saying, "my attendance now would certainly be useless, perhaps injurious."[6]

The division within the Virginia delegation includes General Washington. He reportedly told Mr. Madison he will vote tomorrow to restore the right of the House to originate money bills and bar the Senate from amending. General Washington does not agree with Colonel Mason and Governor Randolph on this issue, but plans to vote with them to prevent them from being "less cordial in other points of real weight."[7]

The Virginia delegation splintering into factions is an ironic development. It was a united Virginia that seized the leadership role when this Convention first convened. It was a united Virginia that put forth the bold blueprint for a revolutionary national government and convinced a reluctant Convention majority to accept critical elements. Now, within sight of achieving its objectives, the Virginia delegation is riddled with disagreement over its own compromised creation.

Monday, August 13, 1787

The question of power over the public purse produced a heated Convention debate today, the lengthy session in the hot, humid hall extending beyond five o'clock and forcing many ill-humored delegates to be late for their normal dinner hour.[1]

Today's stormy session was a reconsideration of a previous Convention action that had denied the national House the right to originate all money bills. Some large State delegates deeply resented the action, for example, Virginia Governor

Edmund Randolph. He demanded today's reconsideration, believing the action was a repudiation by the small States of the Great Compromise between the large and the small States that had saved the Convention from dissolution.[2]

Colonel George Mason of Virginia insists that since the House represents the people and the Senate the States, it is improper that the Senate should have power to tax the people. "The House of Lords does not represent nor tax the people," Colonel Mason argued, because it is not elected by the people of Great Britain. He believes, "If the Senate can originate, they will in the recess of the Legislative Sessions, hatch their mischievous projects for their own purposes. . . ."[3]

James Wilson of Pennsylvania suggested a compromise. The public purse could have two strings, one in the hands of the House and the other in the Senate. "Both houses must concur in untying, and of what importance could it be which untied first, which last . . .?" he asked.[4] James Madison of Virginia and John Dickinson of Delaware made similar suggestions. Mr. Dickinson pointed out that eight States currently have in their constitutions the exclusive right for the popular branch to originate money bills, while allowing the other branch to amend. "Experience must be our only guide. Reason may mislead us," the Delaware delegate warned.[5]

In no mood for compromise, Governor Randolph said he would press for restoring the exclusive right of the House to originate money bills. He said:

> When the people behold in the Senate, the countenance of an aristocracy; and in the president, the form at least of a little monarch, will not their alarms be sufficiently raised. . . . The Senate will be more likely to be corrupt than H. of Reps and should therefore have less to do with money matters.[6]

The charge that the Convention might create a monarchy surfaced today in Philadelphia papers. The *Pennsylvania Gazette* reprinted a circular from Connecticut proposing to send to England for a King. The paper warns the delegates to be on their guard. "The Federal Convention may save us from this worst of curses," the paper wrote.[7]

A majority of Convention delegates took neither the newspapers nor Governor Randolph's concern about a monarchy seriously. By seven States to four, the Convention rejected restoring to the House the power to originate money bills.[8]

The defeat, according to one observer, left Governor Randolph deeply disappointed and humiliated.[9] His only consolation is that the issue remains unresolved, and that General Washington voted with him. The General's gesture may have prevented an angry exit and split of the Virginia delegation.

Tuesday, August 14, 1787

A future crisis for the proposed national government was averted today when nine States voted to pay members of Congress out of the national treasury rather than from the separate States.[1]

The Committee of Detail, contrary to a previous vote by the Convention, had recommended compensation for members of Congress be determined by the States from which they are elected. One observer pointed out that if the provision were left in place, members of the national Congress would be State officers. This would eventually create a conflict with the whole theory of a National Congress under a National Constitution.[2] Colonel George Mason of Virginia spoke of the political implications of the potential conflict:

> It has not yet been noticed that the clause as it now stands makes the House of Represents. also dependent on the State Legislatures; so that both Houses will be made the instruments of the politics of the States whatever they may be.[3]

Major Pierce Butler of South Carolina argued for payment by the States, particularly for Senate members who will be elected by the States. They will be long out of their respective States, he added, and "will lose sight of their Constituents unless dependent on them for their support."[4]

James Madison countered with a razor-like argument. The House and the Senate, he said, will be elected every two and six years respectively, while the States are subject to annual elections—producing the very political instability "which [is] the principal evil in the State Govts."[5]

Mr. Madison's and Colonel Mason's arguments appear to have carried a majority of the Convention. The question then turned to how much members of Congress should be paid out of the national treasury. Roger Sherman of Connecticut proposed five dollars a day with additional compensation provided by the States.[6] John Dickinson of Delaware noted that someone has suggested linking the compensation for members of Congress to the price of wheat. He proposed instead that an act be passed every 12 years setting the wages of national representatives.[7] Oliver Ellsworth of Connecticut favored setting congressional salaries based on the current value of money.[8] The Convention rejected all these proposals with the words "to be ascertained by law."[9]

The Convention also debated but postponed voting on the question of whether members of Congress be allowed to hold other offices and receive compensation. Virginia delegates James Madison and Colonel George Mason have clashed over this and other issues. One observer believes this has led to a serious breach in their friendship.[10]

Colonel Mason, who came to this Convention with high expectations, has in recent weeks become bitter. Today, for example, he sarcastically suggested to the Convention that some delegates favored a corrupt aristocracy.[11]

Like Virginia Governor Edmund Randolph, Colonel Mason finds the emerging constitution something to be feared rather than favored.

Wednesday, August 15, 1787

The Convention was caught today in a cobweb of conflict spun out by three different factions fighting each other to shape a final constitutional document.

James Madison of Virginia for a third time was defeated in his proposal to make all acts passed by Congress subject to joint review by the President and the Supreme Court. Ironically, in opposition, John Francis Mercer of Maryland used Mr. Madison's own argument about the separation of powers, saying that "the Judiciary ought to be separate from [and independent of] the Legislative."[1] Several weeks ago, Mr. Madison had insisted that it was a fundamental principle of free government that the powers of the three branches be "*separately* exercised" and they should also be "*independently* exercised."[2] His later proposal for joint veto power by the President and the Supreme Court over the acts of Congress appears to be a contradiction.

Gouverneur Morris of Pennsylvania renewed his proposal that the President be given *absolute* veto over congressional acts. Mr. Morris said he had no faith in giving the President a qualified veto with Congress able to override it with only a two-thirds vote. A larger percentage, a three-fourths vote, Mr. Morris added, would "prevent the hasty passage of laws."[3]

James Wilson of Pennsylvania agrees that the threat to liberty was not from a powerful President, but from a Congress if unchecked by veto powers of the Executive or the Judicial. In Great Britain, he insisted, "a more pure and unmixed tyranny sprang up in the parliament than had been exercised by the monarch."[4]

As nationalists, Mr. Wilson, Mr. Morris and Mr. Madison still refuse to surrender their view that the national government should have greater powers than now granted by the draft constitution. States' rights delegates such as Mr. Mercer of Maryland believe the draft document has gone too far and argued today for postponement of the presidential veto issue. This visibly irritated delegates who favor the current draft constitution and are impatient to approve the document. John Rutledge of South Carolina, in a rare display of public anger, complained at length that the debates had become tedious. Oliver Ellsworth of Connecticut concurred:

> We grow more & more skeptical as we proceed. If we do not decide soon, we shall be unable to come to any decision.[5]

Clearly, Mr. Rutledge and Mr. Ellsworth regard both the extreme nationalists and the extreme States' rights delegates as an obstructing minority impeding the work of the Convention majority. One unconfirmed report alleges that States' rights delegates from six States have been meeting privately at night after each Convention session to discuss tactics for watering down the draft constitution.[6] Thus, delay is their ally.

John Rutledge of South Carolina understands that the longer the nationalists and the States' rights delegates are allowed to delay final decisions, the less likely there will be any decisions favorable to the draft document. This is apparently why he is expected to ask the Convention to lengthen its daily sessions from four to six hours and that no motions for an earlier adjournment be permitted.[7] Mr. Rutledge is living up to his reputation as "Dictator John."

Thursday, August 16, 1787

Without dissent or debate, the Convention today granted the new Congress the power to levy and collect taxes and to regulate interstate and foreign commerce. It also gave Congress the sole power to coin money and regulate the value of foreign coin, to fix the standard of weights and measures, and to establish post-offices.[1]

By granting Congress the power to tax, the Convention solves a major problem that has hobbled the country under the existing Articles of Confederation. Currently, the Continental Congress in New York has no power to levy taxes on individual citizens, nor can it force the 13 States to pay the nation's debts through the system of voluntary compliance with requisitions for funds.[2]

Today's decisions imply that the States will be forbidden to tax or to restrain interstate or foreign commerce, which amounts to a fundamental shift of power to the proposed new national government.[3] The States will also lose the right to coin money other than gold and silver and will be forbidden to issue "bills of credit" or paper money. On this issue, the Convention was virtually unanimous, mindful of the savage inflation during the last decade. Seven States during the Revolution had printed paper currency and refused to raise taxes. The Continental Congress had issued its own paper currency, leading to the widespread statement, "Not worth a continental."[1]

The memory of the scourge of inflation is so strong that the delegates voted nine States to two prohibiting the new national government from printing paper money. As Gouverneur Morris of Pennsylvania warned: "The Monied interest will oppose the plan of Government, if paper emissions be not prohibited."[5]

Colonel George Mason of Virginia said that while he had a "mortal hatred to paper money," he was unwilling to absolutely tie the hands of the government. " . . . the late war could not have been carried on, had such a prohibition existed," Colonel Mason added.[6] John Mercer of Maryland cautioned that forbidding the new government to emit bills of credit would produce political conflicts between friends and foes of paper money and jeopardize approval of the new government. However, Oliver Ellsworth spoke for the majority when he said:

> ... this [is] a favorable moment to shut and bar the door against paper money. The mischiefs of the various experiments which had been made, were now fresh in the public mind and had excited the disgust of all the respectable part of America. By withholding the power from the new Governt. more friends of influence would be gained to it than by almost any thing else—Paper money can in no case be necessary— ... the power may do harm, never good.[7]

The Convention's strong stand today in favor of hard money underscores Rhode Island's refusal to send a State delegation to Philadelphia. That State is currently in the hands of politicians who favor paper money. They may be forced by the new national government to pay Rhode Island's debts in gold and silver and not inflated paper. The Providence government's paper money policy has earned the State the nickname "Rogue Island."[8]

Friday, August 17, 1787

Turning its back on the traditions of Europe, the Convention today granted Congress the exclusive power to declare war.

This action constitutes an innovation in government: in all other countries, the power to make or declare war is vested in the executive or crowned head of state.[1] In Great Britain, the King is commander-in-chief of the armed forces with exclusive power to raise and regulate fleets, armies and militia. However, in times of peace standing armies in Great Britain are prohibited by law. Parliament, through its power of the purse, can dissolve armies by refusing to appropriate money for their support.[2]

In today's session, Charles Pinckney III of South Carolina

insisted the Senate should have exclusive power to make or declare war. The House would have too many members, he added, while the Senate would be "more acquainted with foreign affairs, and most capable of proper resolutions."[3] Major Pierce Butler of South Carolina proposed vesting war power in the President. " . . . [he] will have all the requisite qualities, and will not make war but when the Nation will support it," the former British military officer added.[4]

James Madison of Virginia and Elbridge Gerry of Massachusetts proposed a significant single-word change that was adopted by the Convention. Rather than the power to "*make*" war, the Congress would have the power to "*declare*" war, leaving the President "the power to repel sudden attacks."[5]

However, the Convention was split right down the center when it was asked to approve the power of the new national government to subdue armed rebellions in any State at the request of that State's Legislature. Luther Martin of Maryland insisted the power was unwarranted and dangerous. Gouverneur Morris of Pennsylvania argued that the new national government should have means to enforce obedience in all cases. He went on:

> We are acting a very strange part. We first form a strong man to protect us, and at the same time wish to tie his hands behind him. The legislature may surely be trusted with such a power to preserve the public tranquillity.[6]

Elbridge Gerry of Massachusetts expressed the belief that much more blood would have been spilled in his State during the recent rebellion by debt-ridden farmers had the general government intervened with armed force. "The States wil be the best Judges in such cases," he added.[7] A 4 to 4 tie vote, with two States absent, led the Convention to drop entirely the power to subdue rebellion in the separate States. Nevertheless, the delegates are expected to return later to the issue.[8]

Mr. Gerry's raising the issue of the recent Shays Rebellion

in Massachusetts was a reminder of public gloom about the inefficiency of current national authority. There is no doubt that last year's mob violence against the State's courts, which were seeking to collect the farmers' debts, had an impact on every delegate. James Madison of Virginia has acknowledged that one of the "ripening incidents" leading to this Convention was the armed rebellion in Massachusetts led by Captain Daniel Shays.[9]

Saturday, August 18, 1787

The military sword was placed in the hands of the new national government today when the Convention unanimously approved congressional power to raise and support armies. However, delegates borrowed from the British Parliament's use of the power of the purse to check that sword by limiting military appropriations to only two-year periods.[1]

Elbridge Gerry of Massachusetts had complained that there was no check against a standing army in time of peace. He pointed out that the existing Congress in New York does not have power to maintain an army and thought the idea "dangerous in time of peace & [he] could never consent to the power to keep up an indefinite number."[2] Mr. Gerry and Luther Martin of Maryland proposed that the number of troops in time of peace be limited to two or three thousand.

The proposal was subjected to ridicule and was overwhelmingly rejected. General Charles Cotesworth Pinckney of South Carolina asked facetiously whether "no troops were ever to be raised until an attack shall be made on us."[3] General George Washington, in a rare display of satirical humor, turned to a delegate who stood near by and whispered that perhaps Mr. Gerry's motion should be amended to read that "no foreign enemy should invade the United States at any time, with more than three thousand troops."[4]

But Convention consensus was shattered when it was proposed that Congress regulate the States' Militia. James Madison of Virginia told the delegates:

> ... the regulation of the Militia naturally [belongs] to the authority charged with the public defence. It did not seem in its nature to be divisible between two distinct authorities. If the States would trust the Genl. Govt. with a power over the public treasure, they would from the same consideration of necessity grant it the direction of the public force.[5]

Today's heated and protracted debate over State militia is the outgrowth of two views. On one hand, the "citizen soldier" militia is viewed as a symbol of the freedom and independence of the States. The existence of the militia has been viewed traditionally as making a national standing army unnecessary. Also, the view is that a national government should not control a military force.[6]

Elbridge Gerry of Massachusetts spoke for the States' rights delegates when he denounced national control of the militia. "The plan will have as black a mark as was set on Cain," Mr. Gerry passionately proclaimed.[7]

On the other hand, as General Pinckney pointed out, the dissimilarity in the militia of the different States during the War of Independence compromised conduct of that conflict. "Uniformity was essential. The States would never keep up a proper discipline of their militia," claimed the former aide to General Washington.[8]

Rather than impede the progress of the Convention, delegates voted to refer the matter of the militia to the Grand Committee of Eleven that was formed today to consider twenty other powers to be delegated to the national Congress. The Committee was also charged with the task of deciding whether the new national government would assume State debts, which have become a chronic economic and political problem since the War of Independence.[9]

Sunday, August 19, 1787

Reviving melancholy memories of a military defeat a decade ago, General George Washington today visited his old encampment White Marsh, near Germantown, Pennsylvania, and, in his own words, "contemplated on the dangers which threatened the American Army at that place."[1]

General Washington made the trip with his close personal friend Samuel Powell, while the Convention was in recess for the day. One observer reported later that the entire trip was a somber one, recalling the days in 1777 and 1778 when Philadelphia was occupied by the British and hunger hung over Valley Forge like a vulture. General Washington visited one house scarred from musket balls and revived his memory of the pitched battle between the British and the Americans.[2]

The lawn around the house had been littered with American and British dead and wounded. Germantown in October 1777 was regarded by General Washington as a military defeat, made more humiliating when some of his troops panicked and fled. Paradoxically, the French were influenced, in part, to aid the Americans because General Washington's troops nevertheless refused to criticize his poor tactics and maintained a high state of morale after their defeat.[3]

One of the senior American officers at Germantown was chief of artillery General Henry Knox. In a letter to General Knox today, a copy of which has been obtained by this correspondent, General Washington wrote that while the business of the Convention is slow, it is sure. He wryly observes that if any good comes from the Convention after three months it will not be because delegates have been in a hurry. In an apparent effort to use his prestige to gain ratification of the draft constitution, he told General Knox:

> . . . I wish a disposition may be found in Congress, the several State Legislatures—and the community at large to adopt the Government which may be agreed on in Convention because I

am fully persuaded it is the best that can be obtained at the present moment under such diversity of ideas as prevail.[4]

During the last few days, the Convention approved a peace-time army for the new national government but became bogged down on control of State militia. How much the debate this week on the creation of the army and control of the militia prompted General Washington to make today's trip to White Marsh and Germantown is not known. In the coming week, this correspondent has learned, the Convention is expected to debate the fate of State militia. Roger Sherman of Connecticut told the delegates at yesterday's session that just as States retain the power to tax, so States must retain their militia for defense. "They will not give up on this point," he warned.[5]

The fight over the militia is a sharp contrast to the almost spectacular ease with which the Convention approved the creation of a national army without any real debate.[6] James Madison of Virginia and a few others want national authority over the State militia with an eye toward making a large regular military force unnecessary. General Charles Cotesworth Pinckney of South Carolina was a military aide to General Washington during the War of Independence and his objection to the national government using State militia may have carried the debate. He cited his experience with the different State militia and their dissimilarities that produced "serious mischiefs."[7]

Most delegates desire a small, well-regulated army for national security and as a way of providing "uniformity" and "proper discipline." Yet they hope to avoid the European evil of maintaining a large standing army in time of peace.[8]

Monday, August 20, 1787

Reaching back to 14th-century England, the Convention today narrowly defined the crime of treason and gave Congress the power to punish anyone who, in open court confesses or with the testimony of two witnesses, is convicted of treason. The definition is: " . . . levying war against them [the United States], or in adhering to their enemies giving them aid and comfort."[1]

The wording of today's treason section is taken in part from the old statute of 1352 by Edward III of England and the English statute of Edward VI's in 1552 requiring two witnesses to an act of treason.[2] One observer noted that today's session involved semantic hair-splitting and gave lawyer delegates an opportunity to display their legal learning.[3] Lawyer James Wilson of Pennsylvania summed up the legal and political thicket of the treason issue:

> . . . much may be said on both sides. Treason may sometimes be practiced in such a manner, as to render proof extremely difficult—as in a traitorous correspondence with an Enemy.[4]

Dr. Benjamin Franklin noted that, in the past, prosecutions for treason were used for political reasons and often involved perjured testimony against innocent defendants. In England, the King's political enemies were charged with treason and a person's religion was often regarded as treason. In the last 10 years in States such as North Carolina, treason prosecutions have been numerous, for offenses ranging from being an officer under the King to petty treason offenses of murder and robbery.[5]

Gouverneur Morris of Pennsylvania warned: " . . . it is essential to the preservation of liberty to define precisely and exclusively what shall constitute the crime of Treason."[6]

Colonel George Mason of Virginia compounded the complexity of the treason issue when he insisted that an act of treason may be against a single State but not the entire

United States. He pointed to the rebellion in Virginia by Nathaniel Bacon in 1676, a century before the American colonial rebellion against Great Britain.[7] James Madison of Virginia warned that treason against a State and treason against the United States meant "the same act may be twice tried & punished by the different authorities."[8] John Dickinson of Delaware insisted that treasonous war and insurrection against one State must be defined as against the whole nation. "The Constitution should be made clear on this point," he added.[9]

It took seven separate votes to arrive at the precise language for the 54 words of the treason section. One observer later pointed out that by laboring so long over the precise language, the delegates hope to keep treason from becoming a weapon in the arsenal of tyranny.[10]

Besides limiting the power of Congress to use the issue of treason as a political weapon, the Convention also limited the new national legislature in six other areas. In one area it forbade Congress's suspending the writ of *habeas corpus* except in cases of rebellion or invasion.[11] The Convention also unanimously agreed to give the new government the power "to make all laws necessary and proper for carrying into execution the powers vested by this constitution in the government of the United States, or in any department or office thereof."[12]

Tuesday, August 21, 1787

The long delayed debate over slavery erupted among delegates today, producing one of the angriest sessions of the entire Convention.[1]

Debate began on a deceptive note of harmony when delegates agreed, with only one dissenting State, to authorize direct federal taxation. Delegates had earlier agreed that Congress could levy taxes and today's provision is to ensure that the proposed national government will possess the resources and financial credit needed to maintain itself in an emergency.[2] Luther Martin of Maryland, perhaps mindful of the part direct taxation had played in the recent armed rebellion of farmers in Massachusetts, issued a warning to fellow delegates that the public would be hostile to the proposal. "Direct taxation should not be used but in cases of absolute necessity; and then the States will be best Judges of the mode," he added.[3]

Mr. Martin also sought, but failed to gain, adoption of a plan that would impose revenue quotas on the States when direct taxation was imposed. The delegates then launched into a long and heated debate on taxing exports. Two New England States joined with the five most Southern States to deny Congress power to tax exports.

Mr. Martin then lit the fuse of anger by proposing a tax on the importation of slaves.[4] He gave three reasons for his proposal:

1. As five slaves are to be counted as 3 free men in the apportionment of Representatives; such a clause wd. [would] leave an encouragement to this trafic.

2. slaves weakened one part of the Union which the other parts were bound to protect: the privilege of importing them was therefore unreasonable—

3. it was inconsistent with the principles of the revolution and dishonorable to the American character to have such a feature in the Constitution.[5]

John Rutledge of South Carolina in reply said "Religion & humanity had nothing to do with this question—Interest alone is the governing principle with Nations—The true question at present is whether the Southn. States shall or shall not be parties to the Union." Mr. Rutledge added, "If the Northern States consult their interest, they will not oppose the increase of Slaves which will increase the commodities of which they will become the carriers."6

Oliver Ellsworth of Connecticut insisted that "the morality or wisdom" of slavery should be left to the States. "The old confederation had not meddled with this point," he added, and he did not "see any greater necessity for bringing it within the policy of the new one."7

Today's stormy session was more a clash over the power to tax and to regulate commerce than over slavery. Northern delegates are reported alarmed that the Committee of Detail in its draft constitution has granted concessions to the Southern States on matters of commerce. "The States will never give up all power over trade," warned Roger Sherman of Connecticut during today's session.8 But Colonel George Mason of Virginia pointed out that the eight Northern States have different interests from those of the five Southern States and the South could be outvoted in the House of Representatives on commercial and tax issues. "The Southern States [have] therefore ground for their suspicions," Colonel Mason observed.9

Thus, the Convention is confronted with a new deadlock between North and South over the regulation of commerce, of which slaves are one component.

Wednesday, August 22, 1787

Debate over the regulation of commerce and the slavery issue continued today and grew so bitter that Convention leaders sought to smother passions by appointing a Committee of Eleven to devise a compromise before anger led to a permanent Convention deadlock.1

One delegate from each State was appointed to the Committee, charged with finding a formula to resolve two inflammatory interrelated issues: one, whether Congress should be given the power to impose export duties; and two, taxation on the importation of slaves. The Committee of Detail had recently recommended to the full Convention a prohibition against such taxation and a ban on any regulation of navigation by the new government unless passed by two-thirds in both the House and the Senate.[2]

The critical issue is the Northern States' control (as a majority) of commerce, with the slavery importation trade complicating any Southern compromise.

The debate today centered on the issue of slavery. Roger Sherman of Connecticut said that, while he disapproved of the slave trade, he favored leaving matters as they stood. The States are now possessed of the right to import slaves and the public good did not require this right be denied, he said. The deeply religious Yankee from Connecticut added that: "... the abolition of slavery seemed to be going on in the U.S. & ... the good sense of the several States would probably by degrees compleat it."[3]

Colonel George Mason of Virginia delivered the most passionate denunciation of slavery of the Convention. The "infernal traffic" was born in the avarice of British merchants, Colonel Mason charged, and the British government had prevented Virginia from putting a stop to it. Virginia, Maryland and North Carolina have banned the importation of slaves, yet, the author of the first Bill of Rights in America added, South Carolina and Georgia are to be permitted to import slaves who will be sold to the frontier West, clamoring for this "nefarious traffic." The tall, white-haired Virginian, his black eyes burning,[4] issued this warning:

> Every master of slaves is born a petty tyrant. They bring the judgement of heaven on a Country. As nations can not be rewarded or punished in the next world they must be in this. By an inevitable chain of causes & effects providence punishes national sins, by national calamities.[5]

Oliver Ellsworth of Connecticut was apparently stung by Colonel Mason's charge that some Eastern delegates with shipping interests had a "lust of gain" by profiting from slavery. Mr. Ellsworth replied that since he never owned a slave he could not judge the effects of slavery on character. An obvious reference to a fact every delegate knows: Colonel Mason owns slaves.[6] Charles Pinckney III of South Carolina offered the only defense of the South during today's occasion. "If slavery be wrong, it is justified by the example of all the world," Mr. Pinckney said, referring to slavery in other modern nations and its existence in ancient Greece and Rome.[7]

With Georgia and South Carolina threatening to oppose the constitution, the Convention compromised with a Committee of Eleven to take up the power of Congress to tax exports and impose duties on the importation of slaves. Despite weariness, the continuing humidity, and the long sessions, every delegate understands that without a compromise between the shipping States of the North and the planter States of the deep South, the constitution will be stillborn.[8]

Thursday, August 23, 1787

A majority of the States today reluctantly gave up absolute authority over their militia and agreed to supremacy of the new national government. The surrender on the issue of State militia control, however, was not without bitter debate.

Elbridge Gerry of Massachusetts complained, for instance, that national control for organizing, arming and disciplining State militia amounted to "making the States drill-sergeants."[1] James Madison and Edmund Randolph both from Virginia countered that the militia was a national concern and required national control. " . . . the Militia were every where neglected by the State Legislatures, the members of which courted popularity too much to enforce a proper discipline," Mr. Randolph added.[2]

During the War of Independence, General George Washington and the Continental Congress had no end of grave difficulties dealing with the State militia.[3] According to one observer, a majority of delegates have nothing but contempt for the militia, and no one more silently contemptuous than Convention President Washington.[4] Despite this, Mr. Gerry warned, the Convention was pushing the experiment of a national government too far:

> Some people will support a plan of vigorous Government at every risk. Others of a more democratic cast will oppose it with equal determination. And a Civil war may be produced by the conflict.[5]

James Madison of Virginia, in rebuttal to Mr. Gerry, insisted that the most likely source of disunion is from the States. It is, therefore, necessary that the national government be granted sufficient powers to deal with such danger. ". . . and as the greatest danger to liberty," Mr. Madison added, "is from large standing armies, it is best to prevent them by an effectual provision for a good Militia."[6] The Virginian was partially successful with his incisive argument.

A Convention majority decided to reserve to the States the appointment of militia officers and authority to train the State militia, according to discipline prescribed by the national government.[7] After this compromise, it was unanimously agreed that the proposed constitution, and the treaties and acts of Congress, be made the "supreme law of the several States and of their citizens and inhabitants."[8]

General George Washington is reported pleased and relieved at this surrender of the States to the supremacy of the proposed national government. During the War of Independence he had vainly pleaded with the States for such power.[9]

The States' rights delegates were visibly angered, however, when it was proposed the new government be given the power to veto all State laws. James Wilson of Pennsylvania, who has persisted with this proposal, said it was the "keystone" to the government the Convention was constructing. The proposal was defeated by a narrow one-vote margin when John Rutledge of South Carolina warned nothing would damn the new constitution to defeat more than national veto power over all State laws. "Will any State ever agree to be bound hand & foot in this manner," he asked.[10]

Friday, August 24, 1787

The method of electing the President became the focus of the Convention battle today, with the large States seeking to free the chief executive from the control of Congress that is favored by the small States.[1]

As it now stands, the Convention has given Congress the power to elect a single person as President for a seven-year term but he is barred from seeking re-election.[2]

John Rutledge of South Carolina triggered today's debate when he proposed election of the President by a *joint* congressional ballot. The small States counterattacked, claiming that the House with its more numerous members from the large States would outvote the small States, since representation in the Senate was equal.[3]

The dispute apparently gave the large States the opportunity then to propose election of the President by the people rather than by the Congress. The move was decisively defeated 9 to 2, and the Convention went on to approve the joint ballot election.[4] It was here that Gouverneur Morris of Pennsylvania delivered what may prove to be the decisive death blow to congressional election of the President. It will lead to legislative tyranny, Mr. Morris insisted; with the President dependent on the Congress they can conspire together in cabals of corruption "and support their usurpations by the influence of tax-gatherers and other officers." He went on, adding:

> Hence, the Executive is interested in Courting popularity in the Legislature by sacrificing his Executive rights; & then he can go into that Body, after the expiration of his Executive Office, and enjoy there the fruits of his policy.[5]

Mr. Morris proposed that the election of the President be made by a college of electors chosen by the people of the States. Much to everyone's surprise, the proposal lost by only one vote. A subsequent vote on the President being "chosen by electors" as an abstract ended in a tie,[6] illustrating the degree of frustration felt by most delegates over the office of the President since the Convention first began debating the question over two months ago.

The degree of distrust of a powerful President was illustrated today by Roger Sherman of Connecticut. When the Convention debated the President's appointment powers, Mr. Sherman objected to the wording giving the President the power to "appoint officers," believing it meant military officers. Corruption in Great Britain is possible, Mr. Sherman went on, by such power and an American President "may set up an absolute Government; taking advantage of the close of a war and an army commanded by his creatures."[7]

The Convention agreed today to change the wording of "officers" to "offices" and to postpone debate on the election of the President. The difficulty the delegates have had regarding the office stems from two reasons. First, the entire history of the separate States has been chief executives with narrow powers and beholden to the State Legislatures.[8] Second, under the Articles of Confederation and in Europe, the office of a single chief executive has few parallels to guide the delegates.

No wonder they are baffled about deciding the powers and election of an American President.[9]

Saturday, August 25, 1787

Political expediency prevailed over moral righteousness today when the Convention diffused the explosive slavery issue by agreeing to a compromise formula fashioned by the Committee of Eleven.[1]

At yesterday's session the Committee report recommended that the importation of slaves be permitted until 1800 and the slave traffic be taxed "at a rate not exceeding the average of the Duties laid on Imports."[2] The current market value for a single slave is an average of $200.[3]

Today, General Charles Cotesworth Pinckney of South Carolina proposed that the date to an end to the slave trade be extended from 1800 to 1808. The change was seconded by Nathaniel Gorham of Massachusetts.[4] Unlike General Pinckney, Mr. Gorham does not own slaves, but he has ships that carry such human cargo.[5] The only delegate to speak against extending the slave trade 20 years was James Madison of Virginia:

> Twenty years will produce all the mischief that can be apprehended from the liberty to import slaves. So long a term will be more dishonorable to the National character than to say nothing about it in the Constitution.[6]

Seven States against four voted for the compromise of extending the date to permit slave trade in exchange for levying duty on that cargo. One observer points out that the behind-the-scenes bargain struck on the slave issue was a strange one: 3 New England States joined with Maryland and 3 Southern States for a majority; 3 Middle Atlantic States joined with Virginia to form a dissenting minority.[7] Gouverneur Morris of Pennsylvania, as a protest gesture, sought to have the word "slaves" inserted in place of the importation of "persons" along with the name of the slave-importing States of North Carolina, South Carolina and Georgia. Mr. Morris said such wording would make it clear the compromise on slavery was in compliance with those States. "If the change of language however should be objected to by the members from those States, [I] should not urge it," Mr. Morris added.[8] Colonel George Mason of Virginia said he was not against using the term "slaves" in the Constitution but opposed naming the three States "lest it should give offence to the people of those States."[9]

Roger Sherman of Connecticut raised the issue that taxing the importation of slaves implied a human being to be a form of property. Mr. Morris joined in, insisting that using the word "persons" and not "slaves" implied Congress could tax imported free men. Mr. Madison thought it wrong to admit in the Constitution the idea that men could be property. To get around this, the Convention agreed to amend the compromise to read that Congress could impose a tax, or duty, "not exceeding ten dollars for each person," thus avoiding the specifics of the importation by mentioning only the sum of money.[10]

This correspondent has learned that in return for the slavery compromise the South will agree to eliminate the two-thirds vote for the passage of any navigation act by Congress. If accepted by the full Convention, this will be a victory for the Northern shipping States.[11] General George Washington is reported to view this week as the most productive of the Convention.[12] It clearly avoids a deadlock and possible dissolution. However, Colonel Mason and Governor Randolph are reported to be infuriated with the compromise, principally since it involves regulation of commerce as well as slave importation.[13] They may withhold their signatures from any final document as a demonstration of deep discontent. A majority of delegates view the North/South compromise as one with all winners and no losers.[14] Such a judgment remains to be vindicated by events.

Sunday, August 26, 1787

General George Washington, with the Convention in recess today, went for a solitary 10-mile horseback ride in the countryside this morning and was reported by one observer as extremely pleased that the progress of the Convention had overcome several major obstacles, rekindling his hopes for a successful conclusion.[1]

His optimism is shared by a few other delegates. Oliver Ellsworth of Connecticut, privately told a friend that the Convention will probably adjourn in another three weeks.[2] But Alexander Martin of North Carolina is reported to have written recently to the Governor of his State saying that the business of the Convention may not be finished by mid-September.[3] Most of the delegates are impatient to return to their States to attend neglected professional and personal matters. Although 55 delegates agreed to serve at this Convention, only 29 have attended every session thus far. The periodic or permanent absence of 26 delegates has been due to a variety of causes: personal and family illness, private business, service in the Continental Congress, boredom, or disagreement with the formation of a new national government.[4] With so many delegates traveling to and from the Convention, concern has been voiced that the secrecy rule might be violated.

Nevertheless, in the three months that this Convention has met, the rule of secrecy has been maintained with remarkable success. This week Convention leaders did authorize the release of a statement flatly denying persistent rumors that the delegates are planning to establish a monarchy. The *Pennsylvania Journal* reported Convention leaders as saying:

> We are informed, that many letters have been written to the members of the foederal convention from different quarters, respecting the reports idly circulating, that it is intended to establish a monarchical government . . . tho' we cannot, affirmatively, tell you what we are doing, we can, negatively, tell you what we are not doing—we never once thought of a king.[5]

On the day the denial was issued, most of the Convention delegates took time out to watch a demonstration on the Delaware river of a new invention: a steamboat built by John Fitch. Governor Edmund Randolph of Virginia says he supports such an invention, as do Dr. William Johnson and Oliver Ellsworth of Connecticut. Surprisingly, Dr. Benjamin Franklin, the most preeminent inventor of recent times, says he has no faith in the practical application of Mr. Fitch's steamboat.[6] Most of Philadelphia find the new invention laughable, while others think Mr. Fitch is only one of numerous opportunists who have flocked to Philadelphia since the Convention began.[7]

Tomorrow when the Convention reconvenes, it will no longer adjourn at four o'clock, as it has been doing. John Rutledge of South Carolina had urged the Convention to lengthen its hours in order to speed up the pace of deliberations. But the Convention voted to begin meeting at ten in the morning and adjourn at three, instead of four.[8] Many delegates complained that such late sessions interfered with their dinner hour.

Monday, August 27, 1787

With surprising dispatch and almost no debate, today's session, with a majority of lawyer delegates in attendance, approved major elements of the Judicial branch of the new national government.

The only disagreement arose when John Dickinson of Delaware objected to life tenure for judges who would serve on the bench "during good behavior."[1] Mr. Dickinson proposed that the President have the power to remove judges with the sanction of the House and Senate. Gouverneur Morris of Pennsylvania objected:

> . . . it [is] a contradiction in terms to say that the Judges should hold their offices during good behavior, and yet be removeable without a trial. Besides it [is] fundamentally wrong to subject Judges to so arbitrary an authority.[2]

Roger Sherman of Connecticut countered, seeing no such contradiction for regulating the judiciary. He pointed out that in Great Britain a provision for summary removal of judges existed. James Wilson of Pennsylvania objected by pointing out that that power to remove a judge in Great Britain was less dangerous than in America—principally because the House of Commons and the House of Lords rarely agree on issues. "The Judges would be in a bad situation if made to depend on every gust of faction which might prevail in the two branches of our Govt.," Mr. Wilson added.[3] Governor Edmund Randolph of Virginia said he opposed Mr. Dickinson's motion because it would weaken the independence of judges. In the separate States and under the British in the colonial era, independence of judges had long been a cardinal principle.[4]

Perhaps this is why Mr. Dickinson's motion was defeated. However, during today's debate four States were absent.

The delegates then turned to defining the jurisdiction of the Supreme Court. They gave the court a sweeping grant of power to hear and decide all cases arising under the proposed constitution, as well as all laws enacted by the national Legislature. James Madison of Virginia warned it was "going too far" to give the Supreme Court jurisdiction in all cases.[5] It was then proposed and adopted that the court would not decide a constitutional issue until a disputed case was actually brought before it by two contesting parties.[6] Thus, the Convention precisely defined today the role of the Supreme Court. It will decide cases and not issues or questions of law. It will have no power to act except when two contending parties present the Court with adversarial arguments—one basing his right on the constitution, the other contending it.[7]

Besides authorizing Congress to create a system of national courts, the Convention also subordinated the Supreme Court to Congress by giving Congress the power to determine the number of justices. It also limited the Supreme Court's jurisdiction by defining its role as a tribunal of final appeal.[8] The Convention has deliberately made it the duty of Congress to exercise oversight of the Judiciary for reasons of practicality. By granting to the States jurisdiction over cases properly theirs, the large number of lawyers at this Convention hope to prevent the national Judiciary from being buried in a mass of unmanageable legal business.[9]

The fact that so many lawyers could agree with so little dissent over a new national Judiciary must be regarded as a minor miracle of this Convention.

Tuesday, August 28, 1787

A majority of States voted today to surrender their power over commerce, contracts and currency in the belief the new national government could better protect life, liberty and property.

The first power surrendered earlier during the Convention was the right to print paper money or bills of credit. It was proposed today that the ban on the power of the States to print paper money be made absolute, rather than provisional with the consent of Congress. In objecting, Nathaniel Gorham of Massachusetts said, " . . . an absolute prohibition of paper money would rouse the most desperate opposition from its partizans."[1]

But invoking the bitter memories of runaway inflation during the last decade, Roger Sherman of Connecticut carried the Convention by stating:

> . . . [I think] this a favorable crisis for crushing paper money. If the consent of the Legislature could authorize emissions of it, the friends of paper money would make every exertion to get into the Legislature in order to license it.[2]

Only Virginia voted against the absolute ban, with the other States approving that the States may use only gold and silver as tender in payment of debts. The delegates hope that the new constitution will ban forever paper money, whether issued by the separate States or by the new national government. Many States have enforced the payment of debts in paper money.[3] In an observation prior to the Convention, General George Washington had expressed the view that paper money in Rhode Island had ruined its commerce, oppressed the honest and "open[ed] a door to every species of fraud and injustice."[4] His views are held by nearly all the delegates to this Convention.

Rufus King of Massachusetts then sought to have the States denied the power to interfere with private contracts. Mr. King pointed out that six weeks ago the Continental Congress in New York had included such a safeguard for contracts when it approved the Ordinance of 1787, that provides for the creation of new States in the frontier Northwest Territory.[5] In the past, State Legislatures favored special individuals by enacting laws that altered contracts, set aside court judgments and allowed payment of debts in tender other than what was called for in contracts.[6]

To put an end to such practices, the Convention agreed by a narrow margin to prohibit the States from passing retroactive or *ex post facto* laws.[7] A similar prohibition against the new national government enacting similar statutes, as a means of avoiding contractual and financial obligations, was approved by the Convention six days ago.[8]

The Convention today also prohibited the States from taxing or restraining interstate and foreign commerce. In giving up this important power, as well as others, most of the delegates believe they have voted to protect private property rights.[9] This Convention of the separate States was originally called out of the belief that order is necessary in the nation's commerce, currency and private contracts. A majority of the delegates hold as a fundamental article of political faith that the most important role of government is the protection of life, liberty and property.[10] As Mr. Sherman told the Convention in its early days: "The two objects of this body are permanency and safety to those who are to be governed."[11]

Wednesday, August 29, 1787

A handful of diehard delegates failed today to drive a wedge between Northern and Southern States over the power to regulate commerce, in their effort to wreck the work of this Convention.[1]

Charles Pinckney III of South Carolina proposed that no act regulating foreign and domestic commerce be passed by Congress without the approval of two-thirds of the House and Senate.[2] The five Southern States lack ships and fear a monopoly on all commerce by the eight Northern States.[3] Luther Martin of Maryland supported Mr. Pinckney. Both have held nightly sessions with other disenchanted delegates to devise a strategy to frustrate approval of the new constitution as currently drafted.[4]

Mr. Pinckney argued at today's session that without a two-thirds vote on all commerce and navigation acts, the five sections of the nation, each with different commercial interests, could pass "oppressive regulations" with a simple majority in the two houses. Sectional commercial conflict would result, he warned, because "States pursue their interests with less scruple than individuals."[5]

George Mason of Virginia agreed with Mr. Pinckney, making the point that the slave-owning Southern States will be a minority in both houses of the new Congress. He then asked rhetorically, "Is it to be expected that they will deliver themselves bound hand & foot to the Eastern States, and enable them to exclaim, in the words of Cromwell on a certain occasion—'the lord hath delivered them into our hands.' "[6]

A majority of the delegates saw the proposal as a potential danger to the compromise worked out by South Carolina and Connecticut whereby the South would support protection of New England trade if in return the South could keep its slaves.[7] In rapid-fire succession, both Northern and Southern delegates supporting the compromise smothered Mr. Pinckney's proposal with polite rhetoric. John Rutledge of South Carolina, the major architect of the compromise with New England, told the delegates:

> It did not follow from a grant of power to regulate trade, that it would be abused. . . . As we are laying the foundation for a great empire, we ought to take a permanent view of the subject and not look at the present moment only.[8]

Major Pierce Butler of South Carolina said he would vote against his colleague's proposal even though the interests of the Southern States and of the Eastern States are "as different as the interests of Russia and Turkey."[9]

Governor Randolph stated he was so dismayed at the

increasing deformities of the draft constitution that he doubted he could agree to it. "A rejection of the motion would compleat deformity of the system," he observed with obvious bitterness.[10] Nevertheless, Mr. Pinckney's proposal was defeated 7 to 4.

This was swiftly followed by unanimous approval of a fugitive slave provision, calling for the States to return runaway slaves.

Today's session sealed the compromise on the slave and trade issues and crushed the last effort to change the course of the Convention. One observer points out that without reaffirming the slavery compromise the entire document devised by the delegates would have been smashed to ruins and with it the work of many heads and hands over many weeks.[11] Predatory foreign powers wait in the wings to enroll slaves for the consolidation of their own power.[12]

Thursday, August 30, 1787

A fear of the potential political power in the vast frontier West has led a majority of Southern and Eastern States to grant the Congress power to admit new States without specifying equality with the original 13. And no new State shall be erected within the limits of any present State (thus increasing its size and voting power) without consent of the national Legislature.[1]

Yesterday's decision was a victory for Gouverneur Morris of Pennsylvania. For weeks he has waged a campaign against the frontier West, warning that its growing poor population will in the future have the political power "to destroy the Atlantic States," their prosperity, and their property rights.[2]

Dissenting from this view, Colonel George Mason of Virginia said:

If it were possible by just means to prevent emigrations to the Western Country, it might be good policy. But go the people will as they find it for their interest, and the best policy is to treat them with that equality which will make them friends not enemies.[3]

The future role of the frontier West has concerned this Convention because of domestic and foreign issues. One observer points out several reasons for the domestic concerns. For one, frontier farmers are regarded as "wild men" with their strange ways, foreign to the older Eastern parts of the country. Another reason is that since the War of Independence the most persistent demands for paper money and other "evils" have come from the frontier West.[4]

A majority of delegates frankly believe that admitting the Western provinces on an equal basis would place the national government in the hands of wild men and bring about evil days.[5] As Gouverneur Morris of Pennsylvania earlier put it, he does not wish "to throw the power into their hands."[6]

Virginians are expansionists; they and other Southerners believe that new States from the agrarian Southwest would increase their support in Congress.[7] At present the settlement of Vermont, Kentucky and regions on the Tennessee River have been agitating for admission to the Union.

But yesterday, Hugh Williamson of North Carolina expressed concern about new States: "The existing *small* States enjoy an equality now, and for *that* reason are admitted to it in the Senate. This reason is not applicable to ⟨new⟩ Western States."[8]

In today's vote, a majority voted to guarantee each State a republican form of government and protection against domestic and foreign violence.[9]

Also in today's session, nine States to two voted to authorize sending national troops into a State in the event of "domestic violence," when requested by its Legislature or Executive. How much delegates' fear of the frontier played in this decision is unknown. In the early days of the Convention few delegates would have consented to sending federal forces into a State beset with serious disorders.[10]

The potential danger of violence has been an influential force in the deliberations of the delegates. The New England States worry about the reoccurrence of a farmers' rebellion in Massachusetts, and they cast a wary eye toward British Canada. The Southern States remain frustrated about their powerlessness to force Spain to reopen the Mississippi River to American navigation. Even more troubling is that the Western provinces may choose to form alliances with a foreign power.[11]

Friday, August 31, 1787

In one of the most revolutionary actions of this Convention, a majority of delegates voted today to have the new constitution ratified by conventions elected by the people in the States rather than by the State Legislatures.[1]

The Convention is also requiring only nine States to ratify the document, rather than all 13 now operating under the existing Articles of Confederation. Today's action amounts to a death sentence for the Confederation, which requires approval of *all* States if any changes in the Articles are to be made.[2]

Rhode Island's refusal to attend this Convention and New York's walkout in early July make it impossible to abide by the unanimous consent rule. In agreeing to ratification of the new constitution by less than 13 States, a majority of delegates have worked a bloodless revolution in government, overthrowing the existing Articles of Confederation.[3] This Convention had originally met *only* to *amend* the Articles, not to create an entirely new constitution.

A vain effort was made today to postpone debate on the

question of ratification. Failing in this, a handful of delegates bitterly denounced the decision of the majority. James McHenry of Maryland reminded the delegates that he and his colleague Luther Martin had sworn an oath to uphold the unanimous consent provision in the Articles. Mr. Martin insisted that the people would be against the new constitution "unless hurried into it by surprise."[4] Colonel George Mason, in a display of temper, said he " . . . would sooner chop off his right hand than put it to the constitution as it now stands."[5] He and Governor Edmund Randolph said they favored a new Convention rather than accept the creation of the present one that has, in their judgment, gone too far.

But Gouverneur Morris of Pennsylvania proposed another convention with the argument that the Convention had not gone far enough.

Elbridge Gerry of Massachusetts denounced the majority for destroying the existing Confederation without the unanimous consent of the parties in it:

> [I object to] . . . the indecency and pernicious tendency of dissolving in so slight a manner, the solemn obligations of the articles of confederation. If nine out of thirteen can dissolve the compact, Six out of nine will be just as able to dissolve the new one hereafter.[6]

Those delegates favoring ratification by State conventions elected by the people refused to reply to the bitter assertions of the minority that what was approved today was illegal, if not unethical. James Wilson of Pennsylvania appealed to a higher law and the principle of national self-preservation. "The House on fire must be extinguished, without a scrupulous regard to ordinary rights," Mr. Wilson asserted.[7] James Madison of Virginia justified today's death sentence for the Articles and the Confederation in the name of the people who "were in fact, the fountain of all power, and by resorting to them, all difficulties [will be] got over. They [the people] could alter Constitutions as they pleased."[8]

The triumph of a new nationalism over the old States' rights order was completed today when the Convention voted that the new constitution need not have the approval of the Continental Congress in New York.[9]

Saturday, September 1, 1787

A Committee of Eleven delegates was reliably reported today to be working on a complex compromise plan for electing a national President, the only major unresolved issue that prevents this Convention from completing almost four months of debating and drafting a new constitution.[1]

Deciding on the method and manner of electing the President has baffled the delegates.[2] Every time the issue has been debated it has been pushed forward and postponed, because of frustration. Yesterday the Convention approved the formation of a Committee of Eleven to deal with all postponed matters, including how the President should be elected and by whom. The Committee, headed by New Jersey jurist David Brearly, is a device to make up the Convention's mind and rescue the delegates from their own disagreement and deadlock.[3]

Today Mr. Brearly submitted to the Convention two reports on postponed minor matters and the Convention adjourned for the next two days without taking action.[4] It is presumed adjournment will give the Committee of Eleven time to work on a compromise plan for electing the President and on three other critical issues dealing with the powers of Congress.[5] Sources report that the Convention is likely to take up the recommendations of the Committee on Postponed Matters next week.

This correspondent has obtained copies of letters that James Madison has written to his father and to Thomas Jefferson. As a member of the Committee of Eleven he writes to his father that the Convention sessions "will probably continue but a short time longer."[6] In his letter to Thomas Jefferson in Paris, Mr. Madison predicts the Convention is likely to finish its work in the next two weeks. But he sourly informs the U.S. Minister to France that he thinks the proposed new national government has not gone far enough to "prevent the local *mischiefs*" of the States. He then went on:

> Reports and conjectures abound concerning the nature of the plan which is to be proposed. The public however is certainly in the dark with regard to it. The Convention is equally in the dark as to the reception wch [which] may be given to it on its publication. . . . it may well be expected that certain characters will wage war against any reform whatever. . . .[7]

There is no doubt that Mr. Madison is referring to his two fellow Virginians, Colonel George Mason and Governor Edmund Randolph. Both in recent days have expressed the belief that the Convention has gone too far and have indicated they may withhold approval of the constitution. Colonel Mason and Governor Randolph have been joined in their discontent by Elbridge Gerry of Massachusetts. One observer reports that the three delegates can be expected in the final days of this Convention to wage an eleventh-hour war of words to curb what they perceive as the dangerous powers given to the new national government. This same observer reports that the three dissident delegates are planning to propose that a Bill of Rights be included in the draft constitution to check the powers of the national government.[8]

However, on August 20 Charles Pinckney of South Carolina proposed a Bill of Rights to protect personal and civil liberties and he could not even muster the support of delegates to bring it to a vote.[9]

Sunday, September 2, 1787

A prominent leader of the Philadelphia Jewish community has appealed to Convention President George Washington and individual delegates to bar religious oaths as the basis for holding public office.

Jonas Phillips, a merchant and veteran of the War of Independence, cited the Pennsylvania Constitution requiring every State Representative to swear he believes in God and acknowledges the Old and New Testaments to be divinely inspired.[1] In his letter to General Washington and Convention delegates, Mr. Phillips insists that such a requirement is against the religious principles of Judaism and of his individual conscience. He said:

> It is well known among all Citizens of the 13 united States that the Jews have been true and faithful . . . and during the late Contest with England. . . . [they] have bravely faught and bleed for liberty which they Can not Enjoy.[2]

Those State constitutions that were adopted between 1776 and 1784 require not only residential and property but also religious qualifications.[3] But unknown to Mr. Phillips, the Convention only two days ago dealt decisively with the issue of religious qualifications for holding office.

On August 30, Charles Pinckney III of South Carolina proposed and it was unanimously adopted without debate that "no religious test shall ever be required as a qualification to any office or public trust under the authority of the U. States."[4]

In the almost four months this Convention has met, the issue of religion has not been discussed. On June 28 when the Convention was on the brink of breaking up, Dr. Benjamin Franklin proposed that each session be opened with prayers. The proposal was turned down because of lack of funds to pay a minister and out of fear that word would leak out revealing the deep divisions in the Convention.

No doubt exists, however, that nearly every delegate has been profoundly influenced by his religious beliefs and training.[5] The delegates to this Convention are overwhelmingly Protestant, with only two Roman Catholics attending. James Madison of Virginia is one of the few delegates to have studied theology and Hebrew at the College of New Jersey, at Princeton, as preparation for a career in the ministry. He reportedly gave up that calling because of poor health.[6]

Virginia Governor Edmund Randolph may have offered an explanation of why the Convention overwhelmingly voted to prohibit religious qualifications for office. "A man of abilities and character" and not his religious creed should be the basis for holding office, Governor Randolph is reported to have said.[7] In banning religious qualifications in the draft constitution, the Convention may have done so at a cost of incurring opposition to ratification in the States that have such laws.

Luther Martin of Maryland has served notice he will use the issue in his State as part of his fight to defeat ratification of the new constitution.[8] Mr. Martin is expected to desert the Convention in the next few days, returning home to sound the alarm against what he perceives is the work of power-hungry pagans.

Monday, September 3, 1787

Fearing corrupt bargains between Congress and the President, the Convention today prohibited elected members of Congress from holding any other civil office. Similarly, no person holding an appointive office in the new national government can serve in Congress.[1]

Today's decision ended a bitterly debated question—its roots in both the American and the British political experience. Early during the Convention, on four separate days, the delegates clashed on the most effective way to control or to reduce in the new national government the kind of corrupt bargains for public office carried on in the British Parliament.[2] As Major Pierce Butler of South Carolina told the delegates:

> Look at the history of the government of Great Britain. . . . A Man takes a seat in parliament to get an office for himself or friends, or both; and this is the great source from which flows its great venality and corruption.[3]

Many of the delegates have held, or currently hold, both elective and appointive offices at the State and national level. It is a custom under the current Articles of Confederation and is believed a method for encouraging qualified individuals to serve in government.[4] The drive by a majority of delegates to prohibit the practice in the new government is believed to stem in part from resentment and jealousy. Some State officials in the last few years have resented the Confederated Congress appointing its own members to executive and diplomatic posts.[5]

In today's debate, Charles Pinckney III of South Carolina sought unsuccessfully to have the practice continued. To bar members of Congress from appointive office, he said, would deny the new government the best qualified and mock the concept of virtue and merit. Colonel George Mason of Virginia bluntly replied: "Instead of excluding merit, the ineligibility will keep out corruption, by excluding office-hunters."[6]

What apparently gave weight to a narrow majority decision today is the fear that the President would have too much power. Roger Sherman of Connecticut said he was in favor of banning members of Congress from appointive office. Otherwise, "their eligibility to offices would give too much influence to the Executive," he said.[7] Gouverneur Morris of Pennsylvania feared that a corrupt bargain could be concluded between the President and the Congress if members were simultaneously appointed to other offices.

To the contrary, James Wilson of Pennsylvania replied. By excluding members of Congress from appointive office, the influence of the President would be increased and at the same time it would "diminish the general energy of the Government."[8]

Today's debate illustrates two points. First, all delegates, in spite of their opposing arguments, fear a powerful President. Second, the delegates have gone to great lengths to insulate the new national government from the corrupt practices of the past. The disagreement today turned on two views of how human beings will act if given power. One view holds that virtue and merit are the basis of good government. The other view holds that men in power will follow their own self-interests and base motives.[9]

A majority decided today that it is wiser to acknowledge human vice and not allow members of Congress to hold two offices at the same time.

Tuesday, September 4, 1787

The Committee of Eleven today submitted to the Convention a complex compromise plan for electing a President and proposed to make the office far more vigorous and independent than many delegates had earlier been willing to accept.[1]

The Committee's report recommends that the President and vice-President be chosen for a four-year term, rather than seven years, as the Convention had previously approved. The President would be eligible for re-election rather than restricted to one term, and elected, not by the State Legislatures or national Congress, but by an Electoral College. Each State would appoint, as its Legislature directs, a number of

Electors equal to its whole number of Senate and House members in the national Congress. The Electors would meet in their respective States and by secret ballot vote for two candidates for President, one of whom shall not be a resident of the same State as the Electors.[2]

Gouverneur Morris of Pennsylvania, a member of the Committee of Eleven, explained one reason for the cumbersome Electoral College:

> As the Electors would vote at the same time throughout the U.S. and at so great a distance from each other, the great evil of cabal was avoided. It would be impossible also to corrupt them.[3]

The ballots of the Electors would be counted, certified, sealed and sent to the seat of the national government. The president of the Senate would then count the ballots before witnesses and the candidate with the greatest number would, if receiving an absolute majority, be declared President. If no such majority was found, the Senate would vote for a President from among the five candidates with the most Electoral ballots. The vice-presidency would go to the candidate who placed second in either the Electors' balloting, or the Senate's voting to break a tie.[4]

The Convention took no action today on the proposed plan for electing the President in order to give the delegates time to study and digest the plan. Delegates with diverse points of view did agree that the plan erased one potential evil that has obsessed them: namely, the corruption of elections by the intrigue of power-hungry factions. "It is in truth the most difficult of all on which we have had to decide," James Wilson of Pennsylvania observed of the weeks of debate on the presidency.[5]

One observer points out that the Electoral College compromise proposal is the only political innovation of this Convention and it overcomes every objection that has been raised against all other methods.[6] It meets, for example, the strong objection of many delegates to direct popular election of the President. At the same time, it satisfies the large States as well as the small States which have a balanced share of power in the Senate. They will share equally in the election of the President when there is an Electoral College tie.[7]

The Committee report today also proposes that the President have the power of appointments, including judges and ambassadors, but subject to the advice and consent of the Senate. The power to make treaties, originally given to the Senate, was shifted to the President but requires the concurrence of two-thirds of the Senate.[8]

In proposing these changes, the Committee is making the President independent of Congress by having the power to initiate appointments and treaties. But at the same time the States, being equally represented in the Senate, would have the power to check the President.[9] If accepted by the delegates, both branches will become co-equals with the responsibility and power to keep an eye on each other.

Wednesday, September 5, 1787

The Senate's role in the election of the President was sharply attacked today as laying the foundation for corruption and risking the danger of transforming that body into a dangerous aristocracy.[1]

Delegates who delivered that verbal indictment today did so out of a general dissatisfaction with major parts of the compromise plan for electing the President. The plan calls for Electors in the States to vote for a President and for the Senate to certify the winner. If none was found to have a majority of electoral votes, the Senate would choose a President from among the five candidates with the most Electoral votes.

Charles Pinckney III and John Rutledge of South Carolina said they were opposed to the entire compromise plan. "It would throw the whole power into the Senate," Mr. Rutledge warned.[2] He proposed instead reconsideration of the original plan for Congress to elect the President for a single seven-year term and be denied re-election. However, eight States opposed reconsideration.[3] Colonel George Mason of Virginia said he preferred "the Government of Prussia to one which will put all power" into the hands of a few in the Senate, creating an aristocracy worse than an absolute monarchy.[4] He stated his objections:

> Considering the powers of the President & those of the Senate, if a coalition should be established between these two branches, they will be able to subvert the Constitution.—The great objection . . . would be removed by depriving the Senate of the eventual election.[5]

Gouverneur Morris of Pennsylvania replied that the danger was being overdrawn. It was likely, he said, that in most elections the votes would fall on characters eminent and generally known, with one man receiving a majority of the ballots for President and therefore the Senate would not have to vote.[6] James Wilson of Pennsylvania and John Dickinson of Delaware proposed that in the event the vote of the Electors deadlocked on a choice, the entire Congress should decide rather than just the Senate. However, seven States voted down that proposal.[7]

Throughout this Convention three words have had an influential impact on the debates: corruption, monarchy and aristocracy. All three were used in today's debate with the effect of creating an impasse on the method of electing the President. Hugh Williamson of North Carolina insisted that election by the Senate "lays a certain foundation for corruption & aristocracy."[8] Governor Edmund Randolph of Virginia bitterly assailed the powers of the President, arguing it was a bold stroke for Monarchy. "We are now doing the same for an aristocracy," he went on, adding that the President's election by the Senate, in addition to its other powers, will "convert that body into a real & dangerous Aristocracy."[9]

Despite such dire predictions, one source reports that the dissenting South Carolina delegation concedes it does not have the votes to prevail and will accept the Electoral College.[10]

Governor Randolph's bitter outburst today is reported by one observer to reflect an accumulative dissatisfaction with the entire instrument of government as drafted by this Convention.[11] The fact he has come to disagree with what he originally proposed, at Mr. Madison's urging, makes the humiliation more intense for the proud Virginian.

Thursday, September 6, 1787

A visible sigh of relief swept over the delegates today when 10 of the 11 States approved a modified plan for electing a President, thus ending one of the most hard-fought, frustrating, and fatiguing decisions of this Convention.[1]

James Wilson of Pennsylvania repeated the assertion some delegates made yesterday about the current plan to allow the Senate to elect a President, in the event of a tie in the Electoral College of the States. He believes it is a dangerous power and a tendency toward aristocracy. Mr. Wilson pointed out that the Senate was given the additional powers to approve Executive and Judicial appointments, to sit as a court of impeachment for the President, and to approve treaties, subject to the evil of foreign influence. The owlish-appearing lawyer then went on:

> ... the Legislative, Executive & Judiciary powers are all blended in one branch of the Government. ... According to

plan as it now stands, the President will not be the man of the people as he ought to be, but the Minion of the Senate. He cannot even appoint a tide-waiter without the Senate. . . .[2]

Gouverneur Morris of Pennsylvania denied Mr. Wilson's declarations that the powers of the Senate were dangerous. "Wherein then lay the dangerous tendency of the innovations to establish an aristocracy in the Senate?" asked the peg-legged Mr. Morris.[3] Colonel Alexander Hamilton of New York today joined the heated debate. He had been in New York on legal, political and personal matters since June 29 and attended the Convention only a few days in July and August.[4] Colonel Hamilton's long absence did not restrain him, however, from expressing a dislike for the scheme of government hammered out during the weeks he was absent. Nevertheless, he said he would vote for it, adding he would "take any system which promises to save America from the dangers with which she is threatened,"[5] referring to foreign influences.

The argument that the Senate's election of the President posed a potentially powerful aristocracy was dealt a death blow by an ingenious proposal by Roger Sherman of Connecticut.[6] Shrewd Mr. Sherman proposed that the House, not the Senate, vote for the President in the event of a tie in the Electoral College voting; each State would have a single vote. Mr. Sherman's proposal was eagerly adopted as a way out of the current impasse.

The delegates then went on to approve a series of proposals to insulate the Electoral College from corruption and intrigue.[7] It was agreed, for example, that the president of the Senate would count the ballots with House and Senate members as witnesses.[8]

Until today, the Executive and Judicial branches of the new national government were no more than extensions of Congress. Today's actions create a three-tiered government, rendering the President independent of Congress.[9] James Madison of Virginia is reported to have confided to a friend that the final agreement for electing the President was possible in some part "by the hurrying influence produced by fatigue and impatience."[10]

One observer points out that an American President chosen by an Electoral College system has only two foreign historical precedents: the Sacred College of Cardinals of the Vatican and the Holy Roman Empire.[11] The Maryland State Senate is the more immediate domestic model for the delegates.

Friday, September 7, 1787

Like an unwanted poor relation in a wealthy family, the vice-President was given the job today of presiding over the upper House of Congress as ex officio President of the Senate.[1]

Until today there had been no discussion by Convention delegates of a necessity or even a desirability for a vice-President. The entirely new proposal surfaced three days ago when the Committee of Eleven recommended the post. Creation of the office is a consolation prize to the person securing the second highest number of votes in the Electoral balloting for the President. And it was agreed that an impartial person should preside over the Senate, without depriving any one State of its two votes.[2]

William R. Davie of North Carolina revealed that the vice-President was given the job of presiding over the Senate in order to break any legislative deadlocks arising over commercial disputes between Eastern and Southern States.[3]

The sparrow-like Elbridge Gerry of Massachusetts was first on his feet to object:

> We might as well put the President himself at the head of the Legislature. The close intimacy that must subsist between the President & vice-president makes it absolutely improper. [I am] against having any vice President.[4]

Gouverneur Morris of Pennsylvania pointed out that the post was pregnant with political ambition. "The vice-President then will be the first heir apparent that ever loved his father," Mr. Morris added with a touch of cynical humor.[5]

Roger Sherman of Connecticut said he did not perceive a danger in the office. "If the vice-President were not to be President of the Senate, he would be without employment," the unsmiling Yankee replied.[6]

Hugh Williamson of North Carolina bluntly insisted that "such an officer as vice-President was not wanted."[7] However, while many delegates believe the office is useless, it does exist in a few States. The vice-President would be a successor to the President if he were removed or incapacitated. And it was with this primary function in mind that a majority voted today to affirm the office despite some delegates' dissent.[8]

Colonel George Mason of Virginia, for example, objected to the vice-President presiding over the Senate, insisting it mixed too much of the Executive and the Legislative. Colonel Mason also objected to Congress and the President having shared powers over appointments and the making of treaties. As a substitute, he proposed a six-person privy Council for the President to decide such matters as a means of keeping the President and Congress "separate & distinct."[9] From the first days of the Convention, the idea of a Council for the Executive had been proposed as a means to check the power of the President. Each time it was proposed, it was rejected. The same fate befell Colonel Mason's proposal today, despite support from Dr. Benjamin Franklin and James Wilson of Pennsylvania and James Madison of Virginia.

However, in its place the Convention unanimously adopted the proposal today authorizing the President "to call for the opinions of the Heads of Departments, in writing."[10] In approving this proposal, the Convention has established the basis for the President to draw advice from his Council appointments.[11]

Saturday, September 8, 1787

In a mood mixed with weariness, impatience and expectation, the Convention today elected by ballot a Committee of Five delegates to re-work the wording and order of the 23 articles of the draft constitution.[1]

The five-member Committee of Style is made up almost exclusively of friends of the new constitution.[2] Although the Committee chairman is the highly esteemed legal scholar Dr. William Samuel Johnson of Connecticut, one source reports that the principal task of improving the literary construction of the draft constitution will fall to Gouverneur Morris of Pennsylvania.[3] Rufus King of Massachusetts, James Madison of Virginia, and Colonel Alexander Hamilton of New York were also elected Committee members because each is known and admired for his exactness of expression.[4]

The creation of the Committee of Style means that the work of the weary delegates is rapidly coming to a welcome conclusion. It is reported that since August 23 James Madison of Virginia has been fighting fatigue and a serious illness. The long ordeal of keeping a detailed daily journal of the Convention proceedings and at the same time participating week after week in the daily debates are said to have taken a heavy physical toll on Mr. Madison.[5]

Today, for example, Mr. Madison was on his feet when the Convention took up the provisions for impeachment trial of the President. Mr. Madison said he feared the power of impeachment in the hands of the House and the Senate could be made into a political weapon against the President. He preferred trial by the Supreme Court or a tribunal of which it was a part.[6]

Gouverneur Morris of Pennsylvania offered this rebuttal:

> ... no other tribunal than the Senate could be trusted. The Supreme Court [are] too few in number and might be warped or corrupted. ... there could be no danger that the Senate would say untruly on their oaths that the President was guilty

of crimes or facts, especially as in four years he can be turned
out [of office].[7]

Colonel George Mason of Virginia proposed that the wording "other high crimes & misdemeanors [against the State]"
be added to the language of the impeachment provision.[8] The
Convention approved the addition. It then, without further
debate, made the President, the vice-President and other
Civil officers of the United States subject to impeachment
trial in the Senate, conviction required by two-thirds of the
members present.[9]

The delegates also approved today the power of the Senate
to amend money bills. Until now the House had been granted
exclusive power to originate money bills and the Senate had
been denied the right to alter them in any manner. Disagreement over the issue had deadlocked the small and large States
and threatened to undo the work of the delegates. Like so
many of the major problems facing them, a compromise was
devised by drawing on past experience. The delegates took
from three State constitutions the provision that the House
would have exclusive power to originate money bills, "but the
Senate may propose or concur with amendments."[10]

As John Dickinson of Delaware told delegates almost a
month ago: "Experience should be our only guide. Reason
may mislead us."[11]

Sunday, September 9, 1787

With delicate diplomatic talks continuing between Spain and
the 13 States over free navigation of the Mississippi River, the
Spanish envoy to the Continental Congress in New York, Don
Diego de Gardoqui, arrived in Philadelphia late yesterday to
meet with Convention President George Washington.[1]

The Spanish envoy's arrival coincided with the climax of a tense Convention debate on the power to make treaties with foreign nations. Underlying the debate is whether Spain will re-open the Mississippi River for the movement of Confederated States' trade through Spanish ports such as New Orleans.[2] The Foreign Secretary of the current Confederated government, John Jay, angered many of the Southern States last year when he endorsed the Spanish envoy's proposal for the Confederation to give up for 25 years rights of navigation on the Mississippi in return for Spain's opening its empire to American commerce.

The offer, in direct violation of Mr. Jay's instructions from the Continental Congress, generated serious discussions for dividing the current Confederation along a North-South split.[3] Fueling additional delegate distrust of Imperial Spain have been persistent rumors that Spain is plotting to make the Kentucky territory a Spanish province.[4]

Colonel George Mason of Virginia has openly expressed the fear that exclusive Senate power to make treaties would be selling the country to foreign powers. He warned last month:

> The Senate by means of treaty might alienate territory &c. without legislative sanction. . . .—If Spain should possess herself of Georgia therefore the Senate might by treaty dismember the Union.[5]

The delegates had shifted the power to make treaties from the Senate to the President. In a later compromise, the President retained the power to make treaties but was required to submit them to the Senate for ratification. A bitter division between North and South developed over whether ratification should be by a simple majority or two-thirds vote. At stake are the conflicting interests of Northern merchants and Southern planters.[6]

After three days of, at times, tense debate, the Convention yesterday agreed on a two-thirds, rather than a majority, Senate vote to ratify treaties concluded by the President. The unanimous vote is reported to have been an effort to calm fears of the Southern States that Eastern and Northern States would surrender navigation rights on the Mississippi.[7]

As Hugh Williamson of North Carolina observed, the Convention apparently did not want to risk in the new Congress another dangerous diplomatic concession to Spain, such as Mr. Jay had nearly concluded in the Continental Congress. Apparently the delegates agree that a two-thirds Senate ratification will be a stronger impediment to foreign concessions than a mere majority vote.[8]

Despite the fear felt by the delegates toward Imperial Spain, General Washington's meetings this week with the Spanish envoy are expected to be cordial. A source reports that the representative of his Imperial Catholic Majesty in Madrid is to be treated to a series of sumptuous dinners in his honor, with General Washington and the city of Philadelphia as hosts.[9]

Monday, September 10, 1787

The Convention defeated a concerted minority effort today to submit the new constitution for approval to the Continental Congress in New York and at the same time it adopted a plan providing for future amendments to the document.

Colonel Alexander Hamilton of New York made a last-minute contribution to the new constitution today when he proposed that the new Congress, not the State Legislatures, initiate any amendments.[1] "There could be no danger in giving this power," Colonel Hamilton insisted.[2]

John Rutledge of South Carolina, however, does see a danger. The amending power might be used, he said, to abolish slavery "by the States not interested in that property and prejudiced against it."[3] Without debate and with only one

State dissenting and another divided, the Convention adopted language stipulating that no amendments would be made prior to 1808 affecting sections of the constitution that relate to the slave trade.[4]

The Convention then went on to approve a cumbersome amending process. Either house of Congress could initiate amendments, but a two-thirds vote is required in both before an amendment can be sent to the States for ratification. Approval of three-fourths of the States, either separately or in Convention, will be required before amendments can become part of the constitution.[5]

Even before the Convention met, advocates of such a political conclave had concluded that the Continental Congress would never approve a new constitution.[6] Throughout the months of debate, most delegates were opposed to the Continental Congress having any role in ratification of a new constitution.[7] Nevertheless, today Colonel Hamilton proposed that not only the Continental Congress approve the document, but also the State Legislatures have a say in its approval prior to submission to State ratifying conventions. Nathaniel Gorham of Massachusetts warned that " . . . the different and conditional ratifications will defeat the plan altogether."[8]

And controlling his anger, James Wilson of Pennsylvania lashed out at Colonel Hamilton's proposal:

> Can it be safe to make the assent of Congress necessary. After spending four or five months in the laborious & arduous task of forming a Government for our Country, we are ourselves at the close throwing insuperable obstacles in the way of its success.[9]

The Convention agreed with Mr. Wilson and voted 10 to 1 to reject Colonel Hamilton's proposal. The States then unanimously rejected any role for the Continental Congress, requiring ratification by nine State conventions.[10]

Virginia Governor Edmund Randolph then stunned the delegates into silence by a slashing attack on the entire document and the weeks of work by the Convention.[11] The plan adopted by the Convention would end in tyranny, he charged. Governor Randolph proposed again the rejected plan of Colonel Hamilton's, of going first to the Continental Congress with the new constitution. Dr. Benjamin Franklin of Pennsylvania broke the awkward silence by seconding the motion. Colonel George Mason of Virginia, an ally of Governor Randolph's, suggested the proposal be tabled so that parts of the system objected to by Governor Randolph might be considered.[12]

Like Colonel Mason, who claims he will not sign the document, Governor Randolph had begun as a warm friend of a new government only now to be one of its coldest critics.

Tuesday, September 11, 1787

For the first time since this Convention began meeting in May, delegates formally convened today and then promptly recessed, explaining: "there being no business before the Convention."[1]

James Madison of Virginia revealed that the five-man Committee of Style and Arrangement, of which he is a member, has not finished refining the language of the draft constitution.[2] Thus, the reason for today's recess. Mr. Madison has said, according to sources, that the entire Committee agreed that the task of actually adding the "*finish*" to the style and arrangement of the document was given to Gouverneur Morris of Pennsylvania. "A better choice could not have been made," Mr. Madison insists.[3]

However, Abraham Baldwin of Georgia says that James Wilson of Pennsylvania, although not a member of the Committee, is playing the role as chief penman, along with Mr. Morris,[4] in preparing the final composition that is expected to be presented to the full Convention tomorrow.

Mr. Morris, who has given the most speeches at this Convention, privately insists he has rejected redundant and equivocal language in order to make the document "as clear as our language would permit."[5] However, it is reliably reported that one radical revision made by Mr. Morris, with the approval of the Committee of Style, was to change the clause relating to laws passed by Congress. The original draft declared that laws passed by the Congress would be "the supreme law of the several States." The change by the Committee of Style is said to read that all such laws shall be "the supreme law of the land." One observer has pointed out that this wording implies judges may have the power to pass on the constitutionality of both national and State laws.[6]

The Committee of Style was handed a draft document consisting of 23 articles divided into 41 sections. In the last few days of rephrasing and organizing sections, the constitution has been compressed and clarified into seven articles and 21 sections.[7] An entirely new preamble has been written, omitting the names of the separate States. In its place is:

WE, the People of the United States, in order to form a more perfect union, to establish justice, insure domestic tranquillity, provide for the common defence, promote the general welfare, and secure the blessings of liberty to ourselves and our posterity, do ordain and establish this Constitution for the United States of America.[8]

One source says that the omission of the individual names of the States was for a specific reason bearing on ratification of the document. Nine States are required to give legal force to the Constitution and at this moment it is uncertain which nine of the 13 will ratify it.[9] The preamble of the Constitution is different from the Articles of Confederation in that nowhere does the older document refer to "We the People." Instead, the preamble to the Articles refers to the "United States in Congress."

The preamble of the proposed Constitution has more in common with the Declaration of Independence, which had spoken of "one people" and "our people," and had acted "by the authority of the good people of these colonies."[10]

Wednesday, September 12, 1787

The ordeal of summer statecraft reached a milestone today when the chairman of the five-man Committee of Style laid before the Convention a document of some four thousand words which is the final composed new Constitution.[1]

Dr. William Samuel Johnson of Connecticut, in presenting the final document to the delegates, also offered a carefully phrased conciliatory letter addressed to the Continental Congress in New York.[2] The letter, a copy of which was obtained by this correspondent, justifies the Convention's revolutionary action by arguing the "Impropriety of delegating such extensive Trust to one Body of Men. . . . Hence . . . the Necessity of a different Organization." The letter goes on to state that during the deliberations, the delegates "kept steadily" in their view "the greatest Interest of every true American," and, it adds, "The Consolidation of our Union in which is involved our Prosperity Felicity Safety perhaps our national Existence."[3]

However, Colonel George Mason of Virginia and Elbridge Gerry of Massachusetts objected that the final Constitution contains no provision for jury trials in civil cases. They also pointed out that there is no provision for a Bill of Rights. Colonel Mason suggested that one could be prepared in a few hours.[4] He had set down his concerns in notes on his copy of the final draft:

> There is no Declaration of Rights, and the laws of the general government being paramount to the laws and constitution of the several States, the Declaration of Rights in the separate States are no security. . . .[5]

At present, eight of the 13 States have a Bill of Rights in their constitutions.[6] Virginia's Declaration of Rights of 1776 was authored by Colonel Mason, and he is credited with influencing Thomas Jefferson's views embodied in the Declaration of Independence.[7]

The proposal for a Bill of Rights suffered a crushing defeat in today's session. Ten States voted no, including Colonel Mason's home State, Virginia. "The State Declarations of Rights are not repealed by this Constitution: and being in force are sufficient," insisted Roger Sherman of Connecticut.[8]

Debating a Bill of Rights at this late hour might delay delegates anxious to take their leave and might also reopen explosive issues already settled. For instance, General Charles Cotesworth Pinckney of South Carolina is reliably reported to believe that a Bill of Rights debate at this late hour would involve rights not only for whites, but for black slaves as well.[9] One observer points out, however, that today's swift and summary rejection of a Bill of Rights is a hasty decision Convention leaders may later regret.[10] The issue may prove to be a powerful political weapon in the hands of those opposed to a new constitution and its ratification.[11]

Today the Convention ordered that the final draft of the Constitution be sent to the Philadelphia printers Dunlap and Claypoole[12] so that by tomorrow the delegates may have copies to begin going over the document line by line for, it may be hoped, the last time.[13]

Thursday, September 13, 1787

With quills in hand and printed copies of the Committee of Style report before them, impatient delegates began today a line-by-line comparison of the document with previous decisions of the full Convention.[1]

A majority of delegates were reported to be pleased and satisfied with most of the stylistic changes of the five-member Committee. One observer describes their work as an adroit and tasteful rendering of the will of the delegates.[2] No objection was raised, for example, to the deletion "his Excellency" as a title for the Executive. He will be known simply as the President of the United States.[3]

However, a change of punctuation in a clause caught the eagle eye of Roger Sherman of Connecticut. A semicolon had been inserted in place of a comma in the enumeration of congressional powers: "To lay and collect taxes, duties, imposts and excises; to pay the debts and provide for the common defence and general welfare of the United States." The semicolon had originally been a *comma*. Mr. Sherman objected to the semicolon following "excises," insisting the change implied an independent power of Congress not granted by the Convention.[4] It is alleged that Gouverneur Morris of Pennsylvania, the principal penman of the Committee, made the punctuation change to suggest a further taxing power of Congress, in line with his own ideas. A reliable source says the change was a "trick" so as to create a distinct power, but after Mr. Sherman discovered it, the original comma was reinstated.[5]

Also today, Committee of Style Chairman William Samuel Johnson reported to the Convention a resolution detailing the necessary six steps to give legal force to the constitution. First, the document, as a matter of strategy, will be laid before the Continental Congress in New York. The resolution does not call for Congress to approve or disapprove. Second, the constitution is to be sent to State ratifying conventions with assent required by nine States. The resolution outlines the third phase:

Resolved . . . the United States in Congress assembled should fix a day, on which Electors should be appointed by the States which shall have ratified the same: and a day on which the Electors should assemble to vote for the President: and the Time and Place for commencing proceedings under this constitution. . . .[6]

The fourth step is for the election of House and Senate members. The fifth is for members of both houses to assemble and count and certify the Electoral College ballots for election of the first President. The sixth and final step would be, in the words of the Resolution: "the Congress together with the President should without delay proceed to execute this Constitution."[7]

Three delegates have indicated a growing discontent with the Constitution. The most respected and prominent is Colonel George Mason of Virginia. Convention leaders are reported concerned that if Colonel Mason refuses to sign the document, it could prove damaging to the cause of ratification. In the few remaining days of this Convention an effort will be made to court Colonel Mason and the two other dissenters, who are Governor Edmund Randolph also of Virginia, and Elbridge Gerry of Massachusetts.[8] However, delegates are in a hurry to return home and what the dissenters want in the way of concessions the Convention may lack the patience to consider.

Friday, September 14, 1787

Worn down by weeks of work, delegates were short on words and long on votes today in their anxious drive to finish framing the new constitution and head for home.[1]

The only substantial change the Convention adopted today concerned method of appointment of the national Treasurer. Earlier the Convention had voted Congress the power to elect by joint ballot a chief financial officer of the new national government.[2] Today John Rutledge of South Carolina proposed that the power of appointment be taken away from Congress and be given to the President. Nathaniel Gorham and Rufus King, both of Massachusetts, objected, insisting the people were accustomed to appointment of Treasurers by State Legislatures. " . . . the innovation will multiply objections to the System," they added.[3] Gouverneur Morris of Pennsylvania argued that presidential appointment of the Treasurer meant " . . . he will be more narrowly watched, and more readily impeached—"[4] Perhaps the most persuasive argument against appointment by the joint Congress came from General Charles Cotesworth Pinckney of South Carolina:

> The Treasurer is appointed by joint ballot in South Carolina. The consequence is that bad appointments are made, and the Legislature will not listen to the faults of their own officer.[5]

In no mood to debate the issue further, a majority voted to make the Treasurer an appointed officer by the President, with approval of the Senate. An effort was also made to require the national Treasurer to publish the treasury's income and expenses on an annual basis. This, however, was turned down as impracticable and the Convention settled for requiring publication "from time to time."[6] In making the Treasurer a presidential appointee, the Convention voted for a unified Executive policy in administering the new national government.[7] Congress will appropriate public funds while the President and his Treasurer will administer their disbursement.

The power of the purse and the power of the sword have been two issues that have troubled delegates like Colonel George Mason of Virginia. Today he and Governor Edmund Randolph also of Virginia proposed that a prohibition against standing armies in time of peace be included in the Constitution.[8] James Madison of Virginia supported the motion, observing, ". . . armies in time of peace are allowed on all hands to be an evil. . . ."[9] Mr. Madison must have realized the motion would be voted down, as it was—9 to 2. It is believed that Virginia voted for the proposal in an effort to appease Colonel Mason and Governor Randolph. Both have given indications that unless certain changes are made in the proposed constitution, they might withhold their signatures. Elbridge Gerry of Massachusetts is also threatening to do the same.

Mr. Gerry and Charles Pinckney III of South Carolina proposed that a declaration guaranteeing press liberty be inserted in the constitution. "It is unnecessary—The power of Congress does not extend to the Press," Roger Sherman of Connecticut bluntly replied.[10] The Convention agreed.

Thus, in rejecting any effort to accommodate the Convention dissenters, a majority of delegates may unwittingly provide ammunition for those who are waiting to ambush the new constitution when it is submitted to the States for ratification.[11]

Saturday, September 15, 1787

In the swiftly fading September light, with the clock tower of the State House striking six, exhausted majorities in all 11 State delegations today gave unanimous approval to a new constitution and ordered that a hand-drafted copy be prepared for signature within the next 48 hours.[1]

After General George Washington, as Convention President, presided over no fewer than 25 motions and votes today, three delegates candidly told the Convention why they could not sign the new constitution.[2]

Governor Edmund Randolph of Virginia, a pained and nervous expression playing across his handsome face, said he could not sign unless a second Convention were convened to correct "the indefinite and dangerous power given by the Constitution to Congress. . . ."[3] Whether he would oppose ratification later, Governor Randolph added, he could not now decide and would leave himself free to decide in his own State. One observer points out that this position is calculated to see which way his constituents in Virginia will jump.[4] After his return home, Governor Randolph is certain to face intense political pressure from Patrick Henry and other opponents of the new constitution.[5]

Colonel George Mason of Virginia was less equivocal. Supporting Governor Randolph in refusing to sign, the tall, white-haired statesman said he would not sign here or in Virginia. He went on to predict that the new government would end either in a monarchy or in a tyrannical aristocracy:

> This Constitution had been formed without the knowledge or idea of the people. A second Convention will know more of the sense of the people, and be able to provide a system more consonant to it. It [is] improper to say to the people, take this or nothing.[6]

Charles Pinckney III of South Carolina, his youthful appearance a contrast to Colonel Mason's age, responded for a

majority of the delegates. Danger and confusion are certain
with a second Convention, which the sword might settle.
"Conventions are serious things, and ought not to be
repeated," Mr. Pinckney added with a trace of frustration and
the ordeal of the last four months in mind.[7]

Elbridge Gerry of Massachusetts, in his nervous manner
and with his nasal New England accent, cited 11 specific
reasons why he could not sign the new constitution. A second
general Convention was the only way to correct the defects of
the document, Mr. Gerry added.[8] The Convention voted a
resounding no to the proposal of a second Convention.

When General Washington asked for a roll call of the States
to agree to the constitution as amended, all States voted "ay."[9]

As the 42 delegates adjourned and streamed out of the
State House in the gathering dusk, they had been sitting in
Convention seven straight hours without food or drink. It was
the longest session of the last four months.[10] The delegates
have been in session 81 continuous days, debated for some 400
hours and voted 566 times. Their ordeal of summer statecraft
has produced a 4,000-word document, consisting of 89 sen-
tences and about 140 provisions.[11]

The delegates made their way down the cobblestone streets
toward a late dinner, as word that a new constitution had been
adopted floated throughout the city on an excited wave of
conversation.[12]

Sunday, September 16, 1787

Dr. Benjamin Franklin is reported to have met secretly with
the entire Pennsylvania delegation today to discuss a plan to
minimize the political impact of the refusal of the dissident
delegates to sign the new constitution.[1]

The ailing 81-year-old Dr. Franklin is reported to have drafted a lengthy speech for tomorrow's formal signing of the document. An advance copy obtained by this correspondent reveals a plea for unanimous agreement by all the States, despite his own disagreement with elements of the document. Dr. Franklin is also expected to make a special plea for *all* delegates to sign the document.[2] Yesterday at least three delegates announced their intention not to sign and several others are reported considering withholding their signature.[3] Dr. Franklin's concern for the negative domestic and foreign political impact is reflected in his speech:

> ... It therefore astonishes me, Sir, to find this system approaching so near to perfection as it does; and I think it will astonish our enemies, who are waiting with confidence to hear that our councils are confounded like those of the Builders of Babel; and that our States are on the point of separation, only to meet hereafter for the purpose of cutting one another's throats.[4]

One informed source reports that Dr. Franklin has approved the draft of a resolution by Gouverneur Morris of Pennsylvania seeking unanimous consent by all the States to the new constitution. The resolution would provide the appearance of Convention unity, overshadowing the fact that individual delegates refused to sign. It is reported that the resolution was approved by the Pennsylvania delegation at Dr. Franklin's home today and will be circulated among other State delegations for their consent prior to tomorrow's formal signing of the document.[5]

Convention President George Washington is reportedly deeply disturbed at the refusal of the three delegates to sign the new constitution, two of them from his own State. However, because of General Washington's position at this Convention it fell to Dr. Franklin to devise a face-saving formula and assume the role of unifier.[6] A majority of delegates are reported to believe that the refusal of some delegates to sign the document will be used by enemies of the new constitution to try and defeat ratification in the States.[7] The bitter fight that lies ahead may be illustrated by one report that the long-time friendship between General Washington and Colonel George Mason of Virginia may be permanently shattered by their disagreement over the new constitution.[8]

The document is being finalized by hand in fine bold lettering on four sheets of parchment; 500 printed copies of the document are also reported rolling off the presses at the Philadelphia printers of Dunlap and Claypoole.[9]

General Washington said at the start of this Convention that a great drama was about to begin. Now, four months later, the drama of the Convention is at an end and the life or death struggle of the Constitution is about to begin.

Monday, September 17, 1787

A majority of delegates fixed their signatures to the new Constitution today and then voted to dissolve this Convention 116 days after its formal opening.[1]

Dr. Benjamin Franklin and Convention President George Washington failed in a last-minute effort to win over the three dissident delegates who refused to sign the document. James Wilson of Pennsylvania read a lengthy conciliatory speech today prepared by Dr. Franklin pleading "for the sake of posterity, we shall act heartily and unanimously in recommending this Constitution. . . ."[2]

Nathaniel Gorham of Massachusetts, allegedly acting on the wishes of General Washington,[3] offered one final amendment to the new Constitution. Mr. Gorham proposed that the population ratio for determining the number of seats for each State in the House of Representatives be lowered from 40,000 to 30,000.[4] The Convention was startled to see Convention President George Washington rise to his full six-feet two-inches and give his one and only speech of this Convention.[5] He told the delegates:

> ... It was much to be desired that the objections to the plan recommended might be made as few as possible— The smallness of the proportion of Representatives had been considered by many members of the Convention, an insufficient security for the rights & interests of the people.[6]

While the change was adopted without debate or opposition, the three diehard delegates still refused to sign. General Washington's last-minute move was obviously aimed at winning over his old friend Colonel George Mason of Virginia. He has been critical that the composition and powers of Congress do not express the will of the people. Today Colonel Mason was sullen and silent, joining Governor Edmund Randolph also of Virginia and Elbridge Gerry of Massachusetts in their iron resolve not to sign. ". . . by opposing or even refusing to sign the Constitution, [they] might do infinite mischief," warned Colonel Alexander Hamilton of New York.[7]

Shortly after three o'clock today 38 of the 41 delegates present[8] affixed their signatures after all States unanimously consented to adopt the new Constitution. General Washington was the first to sign as President of the Convention. He was followed by individual State delegations, starting with New Hampshire and moving South State by State to Georgia.[9] George Read of Delaware signed for himself and then for John Dickinson, who was taken ill a few days earlier and departed for Delaware, leaving a letter authorizing Mr. Read to sign for him,[10] making 39 signatures in all.

As the State House clock struck four, the Convention dissolved itself by adjournment and the exhausted delegates drifted out into the brisk clear autumn air.[11] Most were filled with weary uncertainty, wondering whether months of work would have some meaning and life after this day in September.[12] Dr. Franklin sought to dispel delegate depression with an optimistic observation during today's signing. In spite of his age and ailments, he attended every session, except on May 25, and he pointed out that he had noticed on the back of the Convention President's chair a carved replica of a sun. During the weeks and months of debate he could not determine the sun's movement.

But now, Dr. Franklin added, "I have the happiness to know that it is a rising and not a setting Sun."[13]

Tuesday, September 18, 1787

Major William Jackson, secretary of the Constitutional Convention, left Philadelphia today carrying the original signed copy of the new Constitution with instructions to deliver the document to the Continental Congress in New York.[1]

The Congress is expected to begin debating the new Constitution within the next nine days, although the document does not require its approval.[2] Already there are reports that Richard Henry Lee of Virginia plans to introduce a resolution in Congress censuring the Convention for exceeding its authority.[3] One observer points out that when the 39 delegates signed the new Constitution yesterday they were well aware they had exceeded the authority given to them by the State Legislatures.[4] In creating a new national government, the delegates have signed the death warrant of the old Confederation and its Congress in New York. At least 12 Convention delegates are elected members of the Congress and are expected to be on hand in New York when the heated debate over the new Constitution begins.[5]

Late yesterday Major Jackson met with General George

Washington and turned over the official Journal of the Convention as ordered by the delegates.[6] In the final minutes of the Convention, Rufus King of Massachusetts had proposed that the official records of the Convention be burned or turned over to General Washington. ". . . a bad use would be made of them by those who would wish to prevent the adoption of the Constitution," Mr. King observed.[7] James Wilson of Pennsylvania suggested the records be entrusted to the care of General Washington.[8]

In adopting this course the Convention delegates may have effectively denied opponents of the new Constitution a factual basis from which to argue about what actually transpired during the four months of secret sessions.

General Washington last night attended a cordial farewell dinner with the other delegates at Philadelphia's City Tavern and then retired, in his own words, to "meditate on the momentous wk [work] which had been executed."[9] Today, the General left Philadelphia by carriage for the long journey back to his Mount Vernon plantation after paying a round of courtesy farewells. Most delegates left for their respective States by stage, horseback or packet boat.[10] Before setting out on his journey, General Washington wrote a hurried letter to Marquis de Lafayette in Paris. In the copy obtained by this correspondent, he observed:

> . . . it [the Constitution] is now a Child of fortune, to be fostered by some and buffeted by others. what will be the General opinion on, or the reception of it, is not for me to decide, nor shall I say any thing for or against it: if it be good, I suppose it will work its way good; if bad, it will recoil on the Framers.[11]

Today's Philadelphia newspapers are filled with glowing and enthusiastic accounts of the just concluded Convention. In the next few days and weeks the full text of the new Constitution is expected to be published throughout the separate

States. However, Dr. Benjamin Franklin may have made the most perceptive comment on what was done here. Shortly after the Convention dissolved, a Philadelphia lady asked Dr. Franklin whether America had a republic or a monarchy.

"A Republic," he replied, "if you can keep it."[12]

APPENDIX 1

The Articles of Confederation
Agreed to by Congress November 15, 1777;
ratified and in force, March 1, 1781

Congress resolved June 11, 1776, that a committee should be appointed to draw up articles of confederation between the Colonies. A plan proposed by John Dickinson formed the basis of the articles as proposed to Congress and, after some debate and a few changes, adopted, November 15, 1777. Representatives of the States signed the Articles during 1778 and 1779.

To ALL TO WHOM these Presents shall come, we the undersigned Delegates of the States affixed to our Names send greeting. Whereas the Delegates of the United States of America in Congress assembled did on the fifteenth day of November in the Year of our Lord One Thousand Seven Hundred and Seventy seven, and in the Second Year of the Independence of America agree to certain articles of Confederation and perpetual Union between the States of Newhampshire, Massachusetts-bay, Rhodeisland and Providence Plantations, Connecticut, New York, New Jersey, Pennsylvania, Delaware, Maryland, Virginia, North-Carolina, South-Carolina and Georgia in the Words following, viz. "Articles of Confederation and perpetual Union between the states of Newhampshire, Massachusetts-bay, Rhodeisland and Providence Plantations, Connecticut, New-York, New-Jersey, Pennsylvania, Delaware, Maryland, Virginia, North-Carolina, South-Carolina and Georgia.

ART. I. The Stile of this confederacy shall be "The United States of America."

ART. II. Each state retains its sovereignty, freedom and independence, and every Power, Jurisdiction and right, which is not by this confederation expressly delegated to the United States, in Congress assembled.

ART. III. The said states hereby severally enter into a firm league of friendship with each other, for their common defence, the security of their Liberties, and their mutual and general welfare, binding themselves to assist each other, against all force offered to, or attacks made upon them, or any of them, on account of religion, sovereignty, trade, or any other pretence whatever.

ART. IV. The better to secure and perpetuate mutual friendship and intercourse among the people of the different states in this union, the free inhabitants of each of these states, paupers, vagabonds and fugitives from Justice excepted, shall be entitled to all privileges and immunities of free citizens in the several states; and the people of each state shall have free ingress and regress to and from any other state, and shall enjoy therein all the privileges of trade and commerce, subject to the same duties, impositions and restrictions as the inhabitants thereof respectively, provided that such restriction shall not extend so far as to prevent the removal of property imported into any state, to any other state of which the Owner is an inhabitant; provided also that no imposition, duties or restriction shall be laid by any state, on the property of the united states, or either of them.

If any Person guilty of, or charged with treason, felony, or other high misdemeanor in any state, shall flee from Justice, and be found in any of the united states, he shall upon demand of the Governor or executive power, of the state from which he fled, be delivered up and removed to the state having jurisdiction of his offence.

Full faith and credit shall be given in each of these states to the records, acts and judicial proceedings of the courts and magistrates of every other state.

ART. V. For the more convenient management of the general interests of the united states, delegates shall be annually appointed in such manner as the legislature of each state shall direct, to meet in Congress on the first Monday in November, in every year, with a power reserved to each state, to recall its delegates, or any of them, at any time within the year, and to send others in their stead, for the remainder of the Year.

No state shall be represented in Congress by less than two, nor by more than seven Members; and no person shall be capable of being a delegate for more than three years in any term of six years; nor shall any person, being a delegate, be capable of holding any office under the united states, for which he, or another for his benefit receives any salary, fees or emolument of any kind.

Each state shall maintain its own delegates in a meeting of the states, and while they act as members of the committee of the states.

In determining questions in the united states, in Congress assembled, each state shall have one vote.

Freedom of speech and debate in Congress shall not be impeached or questioned in any Court, or place out of Congress, and the members of congress shall be protected in their persons from arrests and imprisonments, during the time of their going to and from, and attendance on congress, except for treason, felony, or breach of the peace.

ART. VI. No state without the Consent of the united states in congress assembled, shall send any embassy to, or receive any embassy from, or enter into any conference, agreement, or alliance or treaty with any King, prince or state; nor shall any person holding any office of profit or trust under the united states, or any of them, accept of any present, emolument, office or title of any kind whatever from any king, prince or foreign state; nor shall the united states in congress assembled, or any of them, grant any title of nobility.

No two or more states shall enter into any treaty, confederation or alliance whatever between them, without the consent of the united states in congress assembled, specifying accurately the purposes for which the same is to be entered into, and how long it shall continue.

No state shall lay any imposts or duties, which may interfere with any stipulations in treaties, entered into by the united states in congress assembled, with any king, prince or state, in pursuance of any treaties already proposed by congress, to the courts of France and Spain.

No vessels of war shall be kept up in time of peace by any state, except such number only, as shall be deemed necessary by the united states in congress assembled, for the defence of such state, or its trade; nor shall any body of forces be kept up by any state, in time of peace, except such number only, as in the judgment of the united states, in congress assembled, shall be deemed requisite to garrison the forts necessary for the defence of such state; but every state shall always keep up a well regulated and disciplined militia, sufficiently armed and accoutred, and shall provide and constantly have ready for use, in public stores, a due number of field pieces and tents, and a proper quantity of arms, ammunition and camp equipage.

No state shall engage in any war without the consent of the united states in congress assembled, unless such state be actually invaded by enemies, or shall have received certain advice of a resolution being formed by some nation of Indians to invade such state, and the danger is so imminent as not to admit of a delay, till the united states in congress assembled can be consulted: nor shall any state grant commissions to any ships or vessels of war, nor letters of marque or reprisal, except it be after a declaration of war by the united states in congress assembled, and then only against the kingdom or state and the subjects thereof, against which war has been so declared, and under such regulations as shall be established by the united states in congress assembled, unless such state be infested by pirates, in which case vessels of war may be fitted out for that occasion, and kept so long as the danger shall continue, or until the united states in congress assembled shall determine otherwise.

Art. VII. When land-forces are raised by any state for the common defence, all officers of or under the rank of colonel, shall be appointed by the legislature of each state respectively by whom such forces shall be raised, or in such manner as such state shall direct, and all vacancies shall be filled up by the state which first made the appointment.

Art. VIII. All charges of war, and all other expences that shall be incurred for the common defence or general welfare, and allowed by the united states in congress assembled, shall be defrayed out of a common treasury, which shall be supplied by the several states, in proportion to the value of all land within each state, granted to or surveyed for any Person, as such land and the buildings and improvements thereon shall be estimated according to such mode as the united states in congress assembled, shall from time to time direct and appoint. The taxes for paying that proportion shall be laid and levied by the authority and direction of the legislatures of the several states within the time agreed upon by the united states in congress assembled.

ART. IX. The united states in congress assembled, shall have the sole and exclusive right and power of determining on peace and war, except in the cases mentioned in the sixth article—of sending and receiving ambassadors—entering into treaties and alliances, provided that no treaty of commerce shall be made whereby the legislative power of the respective states shall be restrained from imposing such imposts and duties on foreigners, as their own people are subjected to, or from prohibiting the exportation or importation of any species of goods or commodities whatsoever—of establishing rules for deciding in all cases, what captures on land or water shall be legal, and in what manner prizes taken by land or naval forces in the service of the united states shall be divided or appropriated—of granting letters of marque and reprisal in times of peace—appointing courts for the trial of piracies and felonies committed on the high seas and establishing courts for receiving and determining finally appeals in all cases of captures, provided that no member of congress shall be appointed a judge of any of the said courts.

The united states in congress assembled shall also be the last resort on appeal in all disputes and differences now subsisting or that hereafter may arise between two or more states concerning boundary, jurisdiction or any other cause whatever; which authority shall always be exercised in the manner following. Whenever the legislative or executive authority or lawful agent of any state in controversy with another shall present a petition to congress, stating the matter in question and praying for a hearing, notice thereof shall be given by order of congress to the legislative or executive authority of the other state in controversy, and a day assigned for the appearance of the parties by their lawful agents, who shall then be directed to appoint by joint consent, commissioners or judges to constitute a court for hearing and determining the matter in question: but if they cannot agree, congress shall name three persons out of each of the united states, and from the list of such persons each party shall alternately strike out one, the petitioners beginning, until the number shall be reduced to thirteen; and from that number not less than seven, nor more than nine names as congress shall direct, shall in the presence of congress be drawn out by lot, and the persons whose names shall be so drawn or any five of them, shall be commissioners or judges, to hear and finally determine the controversy, so always as a major part of the judges who shall hear the cause shall agree in the determination: and if either party shall neglect to attend at the day appointed, without shewing reasons, which congress shall judge sufficient, or being present shall refuse to strike, the congress shall proceed to nominate three persons out of each state, and the secretary of congress shall strike in behalf of such party absent or refusing; and the judgment and sentence of the court to be appointed, in the manner before prescribed, shall be final and conclusive; and if any of the parties shall refuse to submit to the authority of such court, or to appear to defend their claim or cause, the court shall nevertheless proceed to pronounce sentence, or judgment, which shall in like manner be final and decisive, the judgment or sentence and other proceedings being in either case transmitted to congress, and lodged among the acts of congress for the security of the parties concerned: provided that every commissioner, before he sits in judgment, shall take an oath to be administered by one of the judges of the supreme or superior court of the state, where the cause shall be tried, "well and truly to hear and determine the matter in question, according to the best of his judgment, without favour, affection or hope of reward:" provided also that no state shall be deprived of territory for the benefit of the united states.

All controversies concerning the private right of soil claimed under different grants of two or more states, whose jurisdictions as they may respect such lands, and the states which passed such grants are adjusted, the said grants or either of them being at the same time claimed to have originated antecedent to such settlement of jurisdiction, shall on the petition of either party to the congress of the united states, be finally determined as near as may be in the same manner as is before prescribed for deciding disputes respecting territorial jurisdiction between different states.

The united states in congress assembled shall also have the sole and exclusive right and power of regulating the alloy and value of coin struck by their own authority, or by that of the respective states—fixing the standard of weights and measures throughout the united states—regulating the trade and managing all affairs with the Indians, not members of any of the states, provided that the legislative right of any state within its own limits be not infringed or violated—establishing and regulating post-offices from one state to another, throughout all the united states, and exacting such postage on the papers passing thro' the same as may be requisite to defray the expences of the said office—appointing all officers of the land forces, in the service of the united states, excepting regimental officers—appointing all the officers of the naval forces, and commissioning all officers whatever in the service of the united states—making rules for the government and regulation of the said land and naval forces, and directing their operations.

The united states in congress assembled shall have authority to appoint a committee, to sit in the recess of congress, to be denominated "A Committee of the States," and to consist of one delegate from each state; and to appoint such other committees and civil officers as may be necessary for managing the general affairs of the united states under their direction—to appoint one of their number to preside, provided that no person be allowed to serve in the office of president more than one year in any term of three years; to ascertain the necessary sums of Money to be raised for the service of the united states, and to appropriate and apply the same for defraying the public expences—to borrow money, or emit bills on the credit of the united states, transmitting every half year to the respective states an account of the sums of money so borrowed or emitted,—to build and equip a navy—to agree upon the number of land forces, and to make requisitions from each state for its quota, in proportion to the number of white inhabitants in such state; which requisition shall be binding, and thereupon the legislature of each state shall appoint the regimental officers, raise the men and cloath, arm and equip them in a soldier like manner, at the expence of the united states, and the officers and men so cloathed, armed and equipped shall march to the place appointed, and within the time agreed on by the united states in congress assembled: But if the united states in congress assembled shall, on consideration of circumstances judge proper that any state should not raise men, or should raise a smaller number than its quota, and that any other state should raise a greater number of men than the quota thereof, such extra number shall be raised, officered, cloathed, armed and equipped in the same manner as the quota of such state, unless the legislature of such state shall judge that such extra number cannot be safely spared out of the same, in which case they shall raise officers, cloath, arm and equip as many of such extra number as they judge can be safely spared. And the officers and men so cloathed, armed and equipped, shall march to the place appointed, and within the time agreed on by the united stated in congress assembled.

The united states in congress assembled shall never engage in a war, nor grant letters of marque and reprisal in time of peace, nor enter into any treaties or alliances, nor coin money, nor regulate the value thereof, nor ascertain the sums and expences necessary for the defence and welfare of the united states, or any of them, nor emit bills, nor borrow money on the credit of the united states, nor appropriate money, nor agree upon the number of vessels of war, to be built or purchased, or the number of land or sea forces to be raised, nor appoint a commander in chief of the army or navy, unless nine states assent to the same: nor shall a question on any other point, except for adjourning from day to day be determined, unless by the votes of a majority of the united states in congress assembled.

The congress of the united states shall have power to adjourn to any time within the year, and to any place within the united states, so that no period of adjournment be for a longer duration than the space of six Months, and shall publish the Journal of their proceedings monthly, except such parts thereof relating to treaties, alliances or military operations as in their judgment require secrecy; and the yeas and nays of the delegates of each state on any question shall be entered on the Journal, when it is desired by any delegate; and the delegates of a state, or any of them, at his or their request shall be furnished with a transcript of the said Journal, except such parts as are above excepted, to lay before the legislatures of the several states.

ART. X. The committee of the states, or any nine of them, shall be authorized to execute, in the recess of congress, such of the powers of congress as the united states in congress assembled, by the consent of nine states, shall from time to time think expedient to vest them with; provided that no power be delegated to the said committee, for the exercise of which, by the articles of confederation, the voice of nine states in the congress of the united states assembled is requisite.

ART. XI. Canada acceding to this confederation, and joining in the measures of the united states, shall be admitted into, and entitled to all the advantages of this union: but no other colony shall be admitted into the same, unless such admission be agreed to by nine states.

ART. XII. All bills of credit emitted, monies borrowed and debts contracted by, or under the authority of congress, before the assembling of the united states, in pursuance of the present confederation, shall be deemed and considered as a charge against the united states, for payment and satisfaction whereof the said united states, and the public faith are hereby solemnly pledged.

ART. XIII. Every state shall abide by the determinations of the united states in congress assembled, on all questions which by this confederation are submitted to them. And the Articles of this confederation shall be inviolably observed by every state, and the union shall be perpetual; nor shall any alteration at any time hereafter be made in any of them; unless such alteration be agreed to in a congress of the united states, and be afterwards confirmed by the legislatures of every state.

AND WHEREAS it hath pleased the Great Governor of the World to incline the hearts of the legislatures we respectively represent in congress, to approve of, and to authorize us to ratify the said articles of confederation and perpetual union. KNOW YE that we the under-signed delegates, by virtue of the power and authority to us given that purpose, do by these presents, in the name and in behalf of our respective constituents, fully and entirely ratify and confirm each and every of the said articles of confederation and perpetual union, and all and singular the matters and things therein contained: And we do further solemnly plight and engage the faith of our respective constituents, that they shall abide by the determinations of the united states in congress assembled, on all questions, which by the said confederation are submitted to them. And that the articles thereof shall be inviolably observed by the states we respectively represent, and that the union shall be perpetual. In Witness whereof we have hereunto set our hands in Congress. Done at Philadelphia in the state of Pennsylvania and ninth Day of July in the Year of our Lord one Thousand seven Hundred and Seventy-eight, and in the third year of the independence of America.

JOSIAH BARTLETT JOHN WENTWORTH Junr August 8th 1778	On the part and behalf of the State of New Hampshire
JOHN HANCOCK SAMUEL ADAMS ELBRIDGE GERRY FRANCIS DANA JAMES LOVELL SAMUEL HOLTEN	On the part and behalf of the State of Massachusetts Bay
WILLIAM ELLERY HENRY MARCHANT JOHN COLLINS	On the part and behalf of the State of Rhode-Island and Providence Plantations
ROGER SHERMAN SAMUEL HUNTINGTON OLIVER WOLCOTT· TITUS HOSMER ANDREW ADAMS	On the part and behalf of the State of Connecticut
JAS DUANE FRAS LEWIS WM DUER GOUV MORRIS	On the part and behalf of the State of New York
JNO WITHERSPOON NATHL SCUDDER	On the part and behalf of the State of New Jersey Novr 26, 1778—

Robt Morris
Daniel Roberdeau
Jon^a Bayard Smith
William Clingan
Joseph Reed
22^d July 1778

On the part and behalf of the State of Pennsylvania

Tho M:Kean
Feby 12 1779
John Dickinson
May 5th 1779
Nicholas Van Dyke

On the part and behalf of the State of Delaware

John Hanson
March 1 1781
Daniel Carroll d^o

On the part and behalf of the State of Maryland

Richard Henry Lee
John Banister
Thomas Adams
Jno Harvie
Francis Lightfoot
Lee

On the part and behalf of the State of Virginia

John Penn
July 21st 1778
Corn^s Harnett
Jno Williams

On the part and behalf of the State of N^o Carolina

Henry Laurens
William Henry
Drayton
Jno Mathews
Richd Hutson
Thos Heyward Junr

On the part and behalf of the State of South-Carolina

Jno Walton
24th July 1778
Edwd Telfair
Edwd Langworthy

On the part and behalf of the State of Georgia

APPENDIX 2

The Constitution
of the United States, 1787

WE THE PEOPLE of the United States, in Order to form a more perfect Union, establish Justice, insure domestic Tranquility, provide for the common defence, promote the general Welfare, and secure the Blessings of Liberty to ourselves and our Posterity, do ordain and establish this Constitution for the United States of America.

ART. I

Sec. 1. All legislative Powers herein granted shall be vested in a Congress of the United States, which shall consist of a Senate and House of Representatives.

Sec. 2. The House of Representatives shall be composed of Members chosen every second Year by the People of the several States, and the Electors in each State shall have [the] Qualifications requisite for Electors of the most numerous Branch of the State Legislature.

No Person shall be a Representative who shall not have attained to the Age of twenty five Years, and been seven Years a Citizen of the United States, and who shall not, when elected, be an Inhabitant of that State in which he shall be chosen.

Representatives and direct Taxes shall be apportioned among the several States which may be included within this Union, according to their respective Numbers, which shall be determined by adding to the whole Number of free Persons, including those bound to Service for a Term of Years, and excluding Indians not taxed, three fifths of all other Persons. The actual Enumeration shall be made within three Years after the first Meeting of the Congress of the

United States, and within every subsequent Term of ten Years, in such Manner as they shall by Law direct. The Number of Representatives shall not exceed one for every thirty Thousand, but each State shall have at Least one Representative; and until such enumeration shall be made, the State of New Hampshire shall be entitled to chuse three, Massachusetts eight, Rhode-Island and Providence Plantations one, Connecticut five, New-York six, New Jersey four, Pennsylvania eight, Delaware one, Maryland six, Virginia ten, North Carolina five, South Carolina five, and Georgia three.

When vacancies happen in the Representation from any State, the Executive Authority thereof shall issue Writs of Election to fill such Vacancies.

The House of Representatives shall chuse their Speaker and other Officers; and shall have the sole Power of Impeachment.

Sec. 3. The Senate of the United States shall be composed of two Senators from each State, chosen by the Legislature thereof, for six Years; and each Senator shall have one Vote.

Immediately after they shall be assembled in Consequence of the first Election, they shall be divided as equally as may be into three Classes. The Seats of the Senators of the first Class shall be vacated at the Expiration of the second Year, of the second Class at the Expiration of the fourth Year, and of the third Class at the Expiration of the sixth Year, so that one third may be chosen every second Year; and if Vacancies happen by Resignation, or otherwise, during the Recess of the Legislature of any State, the Executive thereof may make temporary Appointments until the next Meeting of the Legislature, which shall then fill such Vacancies.

No Person shall be a Senator who shall not have attained to the Age of thirty Years, and been nine Years a Citizen of the United States, and who shall not, when elected, be an Inhabitant of that State for which he shall be chosen.

The Vice President of the United States shall be President of the Senate, but shall have no Vote, unless they be equally divided.

The Senate shall chuse their other Officers, and also a President pro tempore, in the Absence of the Vice President, or when he shall exercise the Office of President of the United States.

The Senate shall have the sole Power to try all Impeachments. When sitting for that Purpose, they shall be on Oath or Affirmation.

When the President of the United States is tried, the Chief Justice shall preside: And no person shall be convicted without the Concurrence of two thirds of the Members present.

Judgment in Cases of Impeachment shall not extend further than to removal from Office, and disqualification to hold and enjoy any office of honor, Trust or Profit under the United States: but the Party convicted shall nevertheless be liable and subject to Indictment, Trial, Judgment and Punishment, according to Law.

Sec. 4. The Times, Places and Manner of holding Elections for Senators and Representatives, shall be prescribed in each State by the Legislature thereof; but the Congress may at any time by Law make or alter such Regulations, except as to the Places of chusing Senators.

The Congress shall assemble at least once in every Year, and such Meeting shall be on the first Monday in December, unless they shall by Law appoint a different Day.

Sec. 5. Each House shall be the Judge of the Elections, Returns and Qualifications of its own Members, and a Majority of each shall constitute a Quorum to do Business; but a smaller Number may adjourn from day to day, and may be authorized to compel the Attendance of absent Members, in such Manner, and under such Penalties as each House may provide.

Each House may determine the Rules of its Proceedings, punish its Members for disorderly Behaviour, and, with the Concurrence of two thirds, expel a Member.

Each House shall keep a Journal of its Proceedings, and from time to time publish the same, excepting such parts as may in their Judgment require Secrecy; and the Yeas and Nays of the Members of either House on any question shall, at the Desire of one fifth of those Present, be entered on the Journal.

Neither House, during the Session of Congress, shall, without the Consent of the other, adjourn for more than three days, nor to any other Place than that in which the two Houses shall be sitting.

Sec. 6. The Senators and Representatives shall receive a Compensation for their Services, to be ascertained by Law, and paid out of the Treasury of the United States. They shall in all Cases, except Treason, Felony and Breach of the Peace, be privileged from Arrest during their Attendance at the Session of their respective Houses, and in going to and returning from the same; and for any Speech or Debate in either House, they shall not be questioned in any other Place.

No Senator or Representative shall, during the Time for which he was elected, be appointed to any civil Office under the Authority of the United States which shall have been created, or the Emoluments whereof shall have been encreased during such time; and no Person holding any Office under the United States, shall be a Member of either House during his Continuance in Office.

Sec. 7. All Bills for raising Revenue shall originate in the House of Representatives; but the Senate may propose or concur with Amendments as on other Bills.

Every Bill which shall have passed the House of Representatives and the Senate, shall, before it become a Law, be presented to the President of the United States; If he approve he shall sign it, but if not he shall return it, with his Objections to that House in which it shall have originated, who shall enter the Objections at large on their Journal, and proceed to reconsider it. If after such Reconsideration two thirds of that House shall agree to pass the Bill, it shall be sent, together with the Objections, to the other House, by which it shall likewise be reconsidered, and if approved by two thirds of that House, it shall become a Law. But in all such Cases the Votes of both Houses shall be determined by Yeas and Nays, and the Names of the Persons voting for and against the Bill shall be entered on the Journal of each House respectively. If any Bill shall not be returned by the President within ten Days (Sundays excepted) after it shall have been presented to him, the Same shall be a Law, in like Manner as if he had signed it, unless the Congress by their Adjournment prevent its Return, in which Case it shall not be a Law.

Every Order, Resolution, or Vote to which the Concurrence of the Senate and House of Representatives may be necessary (except on a question of Adjournment) shall be presented to the President of the United States; and before the Same shall take Effect, shall be approved by him, or being disapproved by him, shall be repassed by two thirds of the Senate and House of Representatives, according to the Rules and Limitations prescribed in the Case of a Bill.

Sec. 8. The Congress shall have Power To lay and collect Taxes, Duties, Imposts and Excises, to pay the Debts and provide for the common Defence and general Welfare of the United States; but all Duties, Imposts and Excises shall be uniform throughout the United States;

To Borrow Money on the credit of the United States;

To regulate Commerce with foreign Nations, and among the several States, and with the Indian Tribes;

To establish an uniform Rule of Naturalization, and uniform Laws on the subject of Bankruptcies throughout the United States;

To coin Money, regulate the Value thereof, and of foreign Coin, and fix the Standard of Weights and Measures;

To provide for the Punishment of counterfeiting the Securities and current Coin of the United States;

To establish Post Offices and post Roads;

To promote the Progress of Science and useful Arts, by securing for limited Times to Authors and Inventors the exclusive Right to their respective Writings and Discoveries;

To constitute Tribunals inferior to the supreme Court;

To define and punish Piracies and Felonies committed on the high Seas, and Offences against the Law of Nations;

To declare War, grant Letters of Marque and Reprisal, and make Rules concerning Captures on Land and Water;

To raise and support Armies, but no Appropriation of Money to that Use shall be for a longer Term than two Years;

To provide and maintain a Navy;

To make Rules for the Government and Regulation of the land and naval Forces;

To provide for calling forth the Militia to execute the Laws of the Union, suppress Insurrections and repel Invasions;

To provide for organizing, arming, and disciplining the Militia, and for governing such Part of them as may be employed in the Service of the United States, reserving to the States respectively, the Appointment of the Officers, and the Authority of training the Militia according to the discipline prescribed by Congress;

To exercise exclusive Legislation in all Cases whatsoever, over such District (not exceeding ten Miles square) as may, by Cession of particular States, and the Acceptance of Congress, become the Seat of the Government of the United States, and to exercise like Author-

ity over all Places purchased by the Consent of the Legislature of
the State in which the Same shall be, for the Erection of Forts,
Magazines, Arsenals, dock-Yards, and other needful Buildings;—
And

To make all Laws which shall be necessary and proper for carrying into Execution the foregoing Powers, and all other Powers
vested by this Constitution in the Government of the United States,
or in any Department or Officer thereof.

Sec. 9. The Migration or Importation of such Persons as any of the
States now existing shall think proper to admit, shall not be prohibited by the Congress prior to the Year one thousand eight hundred
and eight, but a Tax or duty may be imposed on such Importation,
not exceeding ten dollars for each Person.

The Privilege of the Writ of Habeas Corpus shall not be sus-
pended, unless when in Cases of Rebellion or Invasion the public
Safety may require it.

No Bill of Attainder or ex post facto Law shall be passed.

No Capitation, or other direct, Tax shall be laid, unless in Proportion to the Census or Enumeration herein before directed to be
taken.

No Tax or Duty shall be laid on Articles exported from any State.

No Preference shall be given by any Regulation of Commerce or
Revenue to the Ports of one State over those of another: nor shall
Vessels bound to, or from, one State, be obliged to enter, clear, or
pay Duties in another.

No Money shall be drawn from the Treasury, but in Consequence
of Appropriations made by Law; and a regular Statement and
Account of the Receipts and Expenditures of all public Money shall
be published from time to time.

No Title of Nobility shall be granted by the United States: And no
Person holding any Office of Profit or Trust under them, shall,
without the Consent of the Congress, accept of any present, Emolument, Office, or Title, of any kind whatever, from any King, Prince
or foreign State.

Sec. 10. No State shall enter into any Treaty, Alliance, or Confederation; grant Letters of Marque and Reprisal; coin Money; emit Bills
of Credit; make any Thing but gold and silver Coin a Tender in
Payment of Debts; pass any Bill of Attainder, ex post facto Law, or

Law impairing the Obligation of Contracts, or grant any Title of Nobility.

No State shall, without the Consent of the Congress, lay any Imposts or Duties on Imports or Exports, except what may be absolutely necessary for executing its inspection Laws: and the net Produce of all Duties and Imposts, laid by any State on Imports or Exports, shall be for the Use of the Treasury of the United States; and all such Laws shall be subject to the Revision and Controul of the Congress.

No State shall, without the Consent of Congress, lay any Duty of Tonnage, keep Troops, or Ships of War in time of Peace, enter into any Agreement or Compact with another State, or with a foreign Power, or engage in War, unless actually invaded, or in such imminent Danger as will not admit of delay.

ART. II

Sec. 1. The executive Power shall be vested in a President of the United States of America. He shall hold his Office during the Term of four Years, and, together with the Vice President, chosen for the same Term, be elected, as follows:

Each State shall appoint, in such Manner as the Legislature thereof may direct, a Number of Electors, equal to the whole Number of Senators and Representatives to which the State may be entitled in the Congress: but no Senator or Representative, or Person Holding an Office of Trust or Profit under the United States, shall be appointed an Elector.

The Electors shall meet in their respective States, and vote by Ballot for two Persons, of whom one at least shall not be an Inhabitant of the same State with themselves. And they shall make a List of all the Persons voted for, and of the Number of Votes for each; which List they shall sign and certify, and transmit sealed to the Seat of the Government of the United States, directed to the President of the Senate. The President of the Senate shall, in the Presence of the Senate and House of Representatives, open all the Certificates, and the Votes shall then be counted. The Person having the greatest Number of Votes shall be the President, if such Number be a Majority of the whole Number of Electors appointed;

and if there be more than one who have such Majority, and have an equal Number of Votes, then the House of Representatives shall immediately chuse by Ballot one the them for President; and if no person have a Majority, then from the five highest on the List the said House shall in like Manner chuse the President. But in chusing the President, the Votes shall be taken by States, the Representative from each State having one Vote; A quorum for this Purpose shall consist of a Member or Members from two thirds of the States and a Majority of all the States shall be necessary to a Choice. In every Case, after the Choice of the President, the Person having the greatest Number of Votes of the Electors shall be the Vice President. But if there should remain two or more who have equal Votes, the Senate shall chuse from them by Ballot the Vice President.

The Congress may determine the Time of chusing the Electors, and the Day on which they shall give their Votes; which Day shall be the same throughout the United States.

No Person except a natural born Citizen, or a Citizen of the United States, at the time of the Adoption of this Constitution, shall be eligible to the Office of President; neither shall any Person be eligible to the Office who shall not have attained to the Age of thirty five Years, and been fourteen Years a Resident within the United States.

In Case of the Removal of the President from Office, or of his Death, Resignation, or Inability to discharge the Powers and Duties of the said Office, the Same shall devolve on the Vice President, and the Congress may by Law provide for the Case of Removal, Death, Resignation or Inability, both of the President and Vice President, declaring what Officer shall then act as President, and such Officer shall act accordingly, until the Disability be removed, or a President shall be elected.

The President shall, at stated Times, receive for his Services, a Compensation, which shall neither be encreased nor diminished during the Period for which he shall have been elected, and he shall not receive within that Period any other Emolument from the United States, or any of them.

Before he enter on the Execution of his Office, he shall take the following Oath or Affirmation:—"I do solemnly swear (or affirm) that I will faithfully execute the Office of President of the United

States, and will to the best of my Ability, preserve, protect and defend the Constitution of the United States."

Sec. 2. The President shall be Commander in Chief of the Army and Navy of the United States, and of the Militia of the several States, when called into the actual Service of the United States; he may require the Opinion, in writing, of the principal Officer in each of the executive Departments, upon any Subject relating to the Duties of their respective Offices, and he shall have Power to grant Reprieves and Pardons for Offences against the United States, except in Cases of Impeachment.

He shall have Power, by and with the Advice and Consent of the Senate, to make Treaties, provided two thirds of the Senators present concur; and he shall nominate, and by and with the Advice and Consent of the Senate, shall appoint Ambassadors, other public Ministers and Consuls, Judges of the supreme Court, and all other Officers of the United States, whose Appointments are not herein otherwise provided for, and which shall be established by Law: but the Congress may by Law vest the Appointment of such inferior Officers, as they think proper, in the President alone, in the Courts of Law, or in the Heads of Departments.

The President shall have Power to fill up all Vacancies that may happen during the Recess of the Senate, by granting Commissions which shall expire at the End of their next Session.

Sec. 3. He shall from time to time give to the Congress Information of the State of the Union, and recommend to their Consideration such Measures as he shall judge necessary and expedient; he may, on extraordinary Occasions, convene both Houses, or either of them, and in Case of Disagreement between them, with Respect to the Time of Adjournment, he may adjourn them to such Time as he shall think proper; he shall receive Ambassadors and other public Ministers; he shall take Care that the Laws be faithfully executed, and shall Commission all the Officers of the United States.

Sec. 4. The President, Vice President and all civil Officers of the United States, shall be removed from Office on Impeachment for, and Conviction of, Treason, Bribery, or other high Crimes and Misdemeanors.

ART. III

Sec. 1. The judicial Power of the United States, shall be vested in one supreme Court, and in such inferior Courts as the Congress may from time to time ordain and establish. The Judges, both of the supreme and inferior Courts, shall hold their Offices during good Behaviour, and shall, at stated Times, receive for their Services, a Compensation, which shall not be diminished during their Continuance in Office.

Sec. 2. The judicial Power shall extend to all Cases, in Law and Equity, arising under this Constitution, the Laws of the United States, and Treaties made, or which shall be made, under their Authority;—to all Cases affecting Ambassadors, other public Ministers and Consuls;—to all Cases of admiralty and maritime Jurisdiction;—to Controversies to which the United States shall be a Party;—to Controversies between two or more States;—between a State and Citizens of another State;—between Citizens of different States,—between Citizens of the same State claiming Lands under Grants of different States, and between a State, or the Citizens thereof, and foreign States, Citizens or Subjects.

In all Cases affecting Ambassadors, other public Ministers and Consuls, and those in which a State shall be Party, the supreme Court shall have original Jurisdiction. In all the other cases before mentioned, the supreme Court shall have appellate Jurisdiction, both as to Law and Fact, with such Exceptions, and under such Regulations as the Congress shall make.

The Trial of all Crimes, except in Cases of Impeachment, shall be by Jury; and such Trial shall be held in the State where the said Crimes shall have been committed; but when not committed within any State, the Trial shall be at such Place or Places as the Congress may by Law have directed.

Sec. 3. Treason against the United States, shall consist only in levying War against them, or in adhering to their Enemies, giving them Aid and Comfort. No Person shall be convicted of Treason unless on the Testimony of two Witnesses to the same overt Act, or on Confession in open Court.

The Congress shall have Power to declare the Punishment of

Treason, but no Attainder of Treason shall work Corruption of Blood, or Forfeiture except during the Life of the Person attainted.

ART. IV

Sec. 1. Full Faith and Credit shall be given in each State to the Public Acts, Records, and judicial Proceedings of every other State. And the Congress may by general Laws prescribe the Manner in which such Acts, Records and Proceedings shall be proved, and the Effect thereof.

Sec. 2. The Citizens of each State shall be entitled to all Privileges and Immunities of Citizens in the Several States.

A Person charged in any State with Treason, Felony, or other Crime, who shall flee from Justice, and be found in another State, shall on Demand of the executive Authority of the State from which he fled, be delivered up, to be removed to the State having Jurisdiction of the Crime.

No Person held to Service or Labour in one State, under the Laws thereof, escaping into another, shall, in Consequence of any Law or Regulation therein, be discharged from such Service or Labour, but shall be delivered up on Claim of the Party to whom such Service or Labour may be due.

Sec. 3. New States may be admitted by the Congress into this Union; but no new States shall be formed or erected within the Jurisdiction of any other State; nor any State be formed by the Junction of two or more States, or Parts of States, without the Consent of the Legislatures of the States concerned as well as of the Congress.

The Congress shall have Power to dispose of and make all needful Rules and Regulations respecting the Territory or other Property belonging to the United States; and nothing in this Constitution shall be so construed as to Prejudice any Claims of the United States, or of any particular State.

Sec. 4. The United States shall guarantee to every State in this Union a Republican Form of Government, and shall protect each of them against Invasion; and on Application of the Legislature, or of the Executive (when the Legislature cannot be convened) against domestic Violence.

ART. V

The Congress, whenever two thirds of both Houses shall deem it necessary, shall propose Amendments to this Constitution, or, on the Application of the Legislatures of two thirds of the several States, shall call a Convention for proposing Amendments, which, in either Case, shall be valid to all Intents and Purposes, as Part of this Constitution, when ratified by the Legislatures of three fourths of the several States, or by Conventions in three fourths thereof, as the one or the other Mode of Ratification may be proposed by the Congress; Provided that no Amendment which may be made prior to the Year One thousand eight hundred and eight shall in any Manner affect the first and fourth Clauses in the Ninth Section of the first Article; and that no State, without its Consent, shall be deprived of its equal Suffrage in the Senate.

ART. VI

All Debts contracted and Engagements entered into, before the Adoption of this Constitution, shall be as valid against the United States under this Constitution, as under the Confederation.

This Constitution, and the Laws of the United States which shall be made in Pursuance thereof; and all Treaties made, or which shall be made, under the Authority of the United States, shall be the supreme Law of the Land; and the Judges in every State shall be bound thereby, any Thing in the Constitution or Laws of any State to the Contrary notwithstanding.

The Senators and Representatives before mentioned, and the Members of the several State Legislatures, and all executive and judicial Officers, both of the United States and of the several States, shall be bound by Oath or Affirmation, to support this Constitution; but no religious Test shall ever be required as a Qualification to any Office or public Trust under the United States.

ART. VII

The Ratification of the Conventions of nine States, shall be sufficient for the Establishment of this Constitution between the States so ratifying the Same.

Done in Convention by the Unanimous Consent of the States present the Seventeenth Day of September in the Year of our Lord one thousand seven hundred and Eighty seven and of the Independence of the United States of America the Twelfth. In witness whereof We have hereunto subscribed our Names.

Gᵘ WASHINGTON — Presidᵗ
and deputy from Virginia

New Hampshire	NICHOLAS GILMAN
	JOHN LANGDON
Massachusetts	NATHANIEL GORHAM
	RUFUS KING
Connecticut	Wᵐ SAMᴸ JOHNSON
	ROGER SHERMAN
New York	ALEXANDER HAMILTON
New Jersey	DAVID BREARLEY
	JONA: DAYTON
	WIL: LIVINGSTON
	Wᵐ PATERSON
Pennsylvania	GEO. CLYMER
	THOˢ FITZSIMONS
	B FRANKLIN
	JARED INGERSOLL
	THOMAS MIFFLIN
	GOUV MORRIS
	ROBᵗ MORRIS
	JAMES WILSON
Delaware	RICHARD BASSETT
	GUNNING BEDFORD JUN
	JACO: BROOM
	JOHN DICKINSON
	GEO: READ
Maryland	DANˡ CARROLL
	DAN of Sᵗ THOˢ JENIFER
	JAMES MᶜHENRY

APPENDIX 2

Virginia	JOHN BLAIR
	JAMES MADISON JR
North Carolina	Wᵐ BLOUNT
	RICHᵈ DOBBS SPAIGHT
	HU WILLIAMSON
South Carolina	PIERCE BUTLER
	CHARLES COTESWORTH PINCKNEY
	CHARLES PINCKNEY
	J. RUTLEDGE
Georgia	ABR BALDWIN
	WILLIAM FEW

NOTES

Note: All Farrand references are to the *Records of the Federal Convention of 1787* unless specifically stated *Framing (of the Constitution)*.

May 18, 1787

1. Bowen, 17.
2. Farrand, 3:20. "James Madison to Thomas Jefferson. Philada. May 15th. 1787."
3. Dept. State, 4:75–76.
4. Rakove, 368–380.
5. Brant, *Nationalist*, 408–412.
6. Bowen, 18.
7. Van Doren, *Rehearsal*, 1.
8. Flexner, *G.W. Nation*, 110–111.
9. Warren, 58.
10. Farrand, 3:21. "Benjamin Franklin to Thomas Jordan. Philadelphia, May 18, 1787."
11. Fleming, 481.
12. Dept. State, 4:120. "B. Franklin to H.E. Thomas Jefferson Esq. Philadelphia, April 19, 1787."

May 19, 1787

1. Farrand, 3:18–19. "Several Gentlemen of Rhode Island to the Chairman of the General Convention, Providence May 11, 1787."
2. Bowen, 13.
3. Farrand, *Framing*, 5.
4. Flexner, *G.W. Nation*, 128.
5. Morris, 113.
6. Morris, 115.

7. McDonald, *Hamilton*, 90–91.
8. Dept. State, 3:112–113.
9. Harwell, 538.

May 20, 1787

1. Farrand, 3:22–23. "George Washington to Arthur Lee. Philadelphia, May 20th, 1787."
2. Flexner, *G.W. Nation*, 116.
3. Flexner, *G.W. Nation*, 116.
4. Farrand, *Framing*, 10.
5. Jensen, *Nation*, 421.
6. Morris, 115–116.
7. Dept. State, 4:99–100, "G. Washington to Marquis de la Fayette, Mount Vernon, March 25, 1787."
8. Rakove, 392.
9. Brown, 5–6.
10. Van Doren, *Franklin*, 743.

May 21, 1787

1. Farrand, 3:24–26, "George Read to John Dickinson. Philadelphia, May 21st, 1787."
2. Munroe, 107.
3. Farrand, 3:25, "George Read to John Dickinson. Philadelphia, May 21st, 1787."
4. Adams,1:125–126.
5. Jensen, *Articles*, XXIX.
6. Jensen, *Nation*, 25.
7. Adams, 1:125–126.
8. Adams, 1:125–126.
9. Brant, *Nationalist*, 411.

May 22, 1787

1. Dept. State, 4:116. "Diary: George Washington, Tuesday, May 22, 1787."
2. Farrand, 3:22. "George Washington to Arthur Lee. Philadelphia, May 20th, 1787."
3. Farrand, 3:22–24. "George Mason to George Mason, Jr. Philadelphia, May 20th, 1787."
4. Van Doren, *Rehearsal*, 19.
5. Van Doren, *Rehearsal*, 20.
6. Rutland, x.

7. Bowen, 52.
8. Bowen, 51.
9. Silverman, 570.

May 23, 1787

1. Wright, 238.
2. Dept. State, 166–167. "James Monroe to James Madison in Philadelphia. Fredericksburg, May 23, 1787."
3. Rakove, 346–347.
4. Morris, 113.
5. Wright, 239.
6. Jensen, *Nation*, 250.
7. Flexner, *G.W. Nation*, 108–109.
8. Wright, 239.

May 24, 1787

1. Farrand, 3:26. "Rufus King to Jeremiah Wadsworth. Philadelphia 24 May 87."
2. Ferris, 33–35.
3. Bowen, 4.
4. Farrand, 3:558n.
5. Storing, 208.
6. Storing, 209.
7. Campbell, 323.
8. Dept. State, 94–95. "J. Madison to General Washington. March 18, 1787."
9. Storing, 208.
10. Brant, *Nationalist*, 399.

May 25, 1787

1. Farrand, 1:2.
2. Farrand, 1:4.
3. Bradford, 76, 197.
4. Van Doren, *Rehearsal*, 24.
5. Farrand, 3:381–382. "Gouverneur Morris: Oration Upon Washington." Delivered in New York, December 31, 1799.
6. Farrand, *Framing*, 56.
7. Farrand, 1:4.
8. Munroe, 107.
9. Farrand, 3:575n. "George Read to John Dickinson. New Castle, January 17th, 1787."

10. Farrand, 3:24–26. "Letter: George Read to John Dickinson. Philadelphia, May 21st, 1787."

May 26, 1787

1. Freeman, 89.
2. Farrand, 3:39–45. "Mr. Otto, Chargé d'Affaires de France, au Secrétaire D'etat des Affaires Etrangères, Comte de Montmorin. A New York, le 10 juin 1787."
3. Kohn, 13.
4. Kohn, 52–53.
5. Farrand, 2:114.
6. Flexner, *G.W. Nation*, 113–116.
7. Reardon, 97.

May 27, 1787

1. Farrand, 3:28. "George Mason to George Mason, Jr. Philadelphia, May 27, 1787."
2. Bowen, 22.
3. Van Doren, 28–29.
4. Dept. State, 266.
5. Barry, 321.
6. Barry, 322.
7. Barry, 322.

May 28, 1787

1. Bowen, 34–35.
2. Bowen, 23.
3. Van Doren, *Rehearsal*, 24.
4. Farrand, 3:29. "George Washington: Diary. *Monday*, [May] 28."
5. Farrand, 1:7.
6. Bradford, 12.
7. Farrand, 1:10.
8. Farrand, 1:10.
9. Farrand, 1:9–10.
10. Barry, 321–322.

May 29, 1787

1. Farrand, 1:26.
2. Bowen, 37.
3. Farrand, 1:26.

4. Reardon, 99.
5. Dept. State, 4:171–172. "H. Knox to General Washington. New York 29 May 1787."
6. Conway, 89.
7. Reardon, 99.
8. Farrand, *Framing*, 68.
9. Farrand, *Framing*, 69.
10. Farrand, 1:27.

May 30, 1787

1. Bowen, 41.
2. Farrand, 1:33.
3. Van Doren, *Rehearsal*, 33.
4. Farrand, 1:41.
5. Farrand, 1:42.
6. Warren, 146–147.
7. Farrand, 1:33–34.
8. Farrand, 1:39.
9. Warren, 149–150.
10. Farrand, 1:41–42.
11. Farrand, 1:43.
12. Farrand, 1:43.
13. Van Doren, *Rehearsal*, 34–35.

May 31, 1787

1. Farrand, 1:48.
2. Farrand, 1:48.
3. Warren, 158.
4. Farrand, 1:48.
5. Farrand, 1:48.
6. Farrand, 1:49.
7. Farrand, 1:49.
8. Warren, 163–165.
9. Van Doren, *Rehearsal*, 44.
10. Farrand, 1:53.

June 1, 1787

1. Van Doren, *Rehearsal*, 53–54.
2. Farrand, 1:65.
3. Barry, 324.
4. Williams, 226.

5. Farrand, 1:65.
6. Farrand, 1:66.
7. Farrand, 1:66.
8. Farrand, 1:71.
9. Bancroft, 20–21.
10. Farrand, 1:67.
11. Warren, 173, 176.

June 2, 1787

1. Farrand, 1:81.
2. Farrand, 1:80.
3. Van Doren, *Rehearsal*, 56.
4. Farrand, *Framing*, 78–79.
5. Farrand, 1:82.
6. Van Doren, *Franklin*, 745.
7. Farrand, 1:85.
8. Farrand, 1:87.
9. Farrand, l:86–87.
10. McDonald, *Novus*, 215, 219.

June 3, 1787

1. Warren, 155–156.
2. Farrand, 3:33. "Benjamin Rush to Richard Price. Philadelphia, June 2nd, 1787."
3. Dept. State, 183. "James Madison to Thomas Jefferson. June 6, 1787 Phila."
4. Bowen, 29. Also, Bradford, 140.
5. Bowen, 29.
6. Bowen, 13.
7. Farrand, *Framing*, 68.
8. Barry, 336.

June 4, 1787

1. Farrand, 1:93.
2. Farrand, 1:96.
3. Farrand, 1:97.
4. Farrand, 1:98.
5. Farrand, 1:99.
6. Warren, 185.
7. Bancroft, 25.

8. Warren, 185.
9. Farrand, 1:103.
10. Warren, 188.

June 5, 1787

1. McDonald, *Novus*, 220.
2. Bancroft, 26.
3. Farrand, 1:119.
4. Farrand, 1:119.
5. Farrand, 1:120.
6. Farrand, 1:120.
7. Farrand, 1:124.
8. McDonald, *Novus*, 256.
9. Farrand, 1:125.
10. Rossiter, *Grand*, 149.

June 6, 1787

1. Warren, 191.
2. Farrand, 1:147.
3. Farrand, 1:132.
4. Farrand, 1:133.
5. Farrand, 1:136.
6. Farrand, 1:131.
7. Bradford, 147.
8. Farrand, 1:136.
9. Farrand, 1:137.
10. Farrand, 3:33–34. "Jeremiah Wadsworth to Rufus King. Hartford, June 3, 1787."

June 7, 1787

1. Farrand, 1:149.
2. McDonald, *Novus*, 230–231.
3. Bradford, 103.
4. Farrand, 1:150.
5. Farrand, 1:157.
6. Farrand, 1:151.
7. Farrand, 1:153.
8. Farrand, 3:359. "Anecdote of Washington and Jefferson."
9. Warren, 194.
10. Farrand, 1:158.

June 8, 1787

1. Warren, 165.
2. Farrand, 1:163.
3. Farrand, 3:92. "William Pierce: Character Sketches of Delegates to the Federal Convention."
4. Farrand, 1:167.
5. Farrand, 1:167.
6. Farrand, 1:172.
7. Bowen, 25–26.
8. Bradford, 111–112.
9. Farrand, 1:169.
10. Farrand, 1:37.

June 9, 1787

1. Warren, 199.
2. Farrand, 1:177.
3. Farrand, 1:178–179.
4. Van Doren, *Rehearsal*, 74.
5. Farrand, 1:183.
6. Warren, 200.
7. Bowen, 86.
8. O'Connor, 140.
9. O'Connor, 142.

June 10, 1787

1. Warren, 204–205.
2. Farrand, 3:86–87. "William Pierce: Anecdote."
3. Bowen, 98.
4. Farrand, 3:39–45. "Mr. Otto, Chargé d'Affaires de France, au Secrétaire d'etat des Affaires Etrangères, Comte de Montmorin. No. 91. A New York, le 10 juin 1787."
5. Farrand, 3:294–295. "Luther Martin's Reply to the Landholder. Baltimore, March 19, 1788."
6. Risjord, 272.
7. O'Connor, 145.
8. Flexner, *G.W. Nation*, 124.

June 11, 1787

1. Bowen, 93.

2. Farrand, 1:196.
3. Williams, 229.
4. Dept. State, 4:195. "Franklin's Speech of June 11, 1787."
5. Farrand, 1:202.
6. Farrand, 1:202.
7. Van Doren, *Rehearsal*, 79.
8. Van Doren, *Rehearsal*, 78.
9. Warren, 211.
10. Bowen, 93.

June 12, 1787

1. Farrand, 1:213.
2. Warren, 212.
3. Farrand, 1:221.
4. Farrand, 3:46. "R.D. Spaight to Governor Caswell. Philadelphia, 12th June, 1787."
5. Farrand, 3:46. "North Carolina Delegates to Governor Casell. Philadelphia, June 14th, 1787."
6. Farrand, 3:36. "Edmund Randolph to Beverley Randolph. Philadelphia, June 6, 1787."
7. Reardon, 101.
8. Farrand, 1:218.
9. Warren, 57.

June 13, 1787

1. Farrand, 1:223–232.
2. Warren, 213.
3. Rossiter, *Grand*, 149.
4. Reardon, 103.
5. Bowen, 102.
6. Farrand, 1:234–235.
7. Farrand, 3:611. "The New Jersey Plan or Paterson Resolutions."
8. Farrand, 1:182–183.
9. O'Connor, 144.

June 14, 1787

1. Farrand, 1:240.
2. Van Doren, *Rehearsal*, 81.
3. Warren, 216.
4. Warren, 217–218.
5. Farrand, 1:242n.

6. Farrand, 3:33. "Benjamin Rush to Richard Price. Philadelphia, June 2nd, 1787."
7. Farrand, 3:35. "James Madison to Thomas Jefferson. Philada. June 6th. 1787."
8. Williams, 231.

June 15, 1787

1. Bancroft, 39.
2. Farrand, 1:246.
3. Farrand, 1:249.
4. Farrand, 1:246.
5. Rossiter, *Hamilton*, 45.
6. Warren, 220.
7. Rossiter, *Grand*, 150.
8. Farrand, *Framing*, 89.
9. O'Connor, 149.
10. Farrand, 3:90. "William Pierce: Character Sketches of Delegates to the Federal Convention."

June 16, 1787

1. Warren, 222.
2. Farrand, 1:250.
3. Farrand, 1:266.
4. Farrand, 1:261.
5. Farrand, 1:261.
6. Bradford, 50.
7. Farrand, 1:258.
8. Farrand, 1:255.
9. Warren, 225.

June 17, 1787

1. Harwell, 542–543.
2. Warren, 227.
3. De Pauw, 60.
4. Rossiter, *Hamilton*, 44.
5. Spaulding, 171.
6. Farrand, 3:234. "Liste des Membres et Officiers du Congres. 1788."
7. Farrand, 3:89. "William Pierce: Character Sketches of Delegates to the Federal Convention."
8. Farrand, 3:86–87. "William Pierce: Anecdote."

June 18, 1787

1. Rossiter, *Grand*, 151.
2. Bowen, 113–114.
3. Warren, 228.
4. Farrand, *Framing*, 87.
5. Farrand, 1:283.
6. Van Doren, *Rehearsal*, 93–94. See also: Farrand 1:289.
7. Farrand, 1:301.
8. Farrand, 3:413. "Extracts from Yates' Secret Proceedings."
9. Farrand, 1:293n. "J.C. Hamilton, *History of the Republic of the United States*, III, 283–384."
10. Farrand, 1:363.
11. Rossiter, *Grand*, 152.
12. Farrand, 1:288.

June 19, 1787

1. Warren, 231.
2. Farrand, 1:320.
3. Farrand, 1:326.
4. Ernst, 99.
5. Bowen, 117.
6. O'Connor, 150.
7. Kelly, 128.
8. Lansing, 16.
9. Farrand, 1:328.
10. Farrand, 1:328.

June 20, 1787

1. Rossiter, *Grand*, 156.
2. Bradford, 36.
3. Farrand, 1:335.
4. Farrand, 1:335.
5. Warren, 233.
6. Farrand, 1:347.
7. Farrand, 1:348.
8. Flexner, *G.W. Revolution*, 548.
9. Farrand, 1:347.
10. Farrand, 1:346.

June 21, 1787

1. Rossiter, *Grand*, 157.
2. Bancroft, 54.
3. Farrand, 1:355.
4. Farrand, 1:363.
5. Farrand, 1:355–356.
6. Farrand, 1:363.
7. Barry, 327.
8. Van Doren, *Rehearsal*, 97.
9. Farrand, 1:361.
10. Rakove, 129, 199.

June 22, 1787

1. Farrand, 1:371.
2. Farrand, 1:377.
3. Farrand, 1:372.
4. Farrand, 1:377–378.
5. Farrand, 1:378–379.
6. Farrand, 1:379.
7. Farrand, 1:379.
8. Farrand, 1:379.
9. Farrand, *Framing*, 92.

June 23, 1787

1. Farrand, 1:381.
2. Farrand, 1:385.
3. Farrand, 1:386.
4. Bowen, 120–121.
5. Farrand, 1:391.
6. Farrand, 1:393.
7. Farrand, 1:392.
8. Farrand, 1:388.
9. Farrand, 1:392.
10. Farrand, 1:394.
11. Farrand, 1:393.
12. McDonald, *Novus*, 199–201.

June 24, 1787

1. Ferris, 50.
2. Warren, 225.

3. Bowen, 12.
4. Van Doren, *Rehearsal*, 96.
5. Bowen, 23.
6. Farrand, 3:59n.
7. Farrand, 1:410.
8. Williams, 235.
9. Farrand, 1:411.

June 25, 1787

1. Farrand, 1:406.
2. Farrand, 1:413.
3. Farrand, 1:406.
4. Farrand, 1:407.
5. Farrand, 1:397.
6. Bancroft, 56.
7. Farrand, 1:413.
8. Farrand, 1:414.

June 26, 1787

1. Farrand, 1:420.
2. Farrand, 1:415.
3. Farrand, 1:375, 354.
4. Farrand, 1:422.
5. Farrand, 1:431–432.
6. Farrand, 1:432.
7. Brant, *Nation*, 81.
8. Farrand, 1:432.
9. Wood, 483–499, 523.

June 27, 1787

1. Farrand, *Framing*, 93.
2. Farrand, 3:272. "The Landholder [Oliver Ellsworth], X. To the Honorable Luther Martin, Esq."
3. Bowen, 119.
4. Van Doren, *Rehearsal*, 98–99.
5. Beveridge, 3:186–187. "Biographical Footnote on Luther Martin."
6. Farrand, 1:439–440.
7. Warren, 246.
8. Farrand, 1:441.

9. Farrand, 3:93. "William Pierce: Character Sketches of Delegates to the Federal Convention."

June 28, 1787

1. Brant, *Nation*, 82.
2. Farrand, 1:455.
3. Warren, 249–250.
4. Farrand, 1:457.
5. Farrand, 1:457.
6. Van Doren, *Rehearsal*, 100.
7. Farrand, 1:451.
8. Mitchell, 64.
9. Farrand, 1:452.
10. Farrand, 1:452.

June 29, 1787

1. Farrand, 1:470–474.
2. Bancroft, 59.
3. Farrand, 1:471.
4. Farrand, 1:464–465.
5. Farrand, 1:478.
6. Farrand, 1:473.
7. Farrand, 1:467.
8. Warren, 255.
9. Farrand, 1:469.

June 30, 1787

1. Farrand, 1:483.
2. Farrand, 1:484.
3. Farrand, 1:497.
4. Farrand, 1:497.
5. Farrand, 1:500–501.
6. Bowen, 132.
7. Ernst, 104.
8. Brant, *Nationalist*, 90.
9. McDonald, *Pluribus*, 170.

July 1, 1787

1. Warren, 260.
2. Farrand, 3:50. "George Mason to Beverley Randolph. Philadelphia, June 30, 1787."

3. Dept. State, 4:223–225. "G. Washington to Doct. David Stuart. Philadelphia, July 1, 1787."
4. Dept. State, 4:235. "G. Washington to Alex Hamilton, Esq. Philadelphia, 10th July 87."
5. Farrand, *Framing*, 94.
6. McDonald, *Hamilton*, 105.
7. McDonald, *Hamilton*, 106.
8. Farrand, 1:481.
9. Bancroft, 66.

July 2, 1787

1. Farrand, 1:509.
2. Brant, *Constitution*, 90.
3. Farrand, *Framing*, 97.
4. Van Doren, *Rehearsal*, 106.
5. Warren, 261.
6. Farrand, 1:517.
7. Farrand, 1:519.
8. Rossiter, *Grand*, 160.
9. Brant, *Constitution*, 91.
10. Farrand, 1:515.

July 3, 1787

1. Farrand, 1:526.
2. Farrand, 1:488.
3. Bancroft, 68.
4. Ernst, 104.
5. Mintz, 185*n*.
6. Warren, 265–266.
7. Dos Passos, 136.
8. Farrand, 3:57. "George Washington to Alexander Hamilton. Philadelphia 10th. July 87."
9. Dept. State, 4:226–227. "A. Hamilton to General Washington. Philadelphia, July 3 87."

July 4, 1787

1. Bowen, 139.
2. Van Doren, *Rehearsal*, 107.
3. Warren, 269.
4. Niles, 402. "Text of Address to the People of the United States—By Benjamin Rush, M.D., 1787."

5. Jensen, *Articles*, 109.
6. Wood, 523.
7. Warren, 270 *fn*1. "*Pennsylvania Gazette* of July 18, 1787."

July 5, 1787

1. Warren, 272.
2. Farrand, 1:532.
3. McDonald, *Pluribus*, 171.
4. Farrand, 1:528.
5. Farrand, 1:530.
6. O'Connor, 154.
7. Bancroft, 69.
8. Flexner, *G.W. Nation*, 131.

July 6, 1787

1. Farrand, 1:543.
2. Farrand, 1:544.
3. Farrand, 1:545.
4. Warren, 277.
5. Banning, 21.
6. Farrand, *Framing*, 100.
7. Warren, 275.
8. Farrand, 1:546.
9. Farrand, 1:544.

July 7, 1787

1. Farrand, 1:550.
2. Farrand, 1:550.
3. Farrand, 1:551.
4. Brant, *Constitution*, 93–94.
5. Farrand, 1:554.
6. O'Connor, 154.
7. Warren, 279.
8. Farrand, 1:553.

July 8, 1787

1. Farrand, 3:190. "Luther Martin: Genuine Information. The Genuine Information, delivered to the Legislature of the State of Maryland, relative to the Proceedings of the General Convention, held at Phila-delphia, in 1787, by Luther Martin, Esquire, Attorney-General of

Maryland, and one of the Delegates in the said Convention." For full text, see Farrand, 3:172–232, and 3:172 *fn3*.

2. Farrand, 1:105.
3. Rossiter, *Grand*, 217.
4. Spaulding, 172.
5. Farrand, 3:246. "Robert Yates and John Lansing, Jr. to the Governor of New York."
6. McDonald, *Pluribus*, 172.
7. De Pauw, 63.
8. Farrand, 3:307. "George Mason's Account of certain Proceedings in Convention. Guston hall. Sep. 30 92. ex relatione G. Mason."
9. De Pauw, 63.

July 9, 1787

1. Brant, *Constitution*, 94.
2. Farrand, 1:562.
3. Farrand, 1:560.
4. Van Doren, *Rehearsal*, 116.
5. Farrand, 1:561.
6. Farrand, 1:562.
7. Jensen, *Constitution*, 61.
8. Brant, *Constitution*, 95.
9. McDonald, *Novus*, 52, 220.
10. Bancroft, 75, 78.
11. Farrand, 2:370.

July 10, 1787

1. Harwell, 543.
2. Farrand, 3:56. "George Washington to Alexander Hamilton. Philadelphia 10th. July 87."
3. Dos Passos, 137.
4. Bowen, 140.
5. Ernst, 105.
6. Van Doren, *Rehearsal*, 117.
7. Williams, 240.
8. Farrand, 1:565.
9. Brant, *Constitution*, 96.
10. Farrand, 1:570.
11. Farrand, 1:571.
12. Farrand, 1:565.

July 11, 1787

1. Rossiter, *Grand*, 161.
2. Farrand, 1:579.
3. Williams, 242.
4. Farrand, 1:583.
5. Brant, *Constitution*, 96.
6. Farrand, 1:584.
7. Farrand, 1:587.
8. Farrand, 1:588.
9. Farrand, *Framing*, 103.

July 12, 1787

1. Mitchell, 74.
2. Rossiter, *Grand*, 162.
3. Farrand, 1:592.
4. Farrand, 1:593.
5. Farrand, 1:595–596.
6. Ernst, 106.
7. Farrand, 3:428. "Rufus King in the Senate of the United States." See also: Farrand, *Framing*, 104.
8. Barry, 329–330.

July 13, 1787

1. Farrand, 1:599.
2. Farrand, 1:603.
3. Farrand, 1:604.
4. O'Connor, 155.
5. Warren, 293.
6. Van Doren, *Rehearsal*, 120.
7. Farrand, 1:603.
8. Perry, 387–397. "Northwest Ordinance 1787"
9. Warren, 300.
10. Farrand, 1:605.

July 14, 1787

1. Rossiter, *Grand*, 162.
2. Warren, 305–306.
3. Farrand, 2:4.
4. Farrand, 2:4.

5. Farrand, 2:4.
6. Williams, 243.
7. Farrand, 2:5.
8. Brant, *Constitution*, 99.
9. Farrand, 2:10.
10. Farrand, 2:7.

July 15, 1787

1. Farrand, 2:2.
2. Ernst, 108.
3. Farrand, 2:7.
4. Flexner, *G.W. Nation*, 131.
5. Farrand, 3:56. "George Washington to Alexander Hamilton. Philadelphia 10th. July 87."
6. Warren, 308.
7. Fitzpatrick, 247.
8. Swiggett, 122–123.
9. Bowen, 186.

July 16, 1787

1. Ernst, 108.
2. Warren, 309.
3. Bancroft, 88.
4. Rossiter, *Grand*, 164.
5. Farrand, 2:18.
6. Farrand, 2:18.
7. Farrand, 2:19.
8. O'Connor, 156–159.
9. Farrand, 2:19.

July 17, 1787

1. Freeman, 6:101.
2. Farrand, 2:26.
3. Warren, 316.
4. McDonald, *Pluribus*, 173.
5. Farrand, 2:19.
6. Farrand, 2:27.
7. Rossiter, *Grand*, 169.
8. Brant, *Constitution*, 103.
9. O'Connor, 160.

July 18, 1787

1. Van Doren, *Rehearsal*, 135.
2. Bancroft, 92.
3. Warren, 326.
4. Farrand, 2:46.
5. Farrand, 2:46.
6. Warren, 327.
7. Farrand, 2:44.
8. McDonald, *Novus*, 253.
9. Farrand, 2:42.

July 19, 1787

1. Warren, 336.
2. Farrand, 2:52.
3. Farrand, 2:54–55.
4. Farrand, 2:56.
5. Farrand, 2:56.
6. Reardon, 110.
7. McDonald, *Novus*, 242.

July 20, 1787

1. McDonald, *Novus*, 242.
2. Farrand, 2:61.
3. Farrand, 2:64.
4. Farrand, 2:65.
5. Farrand, 2:65.
6. Farrand, 2:65.
7. Farrand, 2:66.
8. Farrand, 2:67.
9. Farrand, 2:68.

July 21, 1787

1. Warren, 338.
2. Farrand, 2:73.
3. Farrand, 2:73.
4. Farrand, 2:74.
5. Brant, *Constitution*, 107.
6. Farrand. 2:74.
7. Farrand, 2:75.
8. Mitchell, 87.

9. Farrand, 2:76–77.
10. Brant, *Constitution*, 108.

July 22, 1787

1. Gephart, 1230.
2. Bradford, 182.
3. Farrand, 3:61. "Hugh Williamson to James Iredell. Philadelphia, July 22d, 1787."
4. Farrand, 3:61. "Benjamin Franklin to John Paul Jones. Philada. July 22, 1787."
5. Mitchell, 88.
6. Bradford, 1.
7. Bradford, 4.
8. Warren, 342–343.
9. Boatner, 705.
10. Dos Passos, 139.
11. Boatner, 278.
12. Farrand, 4:75. "Benjamin Rush to Timothy Pickering. August 30, 1787."
13. Flexner, *G.W. Nation*, 134.

July 23, 1787

1. Warren, 347.
2. Farrand, 2:91.
3. Farrand, 2:88–89.
4. Farrand, 2:89.
5. Farrand, 2:89–90.
6. Van Doren, *Rehearsal*, 138.
7. Mitchell, 88.
8. Warren, 339.
9. Farrand, 2:96.
10. Williams, 247.

July 24, 1787

1. Farrand, 2:106.
2. Warren, 353.
3. Bancroft, 95.
4. Barry, 337.
5. Brant, *Constitution*, 111.
6. Farrand, 2:103.

7. Farrand, 2:104–105.
8. Farrand, 2:106.
9. Fitzpatrick, 251–254.

July 25, 1787

1. Williams, 247.
2. Farrand, 2:109.
3. Farrand, 2:112.
4. Farrand, 2:112.
5. Farrand, 2:114.
6. Farrand, 3:61. "John Jay to George Washington. New York 25 July 1787."
7. Bancroft, 432.

July 26, 1787

1. Rossiter, *Grand*, 171.
2. Warren, 364.
3. Farrand, 2:119–120.
4. Farrand, 2:120.
5. Farrand, 2:121.
6. McDonald, *Novus*, 221.
7. McDonald, *Novus*, 96.
8. Farrand, 2:125.
9. McDonald, *Pluribus*, 173.

July 27, 1787

1. Barry, 339.
2. Barry, 339.
3. Farrand, 1:401.
4. Williams, 221.
5. Van Doren, *Rehearsal*, 138.
6. Rossiter, *Grand*, 173.
7. Bradford, 197.
8. Barry, 340.

July 28, 1787

1. Warren, 371.
2. Rossiter, *Grand*, 172.
3. Ketcham, 219–220.

4. Farrand, 3:65–66. "James Madison to his Father. Philada. July 28. 1787."
5. Bowen, 192.
6. Warren, 366. A quote from *Pennsylvania Herald,* July 28, 1787.
7. Farrand, 2:115.
8. Farrand, 3:191. "Luther Martin: Genuine Information."

July 29, 1787

1. Banning, 28.
2. McDonald, *Pluribus,* 174.
3. Reardon, 112.
4. Farrand, 2:137. "Committee of Detail, Document IV, in handwriting of Edmund Randolph."
5. Farrand, *Framing,* 128–129.
6. Van Doren, *Rehearsal,* 140.
7. Barry, 338–339.
8. Barry, 338–339.

July 30, 1787

1. Ketcham, 220.
2. Van Doren, *Rehearsal,* 146.
3. Bowen, 191.
4. Brant, *Constitution,* 116.
5. Farrand, 2:101.
6. Reardon, 102.
7. Barry, 340–341.
8. Van Doren, *Rehearsal,* 147.
9. Warren, 372.

July 31, 1787

1. Warren, 373.
2. Freeman, 102.
3. Flexner, *G.W. Nation,* 132.
4. Farrand, 3:94. "William Pierce: Character Sketches of Delegates to the Federal Convention."
5. Warren, 370–371.
6. Warren, 369.

August 1, 1787

1. Warren, 377.
2. McDonald, *Hamilton,* 106.

3. Warren, 341.
4. Spaulding, 173.
5. Farrand, 3:63. "Mr. Otto, Chargé d'Affaires de France, au Secrétaire d'Etat des Affaires Etrangères, Comte de Montmorin. No. 96. A New York, le 25 juillet, 1787."
6. De Pauw, 75.
7. De Pauw, 75.
8. Farrand, 3:64. "Alexander Hamilton to Auldjo. New York, July 26, 1787."

August 2, 1787

1. Barry, 341.
2. Barry, 341.
3. Farrand, 2:114.
4. Warren, 379.
5. Tyler, 420.
6. Storing, 215.

August 3, 1787

1. McDonald, *Novus*, 95.
2. Warren, 380.
3. Malone, 161.
4. Palmer, 24.
5. Durant, 946.
6. Warren, 383.
7. Malone, 162.
8. Bowen, 11.

August 4, 1787

1. Farrand, 2:175.
2. Bradford, 125.
3. Warren, 381.
4. Risjord, 273.
5. Farrand, 2:191.
6. Bowen, 200–201.
7. Jensen, *Constitution*, 72.
8. Van Doren, *Rehearsal*, 140.
9. Warren, 382.
10. Farrand, 3:66. "Nicholas Gilman to Joseph Gilman. Philadelphia, July 31st 1787."

August 5, 1787

1. Freeman, 103.
2. Van Doren, *Rehearsal*, 140.
3. Barry, 344–345.
4. Warren, 384–385.
5. Farrand, *Framing*, 126.
6. Farrand, 3:91–92. "William Pierce: Character Sketches of Delegates to the Federal Convention."
7. McDonald, *Pluribus*, 174.

August 6, 1787

1. Farrand, 2:176.
2. Farrand, 2:177.
3. Van Doren, *Rehearsal*, 140–141.
4. Bancroft, 120.
5. Farrand, 2:177.
6. Bancroft, 121.
7. Warren, 390–391.
8. Farrand, 2:183.
9. Rossiter, *Grand*, 180.
10. Farrand, 2:189.

August 7, 1787

1. Rossiter, *Grand*, 180.
2. Van Doren, *Rehearsal*, 141.
3. Farrand, 2:201.
4. Farrand, 2:202–203.
5. Farrand, 2:210.
6. Farrand, 2:206.
7. Freeman, 103.
8. Bowen, 205.

August 8, 1787

1. Bancroft, 132.
2. Warren, 403.
3. Farrand, 2:220.
4. Ernst, 109.
5. Farrand, 2:220–221.
6. McDonald, *Pluribus*, 177.

7. Farrand, 2:222–223.
8. Williams, 252.
9. Warren, 397.

August 9, 1787

1. Farrand, 2:216.
2. Williams, 252.
3. Farrand, 2:235.
4. Farrand, 2:236.
5. Bradford, 208.
6. Farrand, 2:236.
7. Bowen, 207.
8. Farrand, 2:237.
9. Farrand, 2:237–238.
10. Farrand, 2:236.

August 10, 1787

1. Farrand, 2:248.
2. Williams, 252.
3. Van Doren, *Rehearsal*, 143.
4. Farrand, 2:249.
5. Farrand, 2:249.
6. Farrand, 2:250.
7. Farrand, 1:375, 1:415.
8. Farrand, 1:375.

August 11, 1787

1. Farrand, 2:259.
2. Farrand, 2:260.
3. Farrand, 2:260.
4. Farrand, 2:260.
5. Warren, 430–431.
6. Van Doren, *Rehearsal*, 144.
7. Flexner, *G.W. Nation*, 137.
8. Campbell, 323, 325.
9. Spaulding, 173.
10. Warren, 404.
11. Farrand, 3:68. "R. D. Spaight to James Iredell. Philadelphia, August 12th, 1787."

August 12, 1787

1. Brant, *Constitution*, 122.
2. Reardon, 115.
3. Farrand, 2:225.
4. Farrand, 2:224.
5. Bradford, 174.
6. Farrand, 3:67. "James McClurg to James Madison. Richmond Augt. 5. 87."
7. Farrand, 2:280n.

August 13, 1787

1. Farrand, 3:69. "*Pennsylvania Herald and General Advertiser.* Wednesday, August 15, 1787."
2. Warren, 435.
3. Farrand, 2:273–274.
4. Farrand, 2:275.
5. Farrand, 2:278.
6. Farrand, 2:278–279.
7. Warren, 437.
8. Farrand, 2:280.
9. Reardon, 115.

August 14, 1787

1. Farrand, 2:292.
2. Warren, 446.
3. Farrand, 2:291.
4. Farrand, 2:290.
5. Farrand, 2:291.
6. Farrand, 2:292.
7. Farrand, 2:292.
8. Farrand, 2:292.
9. Farrand, 2:293.
10. Rutland, 85–86.
11. Farrand, 2:284.

August 15, 1787

1. Farrand, 2:298.
2. Farrand, 2:56.
3. Farrand, 2:299.
4. Farrand, 2:301.

5. Farrand, 2:301.
6. McDonald, *Pluribus*, 180.
7. Farrand, 2:328.

August 16, 1787

1. Bancroft, 132.
2. Warren, 465.
3. McDonald, *Novus*, 270.
4. Van Doren, *Rehearsal*, 147–148.
5. Farrand, 2:309.
6. Farrand, 2:309.
7. Farrand, 2:309–310.
8. Bowen, 13.

August 17, 1787

1. Warren, 480–481.
2. McDonald, *Novus*, 247–248.
3. Farrand, 2:318.
4. Farrand, 2:318.
5. Farrand, 2:318.
6. Farrand, 2:317.
7. Farrand, 2:317.
8. Jensen, *Constitution*, 82.
9. Farrand, 3:547. "James Madison: Preface to Debates in the Convention of 1787."

August 18, 1787

1. Bancroft, 147.
2. Farrand, 2:329.
3. Farrand, 2:330.
4. Warren, 483.
5. Farrand, 2:332.
6. Jensen, *Constitution*, 83–84.
7. Farrand, 2:332.
8. Farrand, 2:330.
9. Jensen, *Constitution*, 85–86.

August 19, 1787

1. Warren, 485.
2. Freeman, 104–105.

3. Boatner, 429–430. "Germantown, Pa., Battle of 4 Oct. 77 (Philadelphia Campaign)."
4. Farrand, 3:70. "George Washington to Henry Knox. Philadelphia. August 19, 1787."
5. Farrand, 2:332.
6. Kohn, 78.
7. Farrand, 2:330.
8. Farrand, 2:331.

August 20, 1787

1. Farrand, 2:351.
2. Warren, 489.
3. Jensen, *Constitution*, 89.
4. Farrand, 2:348.
5. Bowen, 221.
6. Farrand, 2:347.
7. Farrand, 2:347.
8. Farrand, 2:349.
9. Farrand, 2:349.
10. Brant, *Constitution*, 124.
11. Jensen, *Constitution*, 89.
12. Bancroft, 149.

August 21, 1787

1. Rossiter, *Grand*, 185.
2. Warren, 498.
3. Farrand, 2:359.
4. Bancroft, 152.
5. Farrand, 2:364.
6. Farrand, 2:364.
7. Farrand, 2:364.
8. Farrand, 2:361.
9. Farrand, 2:362–363.

August 22, 1787

1. Rossiter, *Grand*, 186.
2. Warren, 501.
3. Farrand, 2:369–370.
4. Van Doren, *Rehearsal*, 152.
5. Farrand, 2:370.
6. Rutland, 86.

7. Farrand, 2:370–371.
8. Williams, 261.

August 23, 1787

1. Farrand, 2:385.
2. Farrand, 2:387.
3. Warren, 519.
4. Jensen, *Constitution*, 84.
5. Farrand, 2:388.
6. Farrand, 2:388.
7. Farrand, 2:394.
8. Farrand, 2:389.
9. Freeman, 106.
10. Farrand, 2:391.

August 24, 1787

1. Jensen, *Constitution*, 106–107.
2. Bancroft, 174.
3. Farrand, 2:402.
4. Farrand, 2:402–403.
5. Farrand, 2:403–404.
6. Farrand, 2:404.
7. Farrand, 2:405.
8. Warren, 525–526.
9. Bancroft, 165.

August 25, 1787

1. Ernst, 110.
2. Farrand, 2:396.
3. Bancroft, 158*n*.
4. Williams, 261.
5. Van Doren, *Rehearsal*, 156.
6. Farrand, 2:415.
7. Rossiter, *Grand*, 186–187.
8. Farrand, 2:415.
9. Farrand, 2:415.
10. Jensen, *Constitution*, 92–93.
11. Warren, 579. See also: Farrand, 2:414*n*.
12. Freeman, 106.
13. Dr. Lance Banning, University of Kentucky, in notes to author.
14. McDonald, *Pluribus*, 183.

August 26, 1787

1. Freeman, 106.
2. Farrand, 3:75. "Ezra Stiles: Diary. [August] 27."
3. Farrand, 3:72. "Alexander Martin to Governor Caswell. Philadelphia, August 20th, 1787."
4. Ferris, 33.
5. Farrand, 3:73–74. "Extract from the Pennsylvania Journal. [August 22, 1787.]"
6. Warren, 510–512.
7. Bowen, 50, 163.
8. Farrand, 2:399.

August 27, 1787

1. Bancroft, 197.
2. Farrand, 2:428.
3. Farrand, 2:429.
4. Warren, 532.
5. Farrand, 2:430.
6. Jensen, *Constitution*, 109.
7. Warren, 541.
8. McDonald, *Novus*, 256–257.
9. Bancroft, 200.

August 28, 1787

1. Farrand, 2:439.
2. Farrand, 2:439.
3. Bancroft, 137.
4. Warren, 551.
5. Ernst, 111–112.
6. Warren, 552–553.
7. Ernst, 111–112.
8. Bancroft, 138.
9. McDonald, *Novus*, 270.
10. McDonald, *Novus*, 3.
11. Farrand, 1:431. (Yates: June 26.)

August 29, 1787

1. Warren, 580.
2. Farrand, 2:449.
3. Warren, 580.

4. Farrand, *Framing*, 153.
5. Farrand, 2:449.
6. Farrand, 2:451.
7. Williams, 263.
8. Farrand, 2:452.
9. Farrand, 2:451.
10. Farrand, 2:452.
11. Rossiter, *Grand*, 187.
12. Bancroft, 161.

August 30, 1787

1. Warren, 596–597.
2. Farrand, 1:536.
3. Farrand, 2:454.
4. Jensen, *Constitution*, 98–99.
5. Jensen, *Constitution*, 98–99
6. Farrand, 2:454.
7. Jensen, *Constitution*, 98.
8. Farrand, 2:454.
9. Van Doren, *Rehearsal*, 158.
10. Warren, 602.
11. Bowen, 168–184.

August 31, 1787

1. Van Doren, *Rehearsal*, 159.
2. Warren, 607.
3. Bowen, 226–228.
4. Farrand, 2:478.
5. Farrand, 2:479.
6. Farrand, 2:561.
7. Farrand, 2:469.
8. Farrand, 2:476.
9. Jensen, *Constitution*, 104.

September 1, 1787

1. Farrand, *Framing*, 166–168.
2. Bancroft, 165.
3. Rossiter, *Grand*, 187.
4. Warren, 611.
5. Brant, *Constitution*, 135.

6. Farrand, 3:76. "James Madison to his Father. Philada. Sepr. 4. 1787."
7. Farrand, 3:78. "James Madison to Thomas Jefferson. Philada. Sepr. 6. 1787."
8. Rutland, 89.
9. Williams, 264.

September 2, 1787

1. Bowen, 216.
2. Farrand, 3:79. "Jonas Phillips to the President and Members of the Convention. Philadelphia 24th Ellul 5547 or Sepr 7th 1787.
3. Warren, 412.
4. Farrand, 2:468.
5. Bowen, 215.
6. Bradford, 142.
7. Farrand, 3:310. "Edmund Randolph in the Virginia Convention. June 10, 1788."
8. Farrand, 3:227, para.100. "Luther Martin: Genuine Information."

September 3, 1787

1. Warren, 618.
2. McDonald, *Novus*, 199.
3. Farrand, 1:379. (Yates: June 22, 1787.)
4. Bowen, 120.
5. Warren, 612.
6. Farrand, 2:491.
7. Farrand, 2:490.
8. Farrand, 2:491.
9. McDonald, *Novus*, 199.

September 4, 1787

1. Rossiter, *Grand*, 190.
2. Farrand, 2:494.
3. Farrand, 2:500.
4. Farrand, 2:494.
5. Farrand, 2:501.
6. McDonald, *Pluribus*, 185.
7. Farrand, *Framing*, 166–167.
8. Warren, 623.
9. Jensen, *Constitution*, 107.

September 5, 1787

1. Warren, 628.
2. Farrand, 2:511.
3. Farrand, 2:507.
4. Farrand, 2:515.
5. Farrand, 2:512.
6. Farrand, 2:512.
7. Farrand, 2:507.
8. Farrand, 2:512.
9. Farrand, 2:513.
10. Williams, 265.
11. Reardon, 116.

September 6, 1787

1. Warren, 630.
2. Farrand, 2:522–523.
3. Farrand, 2:524.
4. Brant, *Constitution*, 145.
5. Farrand, 2:531.
6. McDonald, *Novus*, 251.
7. Bancroft, 182.
8. Farrand, 2:528.
9. McDonald, *Pluribus*, 184–185.
10. Farrand, 3:458. "James Madison to George Hay. Montpelier Aug 23, 1823.
11. Beck, 157.

September 7, 1787

1. Farrand, 2:532.
2. Warren, 633.
3. Farrand, 3:343. "William R. Davie in the North Carolina Convention. July 25, 1788."
4. Farrand, 2:536–537.
5. Farrand, 2:537.
6. Farrand, 2:537.
7. Farrand, 2:537.
8. Jensen, *Constitution*, 114.
9. Farrand, 2:537.
10. Farrand, 2:542.
11. Warren, 643.

September 8, 1787

1. Jensen, *Constitution*, 117.
2. Farrand, *Framing*, 179.
3. Mintz, 198.
4. Brant, *Constitution*, 146.
5. Brant, *Constitution*, 147.
6. Farrand, 2:551.
7. Farrand, 2:551.
8. Farrand, 2:550.
9. Farrand, 2:552.
10. Warren, 668–669. See also: Farrand, 2:552.
11. Farrand, 2:278.

September 9, 1787

1. Freeman, 107–108.
2. Warren, 653–654.
3. McDonald, *Novus*, 169.
4. Bowen, 170.
5. Farrand, 2:297–298. "August 15, 1787."
6. Jensen, *Constitution*, 116.
7. Warren, 657.
8. Farrand, 3:306. "Hugh Williamson to James Madison. New York June 2nd 1788."
9. Freeman, 108.

September 10, 1787

1. Warren, 675.
2. Farrand, 2:558.
3. Farrand, 2:559.
4. Farrand, 2:559.
5. Farrand, 2:555.
6. Jensen, *Constitution*, 102.
7. Bancroft, 205.
8. Farrand, 2:560.
9. Farrand, 2:562.
10. Farrand, 2:563. See also: Jensen, *Constitution*, 102–103.
11. Reardon, 117–118.
12. Farrand, 2:564.

September 11, 1787

1. Farrand, 2:581.
2. Farrand, 2:581.
3. Farrand, 3:499. "James Madison to Jared Sparks. Montpellier, April 8, 1831."
4. Farrand, 3:170. "Ezra Stiles: Diary. [December] 21. [1787]." Mr. Stiles records a conversation with Abraham Baldwin, a delegate to the Convention.
5. Farrand, 3:420. "Gouverneur Morris to Timothy Pickering. Morrisania, December 22d, 1814."
6. McDonald, *Novus*, 255.
7. Warren, 686.
8. Farrand, 2:590. "Report of Committee of Style."
9. Bancroft, 208.
10. Van Doren, *Rehearsal*, 161.

September 12, 1787

1. Beck, 161.
2. Farrand, 2:583–584.
3. Farrand, 2:584. (Letter to Congress.)
4. Farrand, 2:587–588.
5. Farrand, 2:637. (Mason: "Objections to This Constitution of Government.")
6. Bowen, 244.
7. Rutland, 66.
8. Farrand, 2:588.
9. Mitchell, 115.
10. Rutland, 89.
11. Rutland, 91.
12. Rossiter, *Grand*, 173.
13. Rossiter, *Grand*, 198.

September 13, 1787

1. Warren, 689–690.
2. Rossiter, *Grand*, 196.
3. Bancroft, 210.
4. Farrand, *Framing*, 182–183. Farrand, 2:594.
5. Farrand, 3:379. "Albert Gallatin in the House of Representatives. June 19, 1798." See also: Farrand, 2:187*n*.

6. Farrand, 2:604.
7. Farrand, 2:605.
8. Brant, *Constitution*, 148.

September 14, 1787

1. Warren, 692–693.
2. Farrand, 2:315.
3. Farrand, 2:614.
4. Farrand, 2:614.
5. Farrand, 2:614.
6. Mitchell, 116.
7. Rossiter, *Grand*, 198.
8. Farrand, 2:617.
9. Farrand, 2:617.
10. Farrand, 2:618.
11. Mitchell, 119.

September 15, 1787

1. Warren, 706.
2. Freeman, 109.
3. Farrand, 2:631.
4. Van Doren, *Rehearsal*, 165.
5. Rossiter, *Grand*, 199.
6. Farrand, 2:632.
7. Farrand, 2:632.
8. Farrand, 2:632–633.
9. Farrand, 2:632–633.
10. Van Doren, *Rehearsal*, 167.
11. Beck, 161.
12. Van Doren, *Rehearsal*, 167.

September 16, 1787

1. Farrand, 3:104. "Letter to Jefferson[?]. Philadelphia 11. Oct. 1787."
2. Farrand, 2:643.
3. Mitchell, 121.
4. Farrand, 2:642–643.
5. Van Doren, *Rehearsal*, 167.
6. Fleming, 485.
7. Fleming, 485.
8. Flexner, *G.W. Nation*, 135.
9. Rossiter, *Grand*, 201.

September 17, 1787

1. Warren, 716.
2. Farrand, 2:643.
3. Bancroft, 219.
4. Farrand, 2:644.
5. Freeman, 111.
6. Farrand, 2:644.
7. Farrand, 2:645.
8. Rossiter, *Grand*, 201.
9. Bowen, 262.
10. Farrand, 3:81. "John Dickinson to George Read. September 15th, 1787."
11. Bowen, 254.
12. Van Doren, *Rehearsal*, 173.
13. Farrand, 2:648.

September 18, 1787

1. Mitchell, 122.
2. Van Doren, *Rehearsal*, 175.
3. Reardon, 121.
4. Warren, 717–718.
5. Ernst, 117.
6. Freeman, 112.
7. Farrand, 2:648.
8. Farrand, 2:648.
9. Farrand, 3:81. "George Washington: Diary. [September], Saturday 17th."
10. Rossiter, *Grand*, 205.
11. Fitzpatrick, 276–277. "Marquis de Lafayette. Philadelphia Sept. 18, 1787."
12. Farrand, 3:85. "James McHenry: Anecdotes."

BIBLIOGRAPHY

This bibliography is not intended to be an inclusive list of reference sources on the subject of the Constitutional Convention. Nevertheless, as noted by the scholars reviewing this work, the latest sources have been consulted in addition to earlier definitive studies of the Convention and other works. The primary source is Max Farrand's Records of the Federal Convention of 1787. *The following is an alphabetical list of the sources cited and abbreviated in the Notes.*

Adams, James Truslow, ed. *The Dictionary of American History.* Vol. 1. New York: Charles Scribner's Sons, 1940.

Bancroft, George. *History of the Formation of the Constitution of the United States of America.* Vol. 2. 2d ed. New York: D. Appleton and Company, 1882.

Banning, Lance. "The Constitutional Convention." 1985 ms. Department of History, University of Kentucky, Lexington.

Barry, Richard. *Mr. Rutledge of South Carolina.* 1942 ed. New York: Books for Libraries Press, Division of Arno Press, Inc., 1971.

Beck, James M. *The Constitution of the United States: Yesterday, Today— and Tomorrow?* New York: George H. Doran Company, 1924.

Beveridge, Albert J. *The Life of John Marshall: Conflict and Construction, 1800–1815.* Vol. 3. Boston and New York: Houghton Mifflin Company, 1919.

Boatner III, Mark Mayo. *Encyclopedia of the American Revolution.* New York: David McKay Company, Inc., 1966.

Bowen, Catherine Drinker. *Miracle at Philadelphia: The Story of the Constitutional Convention May to September 1787.* London: Hamish Hamilton, 1966.

Bradford, M. E. *A Worthy Company: Brief Lives of the Framers of the United States Constitution.* Marlborough, N.H.: Plymouth Rock Foundation, 1982.

291

292 BIBLIOGRAPHY

Brant, Irving. *James Madison: Father of the Constitution 1787–1800.* Indianapolis: Bobbs-Merrill Company, 1950.

———. *James Madison: The Nationalist 1780–1787.* 1st ed. Indianapolis: Bobbs-Merrill Company, 1948.

Brown, Richard D. *The Aftermath of Shays's Rebellion and the Ratification of the Federal Constitution in Massachusetts.* Ms. Department of History, University of Connecticut, Bridgeport, 1985.

Campbell, Norine Dickson. *Patrick Henry: Patriot & Statesman.* Old Greenwich, Conn.: Devin-Adair Company, 1969.

Conway, Moncure Daniel. *Omitted Chapters of History Disclosed in the Life and Papers of Edmund Randolph.* G.P. Putnam's Sons, 1888; New York: Da Capo Press, 1971.

Department of State, Washington, D.C. *Documentary History of the Constitution of the United States of America 1780–1870.* Vol. 4 . 1905.

De Pauw, Linda Grant. *The Eleventh Pillar: New York State and the Federal Constitution.* American Historical Association. Ithaca, N.Y.: Cornell University Press, 1966.

Dos Passos, John. *The Men Who Made the Nation.* Garden City, N.Y.: Doubleday & Company, Inc., 1957.

Durant, Will, and Durant, Ariel. *Rousseau and Revolution,* vol. 10. *The Story of Civilization.* New York: Simon and Schuster, 1967.

Ernst, Robert. *Rufus King: American Federalist.* Chapel Hill: University of North Carolina, 1968.

Farrand, Max. *The Framing of the Constitution of the United States.* New Haven: Yale University Press, 1913; 26th printing, 1976.

Farrand, Max, ed. *The Records of the Federal Convention of 1787.* Rev. ed. in 4 vols. New Haven and London: Yale University Press, 1966.

Ferris, Robert A., ed. *Signers of the Constitution.* Washington, D.C.: United States Department of Interior, National Park Service Publication, 1976.

Fitzpatrick, John C., ed. *The Writings of George Washington.* Vol. 29. Washington, D.C.: United States Government Printing Office, 1939.

Fleming, Thomas. *The Man Who Dared the Lightning: A New Look at Benjamin Franklin.* New York: William Morrow and Company, 1971.

Flexner, James Thomas. *George Washington in the American Revolution (1775–1783).* Boston: Little, Brown and Company, 1968.

———. *George Washington and the New Nation (1783–1793).* Boston: Little, Brown and Company, 1970.

Freeman, Douglas S. *George Washington—A Biography: Patriot and President.* Vol. 6. New York: Charles Scribner's & Sons, 1954.

Gephart, Ronald M., ed. *Revolutionary America 1763–1789: A Bibliography.* Vol. 2. Washington, D.C.: Library of Congress, 1984.

Harwell, Richard. *Washington: An Abridgment*, in 1 vol. of 7-vol. *George Washington* by Douglas Southall Freeman. New York: Charles Scribner's Sons, 1968.

Jensen, Merrill. *The Articles of Confederation: An Interpretation of the Social-Constitutional History of the American Revolution 1774–1781.* Madison: University of Wisconsin Press, 1970.

———. *The Making of the American Constitution.* Princeton, N.J.: D. Van Nostrand Company, Inc., 1964.

———. *The New Nation: A History of the United States During the Confederation: 1781–1789.* New York: Vintage Books, Random House, 1950.

Kelly, Alfred H., and Harbison, Winfred A. *The American Constitution: Its Origins and Development.* New York: W. W. Norton & Company, Inc., 1970.

Ketcham, Ralph. *James Madison: A Biography.* New York: Macmillan Company, 1971.

Kohn, Richard H. *Eagle and Sword: The Federalists and the Creation of the Military Establishment in America: 1783–1802.* New York: Free Press, Division of Macmillan Publishing Co., 1975.

Lansing, John. *The Delegate from New York or Proceedings of the Federal Convention of 1787, from the Notes of John Lansing, Jr.* Edited by Joseph Reese Strayer. Princeton, N.J.: Princeton University Press, 1939; Port Washington, N.Y.: Kennikat Press, Inc., 1967.

McDonald, Forrest. *Alexander Hamilton: A Biography.* New York: W. W. Norton & Co., 1979.

———. *E Pluribus Unum: The Formation of the American Republic 1776–1790.* Boston: Houghton Mifflin Company, 1965.

———. *Novus Ordo Seclorum: The Intellectual Origins of the Constitution.* Lawrence: University Press of Kansas, 1985.

Malone, Dumas. *Jefferson and the Rights of Man*, vol. 2. *Jefferson and His Time*, 6 vols. Boston: Little, Brown & Company, 1951.

Mintz, Max M. *Gouverneur Morris and the American Revolution*, Norman: University of Oklahoma Press, 1970.

Mitchell, Broadus, and Mitchell, Louise Pearson. *A Biography of the Constitution of the United States.* New York: Oxford University Press, 1964.

Morris, Richard B., ed. *Encyclopedia of American History.* New York: Harper & Row, Publishers, 1970.

Munroe, John A. *Federalist Delaware 1775–1815.* New Brunswick, N.J.: Rutgers University Press, 1954.

Niles, H. *Principles and Acts of the Revolution in America.* Baltimore, 1822.

Risjord, Norman K., *Chesapeake Politics, 1781–1800*. New York: Columbia University Press, 1978.

Rossiter, Clinton. *Alexander Hamilton and the Constitution*. New York: Harcourt, Brace & World, 1964.

———. *1787: The Grand Convention: The Creation of the United States*. New York: Mentor Books, New American Library, 1966.

Rutland, Robert Allen. *George Mason: Reluctant Statesman*. Baton Rouge: Louisiana State University Press, 1961.

Silverman, Kenneth. *A Cultural History of the American Revolution*. New York: Thomas Y. Crowell Company, 1976.

Spaulding, E. Wilder. *His Excellency George Clinton*. New York: Macmillan Company, 1938.

Storing, Herbert J., ed. *The Complete Anti-Federalist*. Vol. 5, *Maryland and Virginia and the South*. Chicago: University of Chicago Press, 1981.

Swiggett, Howard. *The Extraordinary Mr. Morris*. New York: Doubleday & Company, Inc., 1952.

Tyler, Moses Coit. *The Literary History of the American Revolution: 1763–1783*. Vol. 2. New York: Frederick Ungar Publishing, 1897. 1966 (American Classics Series) ed.

Van Doren, Carl. *Benjamin Franklin*. New York: Viking Press, 1938.

———. *The Great Rehearsal: The Story of the Making and Ratifying of the Constitution of the United States of America*. New York: Viking Press, 1948.

Warren, Charles. *The Making of the Constitution*. Cambridge, Mass.: Harvard University Press, 1937; New York: Barnes & Noble, Inc., 1967.

Williams, Frances Leigh. *A Founding Family: The Pinckneys of South Carolina*. New York: Harcourt Brace Jovancvich, 1978.

Wood, Gordon S. *The Creation of the American Republic, 1776–1787*. Institute of Early American History and Culture, Williamsburg, Va. Chapel Hill: University of North Carolina Press, 1969.

Wright, Chester W. *Economic History of the United States*. New York: McGraw-Hill Book Company, Inc., 1941.

ABOUT THE AUTHOR

★

JEFFREY ST. JOHN is the author of five books, and his work in television has received two Emmys. He has written extensively for *The New York Times, Philadelphia Enquirer, Chicago Tribune, Los Angeles Times* and many other newspapers.

Prior to undertaking *Constitutional Journal* he wrote a weekly syndicated column "Headlines and History" and narrated a radio version for Mutual Network and overseas on The Voice of America.

His experience in broadcasting includes NBC-TV "Today," news commentator for CBS-TV "Morning News," CBS Radio, and also as moderator and producer of public affairs programs for New York and Washington, DC television stations. He resides and works with his wife Kathryn in Randolph, VA.